The Making of Economic Policy

B

Macroeconomics and Finance

A Series under the General Editorship of
Lawrence H. Summers and Robert C. Merton

The important connection between financial processes and macroeconomic environment has been revealed in some of today's most inventive economic analysis. Areas of current interest include stock market rationality, expectations and the term structure of interest rates, financial market volatility, and the business cycles debate. This new series will provide a context for continuing research that not only units financial and macroeconomics, but ramifies into constituent fields themselves. Professors Summers and Merton share editorial responsibility for the series as a whole, while lending individual attention to their respective special areas.

The first two titles in the series are:

The Making of Economic Policy
History, Theory, Politics
Steven M. Sheffrin

Continuous-Time Finance
Robert C. Merton

The Making of Economic Policy

History, Theory, Politics

Steven M. Sheffrin

BLACKWELL
Cambridge MA & Oxford UK

Copyright © Steven M. Sheffrin 1989

First published 1989
First published in paperback 1991

Basil Blackwell Inc.
3 Cambridge Center
Cambridge, Massachusetts 02142, USA

Basil Blackwell Ltd
108 Cowley Road, Oxford, OX4 1JF, UK

Library of Congress Cataloging in Publication Data

Sheffrin, Steven M.
    The Making of Economic Policy: history, theory, politics/Steven M. Sheffrin.
        p.   cm.—(Macroeconomics and finance)
    Bibliography: p.
    Includes index.
    ISBN 1–55786–022–X
    ISBN 1–55786–294–X (Pbk)
    1. United States—Economic policy—1945— 2. Economic stabilization—United States. 3. Business cycles—Political aspects—United States. 4. Keynesian economics. I. Title. II. Series.
HC106.5.S424   1989
338.973—dc20   89–9781
                                                                                      CIP

British Library Cataloguing in Publication Data
A CIP catalogue record for this book is available from the British Library.

Typeset in 10 on 11½ pt. Times with Univers
by Setrite Typesetters Limited, Hong Kong
Printed in the USA

Contents

To Anjali, Meera, and Kiran

Preface

In 1977 Franco Modigliani and Milton Friedman debated the desirability of activist stabilization policy at the San Francisco Federal Reserve. It was a classic confrontation between two giants in the field who disagreed sharply on the key issues. Yet looking back at that debate today, one is struck by the underlying similarities in their vision of the economy. Money mattered because lags prevented the adjustment of wages and prices; business fluctuations were undesirable; and the proper policies, although not necessarily activist, could improve the performance of the economy.

Today there is profound disagreement, not just on the design of economic policy, but on our most fundamental premises for understanding the economy. Unlike the Modigliani–Friedman debates, the protagonists of today do not share a common framework. Leading scholars argue that business fluctuations should be modeled as the outcome of competitive, market-clearing processes; other leading economists scoff at this very premise. Debates also rage on other far-reaching issues from the competing visions of positive versus normative policy analysis to the degree to which the postwar economy has been stabilized.

Stabilization policy, however, is too important to fall victim to academic fragmentation. The purpose of this book is to sort through the debates and alternative perspectives, deflate the academic bravado, and begin the process of developing realistic dialogue on the political economy of stabilization policy. Both the nature of the topic and the scope of the recent debates force this book to treat an extraordinary diversity of issues including economic history, dynamic economic theory, time series econometrics, and US congressional politics.

The sheer diversity of the approaches in this book ensure that no one will find all the analyses, answers, and prescriptions to be definitive. This is the price that must be paid for venturing beyond a narrow focus and grappling with the larger issues. The reader should also keep in mind, as a necessary accompaniment to an expansive vision of macro-economics, the motto of the College of Social Studies at Wesleyan University, "A Tolerance for Ambiguity."

This book is intended for individuals with a serious academic interest in the economics and politics of stabilization policy, including economists, political scientists and economic historians. Although some parts of the book do become technical, every effort has been made to ensure that most of the book is accessible to a wide audience.

The bulk of the work on this project was accomplished on a sabbatical leave from the University of California, Davis. The first half of this sabbatical was spent at the Institute for Governmental Affairs at Davis, the second half in the Economics Department at Princeton University. Both institutions provided stimulating research environments.

The author and publisher would like to thank Elsevier Science Publishers for permission to reproduce material drawn from the author's own work, "Have economic fluctuations been dampened? A look at evidence outside the United States," *Journal of Monetary Economics*, 21/1, January 1988.

Many individuals contributed in important ways to this project. My colleagues at Davis, Kevin Hoover and Tom Mayer, read the entire manuscript in detail and provided an open forum for a variety of ideas. At Princeton, Alan Blinder, Steve Goldfeld, and Ben Bernanke were always willing to discuss a wide range of topics. Kailash Khandke prepared the index. Kathy Miner and Petrina Ho typed the manuscript on two different word processors. Finally, Peter Dougherty and Romesh Vaitilingam of Basil Blackwell were a pleasure to work with throughout all stages of the project.

1

Challenges to Stabilization Policy

Macroeconomics has always been fertile ground for controversies and the 1970s marked the most vigorous intellectual disputes since the 1930s. Yet despite the intellectual warfare, there was actually a *tacit* consensus underlying the debate about macroeconomic stabilization. This consensus was not directly attacked during the rational expectations revolution of the 1970s and survived intact until quite recently.

The consensus encompassed five main themes:

1 Fluctuations in economic activity, that is to say business cycles, were socially undesirable and thus should be reduced if at all possible.
2 The historical record clearly demonstrated that the severity of business cycles in the United States had declined over time, especially since World War II.
3 One of the chief causes of prolonged economic fluctuations was the lack of wage and price flexibility in the face of external shocks.
4 Changes in the supply of money were important determinants of economic fluctuations.
5 Normative exercises in macroeconomics should be conducted by examining the welfare consequences of alternative government policies.

It cannot be emphasized enough how strongly these positions were shared by the participants in macroeconomic debates. Business cycle theory attracted so much attention precisely because both economists and the public thought that the boom−bust cycle was costly to the economy and research was driven by the hope that more informed policy (even noninterventionist) could reduce the severity of fluctuations. The historical record exhibiting reduced severity of fluctuations was apparently clear for all to see. There were, of course, no recessions since World War II comparable to the Great Depression. Moreover, even the period preceding the Great Depression was marked by much more violent fluctuations than the period since World War II.

Limited wage and price flexibility was a component of all theories of economic fluctuations. Keynesian economists preferred to think of contractual rigidities or norm-based wage stickiness as the source of this inflexibility. Robert E. Lucas provided rigorous foundations for a lack of wage and price flexibility due to informational limitations, in particular, an inability to distinguish relative price movements from aggregate price movements. Sometimes it became difficult to separate these two perspectives. If we observe contracts that are not fully contingent primarily because of informational limitations, then the sharp contrast between contract theories and information theories begins to blur. In all theories, however, an increase in wage and price flexibility — either through a reduction of contractual arrangements or improved information — would decrease the severity of economic fluctuations.

At one time, monetarists and Keynesian economists waged war over whether "money mattered," but by the early 1970s, the shared consensus held that monetary policy was an important force in the economy. The best indication of this was that the large econometric models all featured an important role for money. The MPS (MIT–Penn–Social Science Research Council) model, for example, featured changes in the money supply affecting consumption, state and local government spending, as well as the conventional links to investment. While there were certainly debates over the precise multipliers for monetary policy, there was general agreement that Federal Reserve policy had profound effects on the economy.

The debate changed in the 1970s from whether "money mattered" to whether it was only unanticipated or unperceived money that mattered. This became the area of a vast and ultimately disappointing econometric growth industry. All participants in the empirical debate, however, shared the presumption that some component of the money supply mattered. All that was at issue was whether it was only the unanticipated or unperceived component of the money supply that was the source of output and employment fluctuations.

Finally, Lucas's critique of econometric models actually reinforced the view that normative analysis in macroeconomics was an important and valid exercise which should be conducted by examining the consequence of alternative government policies. Lucas challenged the usefulness of existing econometric models for evaluating the consequences of isolated policy interventions. He called for specifying government policy rules and analyzing their effects in models in which the private sector could respond to changes in the rules. Nevertheless, normative policy analysis was still seen to be a valid enterprise, although one which needed to be conducted within the context of more sophisticated models which evaluated the welfare consequences of alternative rules explicitly.

As always, there were few who stood outside this tacit consensus.

Post Keynesian economists, a vocal but small group, continued to insist that independent monetary policy did not matter either because money simply did not matter or because the money supply was endogenous to the economic system. Austrian economists, another small minority, naturally would have objected to the social engineering implicit in the call to evaluate the welfare consequences of alternative government policy rules. Finally, there are always a few proponents of "structural unemployment" theories who contend that special factors, such as material or labor shortages, require an increase in normal unemployment and who thus are hesitant to fight what other economists may term "recessions" but which they view as necessary increases in unemployment.

What better testimony to the strength of the *tacit* consensus than this roster of opposition? Post Keynesians, Austrians, and proponents of structural unemployment were distant voices from the mainstream debates in either academic or policy circles during the 1970s. The great majority of the remaining macroeconomists, despite their profound differences on the desirability and efficacy of activist policies, shared in the tacit consensus.

It is important to stress that the "tacit consensus" did not extend to the desirability of active management of the economy by policymakers. A long monetarist tradition, best exemplified through the writings of Milton Friedman, stressed the uncertainties inherent in both our knowledge of the economy and in the knowledge of policymakers. Moreover, another strand of monetarist thought emphasized the political pressures that often forced policymakers into ill-advised decisions. Thus, there were vigorous debates on stabilization policy between monetarists and Keynesians. However, these debates focused on the practicality and desirability of conducting stabilization policy, not its *feasibility*. Those vigorous debates actually respected the tacit consensus that was outlined above. The new attacks, however, take one further step and challenge the very foundation for stabilization policy, not simply its practice.

Recent research has sharply challenged all five ingredients of the tacit consensus. In some cases, the challenges have gained considerable support while, in others, they remain controversial positions. Still the tacit consensus has now crumbled and the result is heated debate over the most fundamental issues.

The challenges came from a wide variety of sources. The construction of the historical data for the United States was re-examined with surprising results. A thoroughgoing attempt to explain economic fluctuations solely as a function of market-clearing behavior in response to exogenous technological shocks led to the development of real business cycle theory. Theoretical research on the interaction between expectations of inflation and contracts led to skepticism as regards the conventional wisdom concerning wage and price flexibility. Finally, the growth and popularity of game theory applied to macroeconomic policymaking and the interest in constitutional solutions to economic problems led to doubts over traditional normative macroeconomic analysis.

Historians who constructed estimates of GNP for past decades were originally concerned with estimating long-run growth trends. How fast, for example, did real GNP grow in the nineteenth century and how did this compare to twentieth-century growth? Simon Kuznets, the father of GNP accounting and the premiere historian of GNP for the United States, refused to publish his annual estimates of GNP for the late nineteenth century because he doubted their accuracy. Consistent with his aim of studying long-run trends, he only published estimates in five-year moving average form.

However, annual estimates of GNP for the past decades began to be used by economists who were interested not so much in long-run growth trends as in economic fluctuations. Interestingly, the data revealed that the variance of real GNP growth dropped dramatically in the United States after World War II. This change is dramatically illustrated in figure 1.1, which plots the growth rate of real GNP from 1870 to 1983. A glance at the figure clearly indicates that the post World War II economy differs dramatically both from the Great Depression and the period before that. Lessons from this picture, of course, could differ. James Tobin claimed similar pictures showed we must have been doing something right while Robert Lucas more soberly intoned that this indicated the possibility for future progress.

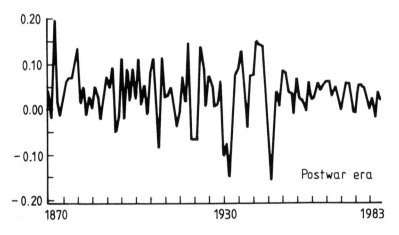

Figure 1.1   Growth rate of real GNP

Recent work by Christina Romer has brought these historical generalizations sharply into question. Romer argues that unemployment and GNP figures before World War I are distorted so as to overstate the true level of economic fluctuations. Essentially, the methods used tend to exaggerate the cyclical fluctuations of those series. When Romer corrects the series for the alleged biases, she finds that the earlier series are only slightly more volatile than the post World War II series. The Great Depression emerges as an even more dramatic event in this analysis because the fluctuations in output during this period now greatly exceed those preceding and following it.

Romer's work has generated considerable controversy, as it should, because the implications of her research are so important. If Romer is correct, it may be difficult to find any positive effect from postwar activist stabilization efforts. The growth of federal government spending, transfer payments and automatic stabilizers, as well as the diminution of the agriculture sector could possibly account for the slightly lower observed volatility of the postwar era, leaving little room in this accounting for a positive effect from stabilization measures.

During the 1970s, the oil price rises engineered by the OPEC cartel forced economists to think seriously about supply factors in macroeconomics, an area which had previously been neglected. Economists began to consider seriously the possibility that potential output could have a cyclical component in addition to the customary exponential trend. Several approaches were taken to this problem. Potential output was made a function not only of the labor force and the capital stock but of energy prices as well. David Lilien developed an intriguing version of the structural unemployment thesis that, in effect, made the natural rate of unemployment very over time. Lilien argued that in periods in which there was considerable structural change there would be a need to reallocate labor across different sectors of the economy. An increased pace of labor reallocation would by its very nature require more frictional or search unemployment and a concomitant increase in the natural rate of unemployment.

Work by Edward Prescott and Finn Kydland took this approach to a radical conclusion. Why not try to explain *all* economic fluctuations as shifts in potential output? Kydland and Prescott, in fact, attempted to explain economic fluctuations as the result of technological shocks in a full neoclassical optimizing model with market clearing. To put in starkly, they looked to see if a particularization of the Arrow–Debreu model could replace Keynes. Instead of just modifying the role of potential output in macro models to allow for technological and other disturbances, their research program led them to develop what has now been termed "real business cycle" theory and to challenge the entire edifice of modern Keynesian economics.

This work, of course, did not develop in a vacuum. In addition to the interest in supply factors as an explanation of macroeconomic fluctuations, Prescott and Kydland's research was driven by the internal logic of theoretical developments in the 1970s. Lucas earned the praise of economic theorists in the 1970s by demonstrating that it was possible to construct market clearing and optimizing models of the business cycles. The fluctuations in Lucas's models, however, were driven by monetary shocks which caused fluctuations because of an inability of agents to distinguish the effects of monetary shocks from the normal movement of relative prices. Yet, the model came under attack by many because of the belief that monetary information was readily available and should be used by fully optimizing agents. Kydland and Prescott decided to investigate the possibility of explaining economic fluctuations in an optimizing model without any monetary factors at all with the sole source of shocks being disturbances to technology. They could thus take up the banner of equilibrium, market-clearing macroeconomics without the assumption of imperfect information with respect to monetary shocks.

Recent work by several time series econometricians has also contributed indirectly to the appeal of real business cycle theory. Conventional macroeconomic thinking is based on the view that potential output follows a smooth trend governed by the growth of factor inputs and technological progress while business cycles are viewed as deviations from this trend. Business cycles are, in a fundamental sense, transitory, that is, eventually the economy returns to the trend of potential output. In the absence of further shocks, the deviation of actual output from potential output will eventually tend towards zero.

However, recent work by some times series econometricians has challenged this interpretation of the data. These econometricians argued that the data support a different characterization of fluctuations in output. Rather than shocks eventually dampening out, they contend that shocks tend to persist or even be magnified in the long run. For example, a 1 percent fall in GNP today would lead these econometricians to predict that twenty years from now, GNP would be at least 1 percent lower than it would have been. In other words, economic fluctuations tend to be permanent.

To the extend that fluctuations in output are permanent, the a priori case for theories based on real disturbances is enhanced. Traditional views of the effects of monetary and fiscal policy describe their effects as transitory. For example, a recession initially induced by tight money would eventually disappear as prices fell to restore the economy to full employment. However, if there are important, permanent technological disturbances to the economy, this could account for permanent movements in GNP which some time series econometricians appear to find.

To the extent that the real business cycle research program proves successful, it will totally change the assumptions underlying conventional thinking about economic fluctuations. In their framework, economic fluctuations are Pareto-efficient responses to technological shocks. It might be possible to devise schemes to reduce these fluctuations but they would necessarily reduce individual welfare. In other words, economic fluctuations are socially desirable. Monetary factors are thought to be unimportant, not because of direct evidence that money does not matter, but indirectly because it is not necessary to include monetary factors in order to explain economic fluctuations. Finally, if market clearing methods work to explain business fluctuations, it strongly suggests that other cyclical phenomena, such as unemployment or capacity utilization, should be explained in terms of optimizing, market clearing models.

Not all challenges to the tacit consensus came from the equilibrium macro theorists. In the *General Theory*, Keynes (1965) had raised the possibility that too much price flexibility could be destabilizing. Tobin (1975) developed a model which echoed the same themes. Consider a fall in autonomous spending which pushes the economy into a recession. The traditional equilibration mechanism is for the aggregate price level to fall thereby increasing real balances and stimulating aggregate demand to restore the economy back to full employment. However, to the extent to which this deflation is anticipated it could lead to an increase in real interest rates through the Mundell–Tobin effect. The rise in real interest rates could, in principle, prevent the economy from being restored to full employment.

Bradford DeLong and Lawrence Summers (1986b) used this line of reasoning to reinterpret the historical stabilization record. Prior to the recent revisionism described above, the historical record on stabilization stressed two themes. First, the severity of economic fluctuations had been greatly reduced following World War II and, second, wages and prices had become less flexible in the postwar period. The growth of multiyear labor contracts as well as the gradual erosion of "casual" labor markets contributed to the greater rigidity of wages and prices. DeLong and Summers argued that if everything else stayed the same, the reduction of wage and price flexibility should have led, according to traditional theory, to an increase in the severity of economic fluctuations, not the decrease that was apparently observed. What can explain this paradox?

There are a wide variety of potential explanations that could reconcile the reduction in wage and price flexibility with the reduction in the magnitude of economic fluctuations. The earlier period could have experienced larger exogenous shocks, greater financial instability in the absence of a central bank or federal deposit insurance, greater induced fluctuations in consumption in the absence of a large tax and transfer system which acts as an automatic stabilizer, or simply higher volatility due to the presence of larger volatile sectors (agriculture). DeLong and Summers reviewed some of these explanations but concluded that they were not sufficient to resolve the paradox.

They argued that the decrease in wage and price stability itself was responsible for the reduction in the volatility of GNP because too much price flexibility can destabilize through the Keynes–Tobin mechanisms. DeLong and Summers originally developed a simple model to demonstrate their claims; subsequent work has investigated these ideas in more sophisticated models with rational expectations and contracts.

The outcome of this debate is important for setting the tone for government policy towards labor market institutions. Should unions and other mechanisms that "regularize" employment and promote attachments of workers to firms be encouraged in the hope that this will reduce aggregate fluctuations? Or should the underlying ideal for the private sector be an atomistic, impersonal labor market in which wages or employment rapidly adjust in the face of exogenous disturbances?

There has always been a tension between positive studies of government behavior and normative policy analysis – a debate mirroring that over free will and determinism. As an example, if the "capture theory" applies to government regulatory agencies, what sense does it make for economists to publish studies and debate about optimal government regulation? In the macroeconomic arena this debate was never really joined because there never was a very serious positive theory to explain either monetary or fiscal policy. The theory of the "electoral business cycle" clearly had merit for some historical episodes (it is still remarkable to contemplate the extent of President Nixon's paranoia about re-election and how this was transmitted to his political and economic policies), but the electoral cycle was clearly refuted in other cases. Southern populists might have felt there was a conspiracy between the Federal Reserve and Wall Street, but this was never translated into a theory that could explain the timing of monetary policy actions. Minsky's financial crisis theories (1982) were also lacking in the specificity required for credible theories. Without theories, the notion of positive economics was just a dream.

The rapid growth of game theory in all areas of economics has changed the situation. As game theory grew in popularity and, in some cases, transformed entire fields (industrial organization), it began to be applied to macroeconomic policymaking. In some sense, it is a natural application. Inflation fighters at the Fed have always felt that they were playing a "game" against the private sector and game-theoretic notions such as credibility were part of the mystique of policymaking activities at the Fed.

Developments in macroeconomic theory also created an opening for the advance of game theory. In Lucas's policy evaluation framework, the private sector responded to rules created by the government. This, however, created two problems. First, how would the private sector handle changes in rules? Would they speculate on the probabilities of rule change? If so, in what sense could the government change a rule if it had been discounted, so to speak, by the private sector? Second, government rules might not be "time-consistent," meaning that the government might have an incentive to change a rule once the private sector had adapted to the initial rule. How should the private sector be expected to respond in this case? Was the initial rule credible? In both these cases, it is clear that the notion of a government following a rule is problematic and there is a need for a richer conceptual framework in which to discuss policy. Game theory can, in principle, provide that framework; and a wide variety of models have been put forth that purport to explain government policy.

The development of game theoretical models of economic policy immediately raises two questions: do they work and, if so, what role do economists have in the policy process? To the extent that game theoretic models of economic policy do have explanatory power, they question the role of the day-to-day policy advice that is so freely given by those attempting to influence policy. Is this advice being evaluated on its merits, ignored, or does it become part of one of the major player's strategies?

A second body of thought also contributed to the challenge to traditional normative analysis. Public choice theory, associated with the work of James Buchanan, stressed that politicians do not necessarily operate for the public interest, but pursue their own personal agendas. The public choice movement has given support to constitutional limitations on economic policy choices. These constitutional solutions to economic problems are not advocated by public choice theorists as first-best solutions to ideal planning or stabilization problems but are purported to be the best, workable solution in a world where politicians and bureaucrats will pursue their own self interests. Public choice theory, therefore, joins company with game theory in challenging the conventional role of policymaking.

The successive chapters in this book will sort through the remains of the crumbled consensus. All new approaches and attacks are inevitably accompanied by excessive claims and bravado. There is nothing inherently wrong with this Madison Avenue approach to scholarship. Weaning scholars and policymakers from old, comfortable truths requires flash as well as substance. Nonetheless, this style of scholarship requires a fresh re-examination of the old views with the new and a special effort to avoid the twin evils of embracing novelty for its own sake and clinging to older ideas which have outlived their usefulness and live only to recall past controversies.

Our examination of the challenges to stabilization policy divides naturally into three parts: history, theory, and politics. Chapter 2 explores the historical questions concerning the scope for stabilization policy. It begins with a review of Christina Romer's work and the controversy it has engendered. Although this debate has focused solely on the interpretation of United States data, the issues raised by the debate reach beyond this one country's experience. I hope to bring a fresh approach to the debate by examining the experience of a variety of countries outside the United States to place the controversy concerning American historical experience into perspective. Chapters 3, 4, and 5 primarily highlight issues in economic theory and statistics. Chapter 3 confronts real business cycle theory. I first present an account of the nature of real business cycle models and an assessment of their strengths and weaknesses. I then turn to two new types of evidence concerning their applicability for the United States economy. The first consists of close examination of the consumption behavior of the unemployed to see if this behavior can be accounted for by any of the existing models. The second concerns the role of monetary policy and, more specifically, whether there is convincing evidence to suggest that changes in the money supply have had pronounced effects on real economic variables.

This chapter also re-examines the evidence put forth by several time series econometricians which purports to demonstrate that fluctuations to output are permanent. First I survey the extensive recent literature on this topic which has increasingly raised doubts concerning the ability to infer long-run movements in data from the relatively short time series which are available. Then I pose a different but related question: are the econometric methods that we currently have available for the analysis of economic time series powerful enough to distinguish the long-run from short-run effects of economic policies? Finally, I explore whether certain features of the historical data actually suggest that stabilization policy has been successful.

Chapter 4 focuses on the effects of changes in wage and price flexibility on the dynamics of stabilization policy. First comes a review of the facts: what have been the changes in wage and price stability from the late nineteenth century to the modern period? The discussion then turns to the question about whether increased price flexibility can be stabilizing and a number of recent models developed to analyze this point are examined. After this review comes an assessment of the explanatory power of the alternative models for the macro time series in order to resolve the stabilizing or destabilizing properties of increased price flexibility.

In the past several years, a self-proclaimed "new Keynesian economics" has become a feature of the policy debate. Chapter 5 evaluates the contributions of the new Keynesian economics at this stage in its development. There are actually a series of different models that fall under the rubric of new Keynesian at this time. The chapter focuses on whether these models provide any new insights for the actual conduct of stabilization policy or merely put old wine in new bottles.

Chapters 6 and 7 turn attention to the interactions between economics and politics. Chapter 6 raises the question of whether recent developments of the application of game theory in economic policy warrant a new conception of policy. The chapter discusses both the theoretical plausibility of existing theories and evaluates some recent attempts to combine insights from traditional political science with game theory.

Chapter 7 examines the issue of constitutional rules in macro policy. It takes a case study approach to the issue by examining the economics and politics of both monetary targeting and the Gramm–Rudman laws. These were two recent episodes in United States monetary and fiscal policy in which policies were taken to limit discretion explicitly. By comparing and contrasting the political economy of the two episodes, it is possible to gain an appreciation of how quasi-constitutional mechanisms work in practice.

As will become apparent in the discussion in the substantive chapters, the demise of stabilization policy is premature. The final concluding chapter puts the debate into perspective. The historical record, upon closer examination and with the aid of cross-country comparisons, reveals considerable dampening of economic fluctuations. Reinterpretation of recent time series evidence also provides some independent support for historical stabilization of the economy. While real factors do seem to play an important role at times, real business cycle theory misses essential elements of the economic story. None of the other theoretical challenges nor the new Keynesian economics adds any fundamental insights to the debate.

On the political front, game theory provides interesting models of the policymaking process but even the most advanced synthesis of political science and game theory has limited explanatory power. Recent experiments in economic constitutionalism fall victim to fundamental problems of definition and fail to put an end to "politics as usual." Policymakers cannot, at this point, successfully put the economy on automatic pilot. The tacit consensus still provides a useful framework for thinking about the scope of policy.

The concluding chapter also takes a broad overview of stabilization policy. Rather than viewing stabilization policy as a technical problem to be solved once and for all, it sketches an alternative view. At key junctures in the economy, fundamentally new issues appear to dominate the horizon and neither economists nor policymakers are fully equipped to handle these. As policymakers grope for solutions, economists devise new conceptual categories and tools to analyze the problems. Finally, I suggest that economists should take a broader, more expansive view of their potential contributions to stabilization policy. Rather than being simply sophisticated interpreters of current economic events or developers of new models, economists should aid in developing the institutional mechanisms to facilitate the successful conduct of policy.

2

Have We Stabilized the Economy?

2.1 Introduction

Before turning to the recent controversies in macroeconomic history concerning the degree to which the postwar economy has been stabilized, it will be valuable to explore briefly a different but related controversy in the philosophy of history. Besides providing some useful background perspective, the arguments of the philosophers echo in the recent cliometric debate and the protagonists in the economic debates find allies in different philosophical camps.

The starting point for philosophical debate about the nature of historical research and explanation begins with the "covering-law-model" of explanation articulated most fully by Carl G. Hempel (1966). According to this view, explanations offered by historians are fundamentally of the same character offered by scientists. All true explanations require that the event to be explained be accounted for by the initial conditions inherent in the situation and a general law which proscribes that whenever the initial conditions are present, the event will follow. The general law or covering-law model provides the unity between explanations in science, the social sciences, and history.

This view implies that explanations of historical events can only be as sound as the covering laws upon which they are based. Of course, this poses some difficulties for historical explanations because the "laws" available from the entire body of social science are not terribly impressive compared to the laws of physics or other sciences. Despite this problem, Hempel and others argue that explanations logically must rely on covering laws, and history and social science are simply in a position to give less convincing arguments than those that are put forward in the sciences. Hempel recognized that history and social sciences (as well as sciences in some cases) may rely on laws which are statistical in nature; that is, they specify that when certain initial conditions are present, a particular event will occur with a "high likelihood." Presumably, explanations in social sciences and history would, at best, satisfy these statistical covering laws.

One implication of this view is that there is nothing inherently different about knowledge in history as compared to knowledge in other fields. While the events or facts to be explained lie in the past, the method or logic of explanations must be the same. Historians may find it useful to engage in imaginative reconstruction of historical events but that is simply a vehicle for generating hypotheses, just as scientist may stare at a coffee cup in order to generate new ideas. Nor are there particular scientific laws which only apply to the past. All true scientific laws have the property that they generate the same outcomes when faced with the same initial conditions. Historians may find different initial conditions but the laws governing explanations must not be unique to history.

Although lamenting the trend, Robert Solow recognized the prevalence of Hempel's views on actual practice in modern economic history. After caricaturing the current practice of some economists, he went on to write:

> As I inspect current work in economic history, I have the sinking feeling that a lot of it looks exactly like the kind of economic analysis I have finished caricaturing: the same integrals, the same regressions, the same substitution of t-ratios for thought. Apart from anything else, it is no fun reading the stuff any more. Far from offering the economic theorist a widened range of perceptions, this sort of economic history gives back to the theorist the same routine gruel that the economic theorist gives to the historian. Why should I believe, when it is applied to thin eighteenth-century data, something that carries no conviction when it is done with more ample twentieth-century data? (1985, p. 330)

A Hempelian could sympathize with Solow's loss of enthusiasm for reading modern economic history as well as his observation that bad social science can be practiced on past as well as current events. But the Hempelian would insist that the aim of historical explanation is no different in character than social scientific explanations for modern phenomena, even if this means that history no longer delivers "special truths" from the past.

Historians naturally resent an account of their discipline which portrays them as amateur social scientists operating with bad data. Philosophers, sympathetic to the notion that historical explanation is *sui generis*, have offered alternative accounts of the nature of explanation in history.

Some alternatives, however, are not satisfactory. Kenneth Arrow

(1985) supported the position of an eminent historian that history sought to study the individual case while social science aspired for generalizations. Unfortunately, as Louis Mink (1966) recounts, this view of history has been rejected by most historians as well as philosophers. The reason for this rejection is simple: historians have always used and continue to use generalizations of different levels and different kinds, for example, labelling events as "revolutions." While some historians may study particular events, their methods of explanation reveal an appeal to a wide variety of general principles.

The most persuasive alternative viewpoint to Hempel's stresses the special role of narrative in historical explanations. According to this position, a historian aims to weave together in a narrative a wide variety of facts and perspective to arrive at an understanding of an event or episode *as a whole*. As Mink (1966, p. 191) described explanations offered in history, "[they] cultivate the specialized habit of understanding which converts congeries of events into concatenations, and emphasizes and increases the scope of synoptic judgment in our reflection on experience." As these philosophers argue, historians often engage in the same activity in explaining historical events as ordinary individuals do in their day-to-day existence. After an account of a person's backgrounds and motives we might suddenly understand why he voted the way he did at a meeting or behaved in what originally had been perceived to be a peculiar manner. It is this type of understanding (which does not rely on valid social-scientific universal laws) which constitutes much of historical explanations. Philosophers who articulate these views do not suggest that there is no role for Hempelian social scientific explanations of particular historical episodes, but insist that the Hempelian mode of explanation is neither universally valid nor widely applied in historical work.

Can these philosophers inspire a new brand of economic history that would rescue Robert Solow from the Hempelians he now sees inhabiting economic history? Probably not. Contemporary economic historians do not generally rely extensively on narratives or the type of arguments or presentations typically found in histories written from a more traditional humanistic perspective. Some types of economic history could rely on narrative explanations. For example, it might be possible to write a narrative on a particular entrepreneur whose motivations stemmed in Weberian fashion from a set of religious beliefs. But this is not the type of economic history we have come to expect from our cliometricians nor, frankly, the type that Solow would want to see.

However, the anti-Hempelian philosophers also stress that the activities of historians and their methods should be taken seriously in analyzing the nature of the historical enterprise. From this perspective, Sir Isaiah Berlin offered an interesting example of the different attitudes scientists and historians have towards evidence and theory. In the face of evidence that appears to disconfirm a well-known and respected scientific theory, scientists would not jettison the theory but would construct explanations to "explain away" the piece of disconfirming evidence. Perhaps the initial conditions were not the same (the *ceteris* not quite *paribus*), the equipment was faulty, the data suspect, or perhaps the investigator simply made an observational error. This type of activity in a scientist is respected, praised and encouraged. Theory, at least at a first pass, takes primacy over data.

Berlin, however, noted that such an approach would be viewed as scandalous in the context of history. If a historian jettisoned an otherwise reliable eyewitness account (say that Napoleon was seen wearing a three-cornered hat in the battle of Austerlitz) because it failed to conform to his theory (one which stated that French generals never wore three-cornered hats in battle), his work would not achieve acceptance. Of course, Berlin recognized that this was a trivial example but he went on to argue:

> It would not be difficult to think of more sophisticated examples, where an historian lays himself open to the charge of trying to press the facts into the service of a particular theory. Such historians are accused of being prisoners of their theories; they are accused of being fanatical or cranky or doctrinaire, of misrepresenting or misreading reality to fit in with their obsessions, and the like. Addiction to theory — being doctrinaire — is a term of abuse when applied to historians: it is not an insult to a natural scientist. We are saying nothing derogatory if we say of a natural scientist that he is in the grip of a theory. (1966, p. 16)

As we will see clearly later in the chapter, this *attitude* towards data is at the heart of the controversy concerning the reassessment of the stabilization record of the United States and provides it with its passion. Assuming Berlin's account of the difference in attitudes towards data between the scientists and historians is correct, what is the fundamental source of the difference in attitudes?

One hypothesis is that this attitude reveals a fundamental difference in the methods applicable to each branch of knowledge and is evidence against the methodological unity of history and the sciences. A second hypothesis is that historians are reluctant to cast away evidence because they have never found any particular social science theory convincing enough to warrant strict adherence to its predictions. Alan Donagan (1966, p. 143) argues that providing convincing covering laws in social science "is *always* difficult; and it has *never* been done." One need not adopt such an extreme position to express skepticism towards social scientific explanations and a corresponding deference to apparent historical evidence.

This second hypothesis offers another reason why the debate about the re-examination of the "facts" of the historical stabilization record has been vehement. Economics is probably the only discipline in the social sciences for which claims that there are valid statistical laws are taken seriously. To the extent that some laws or empirical generalizations are credible, the attitude of Berlin's typical scientists may begin to be applied to historical data in economics. This will ensure that the clash of "two cultures" will be heard loud and clear in the debate over the historical stabilization record.

2.2 Prior Beliefs

Before the recent controversy over the historical stabilization record, economists of widely differing persuasions agreed that the post World War II economy differed dramatically from the economy preceding the war. A few extended quotes can best convey the intensity of these beliefs.

Robert E. Lucas, a stern critic of stabilization policy, described his views on the postwar era:

> Also omitted, but too striking a phenomenon to pass over without comment, is the general reduction in amplitude of *all* series in the twenty five years following World War II. ... Nevertheless, so long a period of relative stability strongly suggests that there is nothing inherent in the workings of market economies which requires living with the level of instability we are now experiencing, or to which we were subject in the pre-World War II years. That is, attempts to document and account for regular cyclical movements need not be connected in any way to a presumption that such movements are an *inevitable* feature of capitalist economies. (1977, p. 10)

In a rare optimistic mood, Lucas envisions a world less volatile than the late 1970s and the pre World War II era. He does not single out the Great Depression for special attention, except, of course, to include it implicitly in the earlier era.

In his 1959 Presidential Address to the American Economic Association, Arthur Burns commented on the radical changes in the economy since World War II:

> It is a fact of the highest importance, I think, that although our economy continues to be swayed by the business cycle, its impact on

the lives and fortunes of individuals has been substantially reduced in our generation. More than twenty-five years have elapsed since we last experienced a financial panic or a deep depression of production and employment. Over twenty years have elapsed since we last had a severe business recession. . . . There is no parallel for such a sequence of mild − or such a sequence of brief − contractions, at least during the past hundred years in our own country. (1960, pp. 1−2)

It is clear from the last sentence that Burns was not restricting his comments to contrasting the Great Depression with the postwar era but also wished to contrast the recent period with the long scope of economic history in the United States.

James Tobin reflected on the historical evidence after his discussion of the "new classical economics" in his Yrjo Jahnsson lecture:

How it [stabilizing the economy] can be done, better than in the past, is a quest that continues to deserve the attention of economic theorists and econometricians. We should not be diverted by the new classical macroeconomics, an intellectually ingenious construct that does not describe the societies in which we happen to live. We can take some encouragement from the economic performance of the advanced democratic capitalist nations since the second world war. On this point, Martin Baily has proved once more that a picture is worth a thousand words. His picture . . . . shows how much more stable real output has been in the United States under conscious policies of built-in and discretionary stabilization adopted since 1946 and particularly since 1961. (1980, pp. 46−8)

Since Baily's picture (1978), similar to figure 1.1 above, presents the rate of growth of real GNP from 1901 through 1979, it is safe to assume that Tobin meant to include this entire period in his characterization of greater instability and not simply the Great Depression.

It would be hard to find another issue upon which three such diverse economists as Lucas, Burns, and Tobin would have agreed. The new classicist, the National Bureau of Economic Research (NBER) practitioner, and the quintessential Keynesian all saw the reduction in the volatility of the business cycle to be fundamentally important for evaluating both potential changes in the economy and the scope for stabilization policies.

Burns's Presidential Address discusses in detail the reasons which he believed accounted for the relative stability of the postwar economy. One of the primary factors was the growing disjunction between fluctuations in production and fluctuations in the personal income available to consumers. Both the government and the private sector contributed to this trend. Large corporations tended to maintain stable dividend policies thereby dampening fluctuations in personal income. The government's tax and transfer system also contributed heavily to the stability of personal income. As Burns noted (1960, p. 6), disposable income of individuals actually rose during the recession of 1954.

The second factor contributing to stability was changes in the nature of employment patterns. After the Civil War, individuals were increasingly drawn off farms and other self-employment into cyclical volatile industries which increased overall employment volatility. However, by 1920 this trend towards increasing concentration of workers in cyclical industries had stopped and growth in the "service sector" came to be important. This growth coupled with the rise of white-collar employment led to increasing stability of overall employment in the postwar era.

Consumption spending and investment spending also, according to Burns, became less volatile. Consumption spending became more stable largely because of the increased stability of personal income but also because of what Burns perceived to be an increased willingness of consumers to change their work patterns to maintain stable consumption. Investment spending became more stable for a number of reasons but primarily because of changes in expectations. As Burns wrote, "In investment circles, as elsewhere, the general expectation of the postwar period has been that government would move with some vigor to check any recession that developed, that its actions would by and large contribute to this objective, and that they would do so in manner, that is broadly consistent with our national traditions" (1960, p. 13). Burns's proclamation of the stability arising from government's willingness to take aggressive action may strike us as a bit exaggerated considering he was primarily discussing the 1950s, a period not identified today with an activist philosophy. But surely Burns's argument about the potential stabilizing effect on investment of government's willingness to take action, later developed formally by Martin Baily (1978), does meet with surface plausibility.

Thus, the belief that the data demonstrated that the postwar economy was more stable was not simply a belief based on staring at historical GNP data. The structural and behavioral changes that Burns discussed also provided foundations for the belief in a more stable postwar economic system.

2.3 Romer's Radical Reconstruction

It was within this background of shared beliefs that Christina Romer argued in a series of papers that available historical data presented a misleading picture and that the volatility of the earlier periods was overstated. To appreciate the radical nature of this position, DeLong and Summers (1986b, p. 684) argue precisely the opposite position in a paper first delivered at a conference in 1984: "It seems likely, however, that the deficiencies in the data lead us to *underestimate* rather than overestimate the extent of cyclical variation in the pre-World War I economy" (emphasis added).

Romer's assault on the conventional wisdom took place on several fronts. In successive papers, she argued that data from earlier periods overstated the volatility of unemployment (1986a), estimates of GNP (1986b), and indices of industrial production (1986c). She also discussed in other papers (1986d, 1987) both the interrelationships of the estimates and related background material. This multi-pronged assault was necessary not only because of the deeply ingrained views on the subject but also because the volatility of real variables in earlier series is apparently evident in a wide range of data including unemployment, GNP, and industrial production.

I will examine Romer's contributions in three steps. First, I will outline her methods and conclusions for the three principal series (unemployment, GNP, and industrial production) which she analyzes. I then turn to the critics of her work and an assessment of the points they raise and how they affect her initial conclusions. I then try to cut through the charges and counter-charges and address the question of how this debate has changed our view on the volatility of real variables in an earlier phase of the economic history in the United States. Finally, data from a variety of other countries is presented to gain some perspective.

Unemployment

The standard historical series for unemployment was created by Stanley Lebergott and presented in detail in his book *Manpower in Economic Growth* (1964). Romer accepted Lebergott's series for the period after 1930 but questioned the estimates from 1890 to 1930. Lebergott derived his unemployment estimates as the difference between independent estimates of the labor force and employment. Romer first presents an a priori case that Lebergott's methods for both series lead to too much volatility in the unemployment series for the earlier years.

According to Romer, the excess volatility arises in Lebergott's series because of faulty methods of interpolation in the estimates of the labor force and the estimates of employment. For both series, Romer accepts Lebergott's estimates in benchmark (census) years but objects to his methods of constructing the data between the benchmark years.

Lebergott's estimates for the labor force were obtained by interpolating participation rates for various groups linearly between benchmark years and then multiplying by annual population estimates. Romer argued that this method ignored the procyclical behavior of the labor force which is evident in postwar data and which she argues is also evident in prewar data. Lebergott's estimates of the labor force, therefore, are too large in recessions and too small in booms and this leads to unemployment estimates which are too large in recessions and too small in booms.

A related problem afflicts Lebergott's estimates of employment. Lebergott first derives benchmark estimates for employment in various sectors from census records and industry reports. He then uses various series to interpolate between the benchmark years. Romer was principally concerned that this method overstated employment fluctuations in construction, manufacturing, and trade. For these series, Lebergott used output measures to interpolate between the benchmark years. In these interpolations, deviations from trend in employment varied one-to-one with variations from trend in output. According to Romer, this was the primary source of excessive volatility of the employment series. In postwar data, employment moves much less than one-to-one with output; this is the basis for the various estimates of Okun's law. If similar relations operated in the prewar era, Lebergott would have created an employment series that was too procyclical. Coupled with the alleged bias in his labor force series, the result would be an unemployment series which would overstate cyclical fluctuations.

While these conjectures appear quite reasonable on the surface, it is not clear the extent to which they are quantitatively important. No one has discovered any additional data which would directly settle the issue. Indeed trends in scholarship suggest that no one will soon duplicate Lebergott's prodigious efforts (accomplished in his spare time in a non-academic position) and settle the issue once and for all. Romer, however, thought of an ingenious, although certainly debatable, approach of providing quantitative significance to her points.

Romer's first step was to create "bad data" for the postwar era. Specifically, she tried to replicate Lebergott's methods on postwar data. This involved interpolating between benchmark years using methods which she believed would be the modern-day equivalent of those used by Lebergott for the earlier period. Her basic finding from this exercise was that the constructed series were substantially more volatile than the true unemployment series. For purposes of comparison, the standard deviations of Lebergott's series for 1900–30 was 2.38; the true postwar unemployment series from 1948–82 had a standard deviation of 1.58; and the various constructed series for the postwar period had standard deviations averaging about 2.15. According to Romer, this provided initial evidence that Lebergott's methods induce excessive volatility in the unemployment rate.

Romer, however, wanted to reconstruct estimates of unemployment for the 1900–30 period. To accomplish this, she related the true unemployment series to the artificially constructed "bad" series and used the relationship which holds statistically between the two series in the postwar era to adjust Lebergott's series between the benchmark years.

In developing the statistical relation between the two postwar unemployment series, she used theory to help specify the relationship. Specifically, she assumed that the true labor force was procyclical while the labor force according to the "bad data" did not have a cyclical component. She assumed that the true employment series was related to current and lagged output deviations from trend but that the "bad" employment series was more highly correlated with current output deviations from trend. These assumptions imply a particular relationship between the actual and constructed unemployment series which she estimated with modest success. This regression was then used to adjust Lebergott's estimates between benchmark years.

The result of this exercise was to create a new unemployment series for the period 1890–1930. By construction, this series exhibited less severe fluctuations than Lebergott's original series. For the period 1890–1930, in which the unemployment rate ranges between 18.4 and 1.4 percent in the original data, the standard deviations of Lebergott's and Romer's series are 4.04 and 2.60 percent respectively. It is important to stress that Romer created her series without using any new prewar data but by adjustments to the data based on the postwar relationship between the true series and a "bad" series created to replicate Lebergott's methods.

Gross national product

Series on gross national product dating back to 1869 originated with the work of Simon Kuznets (1946, 1961). In his 1961 book *Capital in the American Economy*, Kuznets actually developed two historical series for GNP, a "components" series and a "regression" series. Both series were presented in five-year moving averages and only the regression series was published in annual form for the period 1889–1918. Kuznets was quite explicit in his views concerning the annual series:

> For the early years of the period, 1869–1888, the derived annual series, even for the comprehensive aggregates — gross and net

in creating *separate* component series. Since economic investigators are interested in the components of GNP and Kuznets claimed that the aggregate measures did not differ significantly, it is possible to see why the component series has been adopted for historical use.

Romer argues that the regression approach is really the only reliable way to construct GNP estimates but that Kuznets produced inaccurate estimates by including the years of the Great Depression in his regression. Romer (1986b) first illustrates that the coefficient on commodity output is almost always substantially less than 0.9 (0.5−0.7) except when the years of the Great Depression are included. She argues that the severity of the Great Depression created an atypical cyclical pattern between GNP and commodity output which did not appear to hold in either the postwar era or the prewar era excluding the Great Depression. When Romer constructs regression estimates using her preferred regression, which allows for a time-varying coefficient on commodity output, she finds fluctuations in GNP to be substantially less than the standard Kuznets−Gallman estimates. For the period 1869−1918, the standard deviation of percentage changes in the Kuznets−Gallman GNP series is 0.058; for Romers series, the standard deviation is 0.040; and, for comparison, the standard deviation of percentage changes from 1947 to 1983 is 0.027 (see table 2.1).

In addition, Romer (1986d) argues that other cyclical properties of her series differ from the traditional series. For example, it is often argued (DeLong and Summers (1986b)) that economic fluctuations became more persistent in the postwar era in the sense that rates of change of GNP are more highly correlated over time in the postwar era. Romer's revised data do not show as substantial an increase in persistence as measured by first-order autocorrelations between the earlier years and the postwar period.

In summary, Romer argues that a proper application of the regression method reveals that GNP was not as volatile as previously thought and that its cyclical properties have not changed. This argument is totally

Table 2.1   Volatility of GNP

Series	Period	s.d. of % changes
Kuznets−Gallman	1869−1918	0.058
Romer (1986b)	1869−1918	0.040
Commerce	1947−1983	0.027

s.d., standard deviation.
Source: Romer (1986b), table 4

independent of her arguments concerning the volatility of the unemployment series which we reviewed above.

Industrial production

Romer detects the same sort of excessive volatility in historical series
of industrial production. She argues that the series created by Frickey
(1947), which typically is used to extend historical series of industrial
production back from 1914 to 1860, is constructed in such a manner as
to exaggerate fluctuations during that period relative to the postwar
era. The essential problem with Frickey's index, in Romer's view, is.
that it is weighted too heavily with raw materials compared to modern
indices and that since inventories of raw materials are procyclical, this
imparts a bias towards excessive volatility.

To illustrate her case, Romer constructs two "bad" series for the
postwar era. The first is an exact replication of the Frickey index while
the second is an updated version that still emphasizes raw materials but
lets the identity of the materials change to include modern products.
She then compares the volatility of these "bad" postwar indices to the
original Frickey index and shows that they are comparable and more
volatile than the official series for industrial production. She concludes
from this exercise that the Frickey series is too volatile.

To buttress her case, Romer then examines in more detail the
sources of bias in the Frickey index and whether the pre- and postwar
economies are similar enough to justify her procedures. She concludes
that raw materials played essentially similar roles in the pre- and postwar economies. She also argues that the limited historical evidence
suggests that inventories of raw materials were procyclical in the earlier
period as well as in the postwar era.

As a final step, Romer compares the Shaw–Kuznets series on commodity output (described above in the GNP discussion) to modern
equivalents and argues that their volatility properties are similar. In
her view, the Shaw–Kuznets series provided a more comprehensive
and accurate picture of basic commodity production for the prewar
economy and was not subject to the same biases as the Frickey index.
Perhaps for this reason she did not follow her pattern in previous work
and create alternative basic series.

2.4 The Critics

Criticism of Romer's work falls into two patterns. On the one hand,
there are those who fundamentally reject her approach and method-

ology. On the other hand, there are those who, in principle, accept her approach but quarrel with its execution and the conclusions she draws. The criticisms of the first group are less "helpful" but because they are so fundamental they are, perhaps, the most interesting.

Stanley Lebergott questioned the entire logic of Romer's total effort. His criticism is based on his observation: "We had best begin a review of her new series by remembering Archimedes, who declared that he would move the earth — given a fulcrum in other space" (1986, p. 367). Romer's fulcrum is the assumption that empirical relationships that are valid in the postwar era are also valid in earlier periods. Lebergott denies Romer's basic premise:

> Of course, few economists would believe that the ratios and reaction function from 1960—1980 applied to the depression decade. But how many will believe her basic premise — that they applied, by definition to those more remote eras — 1900—1913, 1916—1918, 1921—1929? Did our longest depression plus our greatest war really have no impact on the structure of those pre-1930 economies, leaving their cyclical coefficients to reappear, unchanged, in 1960—1980? (1986, pp. 368—9)

At best, according to Lebergott, we resurrect Solow's nightmare that our study of the past delivers us nothing but our current theories about the present. "For Romer's new series cannot be used to study ... many aspects of economic change. Why not? Because scholars will get back, in distorted form, the elasticity she originally imbedded in her estimating procedures for the earlier decades" (1986, pp. 370—1).

We can illustrate this basic point by looking in more detail at two of the assumptions in Romer's unemployment calculations. First, she assumes that the pre Depression labor force was as procyclical as the postwar labor force. Her primary evidence is a cross-sectional regression of the participation rate by city on the unemployment rate by city for both eras, but she admits that this procedure does have flaws and is far from conclusive. Second, and perhaps more important, is the assumption that the relationship between output and employment is the same in the two eras. David Weir (1986) presents some evidence that this was *not* true for manufacturing. During the 1920s, a census for manufacturing was taken every two years so that interpolation problems for yearly data are much less of a problem and nonexistent for biannual data. Weir shows that on this data, employment and output appear to move one-for-one thereby casting doubt on Romer's basic hypothesis for excess volatility.

Similar doubts can be cast on her criticism of the industrial production indices. The evidence presented that materials were just as important in the economy today as they were in the past and that material inventories were equally procyclical is suggestive but far from persuasive on the normal standards of evidence we demand for controversial assertions today. To put it simply, Frickey's index is heavily weighted by pig iron, but how do we know that the economy at the turn of the century was not reflected by the fortunes of the pig iron industry?[1]

Romer takes an uncompromising Hempelian position to these criticisms. She first observes that the basic data available to her are essentially the same as were available to Kuznets and Lebergott and she differs from them only in their assumptions. Why should we accept her assumptions rather than those of the original constructors of the data? She offers three reasons. First, the data are now being used for different purposes (cyclical analysis rather than long-term trends) and her new assumptions principally concern cyclical behavior. Second, the technology of data creation has changed so it is now trivial to run hundreds of regressions in the time it used to take to do just a few. Third, according to Romer we have learned a great deal about the economy since the original data were created and she cites (1986, p. 351) Okun's law as an example.

It is precisely this last point which is at issue. How do we know if Okun's law (which even varies over the postwar period) holds sixty years earlier in the economy? Romer recognizes this fundamental issue but still asks why the older assumptions should be sacrosanct in the face of the cumulative weight of her evidence.

Lebergott does not offer an explicit defense for his assumption but rather hints at a different notion of the enterprise of data creation. He discusses the large number of individual series he had to construct for employment, the "achingly dull scholarship," and the "serious work, in a different direction, [that] is needed if one wants a plausibly better annual series" (1986, pp. 368–9). What is this "different direction" to which Lebergott hints?

Perhaps the best way to understand Lebergott's alternative vision of data construction is to take an example of his work outlined in his book (1964), particularly the data on unemployment for the 1890s. Without endorsing the particular numbers, it is intriguing to see Lebergott's approach in detail. He first constructs an overall employment series using Frickey's index to extrapolate between 1890 and 1900 and combines this with labor force estimates to derive unemployment estimates. However, he tries to check his series for accuracy and to reconcile it with other estimates. For example, he attempts to check his estimates for 1893 by comparing them to a contemporaneous estimate by an economist based on surveys from more than forty-four cities and finds that his estimate is roughly comparable and also consistent with data on relief recipients in Massachusetts. Lebergott also tries to explain why his estimates differ from previous ones offered by Paul Douglas.

It is the process of constant checking and recalibration with the plethora of historical evidence available (including contemporaneous accounts, related series and economic and political events) that constitutes Lebergott's "different direction." In many ways, it bears some similarity to the narrative mode of historians described by the anti-Hempelian philosophers. All pieces in a narrative must fit together; here, the jigsaw puzzle includes fragments of information from various sources that must be internally consistent.

These same processes are evident in Lebergott's construction of many of his employment series. Explicit choices are made when to use or abandon specific series for guidance or interpolation. These decisions are not made so much with an explicit theory in mind as by the internal consistency of the data and its overall consistency with other perceived facts. Although Lebergott is not a "narrative" historian, he is an excellent example of Berlin's historian, unwilling to jettison a perceived fact to support a theory.

Lebergott and Kuznets could be described as scientists who simply place more faith in cross-checking contemporary evidence than in applying existing "laws" and their methods need not be construed as unscientific or anti-Hempelian. But the key point is that their instincts as historians point them in a different direction from many contemporary practitioners.

But are we painting an idealized picture of the type of work actually conducted by Kuznets and Lebergott? Are there that many other independent pieces of historical evidence to provide checks on the basic estimates? Would the authors of the series use different assumptions if they were making their estimates today? While we may want to accept Lebergott's estimate for 1893, are we prepared to accept the jump in unemployment from 11.7 to 18.4 percent from 1893 to 1894 when the relief recipients series showed only a modest increase?

David Weir (1985) and Nathan Balke and Robert J. Gordon (1986) accepted the basic thrust of Romer's research but challenged specific elements of her implementation. Weir focused on both unemployment and GNP while Balke and Gordon concentrated just on GNP. Both papers contend that Romer's conclusions are overturned when alternative and preferable procedures are employed.

Weir had two substantive criticisms of Romer's procedures for unemployment. As noted above, he contended that the manufacturing series was based on adequate data, and for the data available, the relationship between employment and output was one-for-one. Thus, the manufacturing series did not need corrections. For trade and construction he did accept the need for revision and adjusted Lebergott's series directly using relationships estimated on postwar data. This procedure allows for sectoral shifts in the data which could cause bias in Romer's approach. For the labor force calculations, he again adjusted Lebergott's calculations using sex-specific participation relationships estimated from postwar data. Combining Lebergott's revisions, he constructs unemployment series which he argues are much closer to Lebergott's in volatility than Romer's.

Weir's criticism of Romer's GNP estimates focused on the years included in her regression of GNP and commodity output. Weir argues that the anomalous years are not those of the Great Depression but the period 1909–18. He demonstrates that the regression results are sensitive to including these years and their inclusion is responsible for lowering the coefficient on commodity output. Weir argues that both the Kuznets and Shaw estimates are of lower quality for these years and that Romer has not produced any independent evidence that the relationship between GNP and commodity output changed during the Great Depression.

Balke and Gordon suggest three changes to Romer's procedures. First, they suggest that trend output be estimated by piecewise linear trends rather than moving-averages – a procedure that Romer (1986b) adopts in her latest GNP estimates. Second, they suggest that a Commerce Department series, rather than the original Kuznets series be used for the years 1909–38. In a later paper, Romer (1987) argues that the Kuznets series (which later was embodied into Kendrick's estimates) is actually superior to the original Commerce Department series. Finally, Balke and Gordon suggest that railroad ton miles and an index of construction be included in the regression to explain GNP and then used along with the Shaw series to interpolate GNP estimates between benchmarks. They argue (1986, p. 3) that making these adjustments leads to the conclusion that "there is not a shred of evidence to support the view that the greater volatility of real GNP before 1929 is 'spurious.'"

At this point, even the most devoted Hempelian might despair over the debate surrounding the proper way to adjust the data. It is inherently difficult to justify the exclusion or inclusion of certain years or variables in a regression. It is precisely the inconclusiveness of similar debates in the postwar era over such topics as money demand or investment which has led to great skepticism over the value of econometric work in adjudicating between economic theories. The limited number of annual observations in this debate also poses special problems for the robustness of the results. A final difficulty is that since this is an ongoing research area, revised estimates taking into account some of the critics' points are produced just as the critics' final versions go to press.

Romer's procedures can be defended from some of the charges of her critics. It is not obvious, for example, that railroad miles and construction indices bear a more stable relationship to GNP than does an aggregate measure such as commodity output whose relationship to GNP might be less susceptible to technological change. Moreover, Romer (1987) discusses in great detail why she believes the Commerce Department estimates for the years 1909 through 1921 are not adequate. With respect to the use of the years dating from 1909 in her basic regression, it should be noted that Kuznets felt the data from those years to be reliable enough to use in his regression estimates. While these may be, in some cases, reasonably persuasive arguments, the detached observer will find it difficult to decide some of these issues on a priori grounds.

To gain some perspective on this debate, it will be useful to take another look at the range of estimates produced and to determine whether the range of estimates matches the range of rhetoric. We then turn to new evidence concerning the behavior of GNP and industrial production for countries outside the United States to bring new insights to our domestic debate.

A perspective

The rhetoric in this debate has been heated as a few examples illustrate. The abstract to Romer's unemployment paper reads: "This paper shows that the stabilization of the unemployment rate between the pre-1930 and post 1948 eras is an artifact of improvements in data collection procedures" (1986a, p. 1). Her paper on industrial production states in the introduction that "there is very little stabilization between the pre-1914 and post 1947 eras" (1986c, p. 314). We have already noted that Balke and Gordon found not "a shred of evidence" to support the notion of excessive volatility. The title of David Weir's 1985 paper begins with the words "Stabilization Regained." Finally, Lebergott (1986, p. 369) asks rhetorically why Kuznets and he failed to follow Romer's procedures: "Because we were not ingenious, or because we preferred achingly dull scholarship?"

Despite this rhetoric, a detached look at the final estimates presents a much more modest picture both of the controversy and the degree to which the picture of the prewar economy has been changed. First, table, 2.1 presents the standard deviation of Romer's preferred estimates and comparisons to the Kuznets−Gallman series and postwar series. The Kuznets−Gallman series by this metric is twice as volatile as the postwar series while Romer's series is roughly 50 percent higher. Thus, even for a period which *excludes the Great Depression*, the prewar economy according to Romer still is roughly 50 percent more volatile.

Table 2.2   Comparative volatility measures

Series I	Series II	Ratio of s.d. from trend of I to II
Gallman 1872–1928	Commerce 1950–80	1.91[a]
Romer (based on her 1985 version) 1872–1928	Commerce 1950–80	1.34[b]
Gordon-Balke (incorporating all suggested changes) 1872–1928	Commerce 1950–80	1.43[a]

[a] Detrending based on linear trends.
[b] Detrending based on moving averages.
Source: s.d., standard deviation. Balke and Gordon (1986), tables 3 and 7

The same point can be seen in table 2.2 which is based on the Balke and Gordon paper (1986). The Gallman series has a standard deviation 91 percent higher than their postwar series while their version of Romer's series (based on the procedures in her earlier 1985 work) has a standard deviation 34 percent higher. Balke and Gordon create a number of series reflecting alternative assumptions but taking all their preferred corrections together, their series has a standard deviation 43 percent as large as the Kuznets–Gallman series. This is almost identical in volatility to Romer's preferred series! While some of Balke and Gordon's series are more volatile than this, they are all universally less than the Gallman series.

Even the unemployment series upon closer examination present a picture of a more volatile economy. Table 2.3 presents the key evidence. While the data for 1900–30 show that Lebergott's series is considerably more volatile than Romer's (whose series is even less volatile than the postwar series), including the previous decade changes the picture. Looking at the period 1890–1930, one which again excludes the vast unemployment of the Great Depression, the volatility of unemployment according to either Romer's or Lebergott's measure substantially exceeds the volatility to postwar unemployment. While Weir's estimates are closer to Lebergott's for the smaller sample period, they exhibit almost identical volatility to Romer's for the entire period 1890–1930.

What can we conclude from this comparison of estimates? First, by all measures the prewar period is more volatile than the postwar period even when the Great Depression is excluded. Second, the

Table 2.3 Unemployment volatility (%)

Series	1890–1930	1900–30	1948–82
Lebergott (1964)	4.04	2.38	—
Weir (1985)	2.73[a]	2.10[b]	—
Romer (1986a)	2.60	1.39	—
Postwar	—	—	1.58

[a] 1890–1900 estimates combined with those in (b).
[b] Based on the Weir (1985) series CFL3 for the labor force and EZC3 for employment.
Source: Romer (1986a), Weir (1985)

differences between Romer's estimates and those of her critics who adopted similar methodologies are not that substantial. What is at issue is just the degree to which the prewar economy is more volatile than the postwar economy. Taking GNP as an example and using the standard deviation of percentage changes as a measure, is it more accurate to think of the period 1870–1918 as being 100 percent more volatile than the postwar era or 50 percent more volatile?

Even if we could pin down the precise degree between 50 and 100 percent by which the volatility of the post Civil War pre World War I economy exceeded that of the postwar era, we would still have to determine whether our answer dramatically changed our perception of the prewar economy. To put it starkly, is 50 percent a large number in this context? To gain some perspective, it is useful to take a look at data from other countries.

2.5 A Look at Evidence from Outside the United States

The first question addressed here is the extent to which other countries experienced a decrease in the volatility of economic growth. We then explore the diversity of experience across countries as well as analyze the time-series properties of the data from those countries.

Volatility

There are several reasons why data from other countries could provide perspective on the volatility debate. First, most commentators who discussed the decrease in the severity of the business cycle attributed it both to structural change and perhaps the knowledge on the part of the private sector that the government would intervene in an economic emergency, not the explicit stabilization policies that were actually followed. These structural changes and implicit commitments by governments were common throughout the industrialized countries in the post World War II era and were not restricted to the United States. Thus, if the United States did experience a reduction in the severity of business cycles, one would expect similar patterns in other industrialized countries.

Second, there is reason to believe that, for many European countries, the underlying data for periods before 1914 are better than for the United States. Many of these countries had formal statistical bureaus in place by 1870 whereas, in the United States, the statistical efforts were less frequent. The merits of the European data are discussed in more detail below.

We find that for the most part there was *not* a dramatic decrease in the severity of economic fluctuations for six European countries and Canada using data on GNP (or GDP). For most of these countries, the variance in the growth rate of real economic indicators did not change sharply between the periods 1871−1914 and 1951−84. All countries, however, did experience very severe economic fluctuations during the interwar period.

Tobin (1980) found a picture of real GNP growth more persuasive than tables. This present author concurs and I present graphs of real growth for the countries in the present sample as well as the descriptive statistics.[2] We will then turn to look at one country that did show a dramatic decrease in the severity of the business cycle, Sweden, and examine additional evidence for this case. The decrease in the volatility of economic fluctuations for Sweden does not appear to be an artifact of the data construction.

Before discussing the relative merits of the European versus the United States data, it will be helpful to review the alternative means of calculating national income statistics. There are essentially three different approaches that have been used to compile aggregate income statistics. Most countries now use these methods jointly to refine their estimates but this luxury is generally not available for historical work.

The three methods are the expenditure approach, the income approach, and the value-added approach. The expenditure method uses actual and imputed spending on final goods and services to derive the aggregate series. The income approach adds together factor costs of production plus capital consumption and indirect taxes to arrive at the aggregates. The value-added method subtracts nonfactor costs of production from the value of production or gross sales on an industry basis. This method is used today in many countries for the agricultural sector.

Do the problems identified in US data by Christina Romer afflict the data for the countries examined here? A close look at the methods used to construct the data in the United Kingdom, Denmark, Sweden, Italy, the Canada is somewhat reassuring. There is neither a sharp change in the methods used to construct GNP (unlike the break in methods before and after 1909 in the United States) nor the strong reliance on extrapolative measures such as required to estimate GNP from commodity output for the United States. This fact, coupled with the generally better primary source materials, suggests that historical comparisons for volatility can be taken seriously. Here are the essential features of the earlier GNP estimates for the United Kingdom, Denmark, Sweden, Italy, and Canada:

United Kingdom   The estimates in this chapter are taken from Feinstein (1972). Although the data used are based on the expenditure approach, Feinstein also constructed estimates based on the income approach. The reintroduction of the income tax in 1842 allowed Feinstein the luxury of having two independent estimates of aggregate income. Feinstein discussed in detail the relationship between the two estimates. Prior to 1909, estimates of GNP based on the expenditure approach exceed those based on the income approach. Nonetheless, their cyclical properties are very similar. In fact, the standard deviation of current dollar growth rates of GNP from 1871 to 1909 are virtually identical (0.035 vs 0.036 for the income and expenditure estimates respectively). Since two totally independent measures give such similar results in terms of volatility for the earlier period, we can have reasonable confidence that they give an accurate picture.

Denmark   The estimates for Denmark are based on the work of Bjerke and Ussing (1958) with an earlier discussion in Bjerke (1955). They used an income approach based largely on tax records that extend back to 1870 and also made particular use of annual estimates of assessed income in Copenhagen. Although the authors worried about the effects of tax evasion on their estimates, alternative assumptions on tax evasion would primarily affect the levels but not the cyclical properties of their estimates.

Sweden   The historical data used in this paper come from Johansson (1967). He used the value-added method consistently in producing estimates for 1861–1955. For the period from 1861 to 1930, he relied heavily on the earlier work of Lindahl et al. (1937), which was also based on the same value-added method. The earlier work had the good fortune to be based on a rich body of governmental statistics. The Central Bureau of Statistics was established in Sweden in 1858 and from 1870 onwards there are consistent series on trade and agricultural production. The main deficiency in the estimates is the lack of data on inventory changes. The consequences of this and other potential biases in Swedish data will be discussed in more detail below.

Italy The historical Italian data are derived from *Annali di Statistica* (1957). Estimates for the period 1861–1956 were generated on a detailed sectoral basis by value-added methods. In general, the data on agriculture, mining, and manufacturing are based on a rich body of primary statistics. Estimates for trade and transportation are based on more indirect methods such as the use of employment and census data. This could introduce some biases into the estimates of volatility. However, industrial production statistics, detailed in Sheffrin (1988a) and for which the reliability is high, exhibit a similar pattern to the GNP data.

Canada M. C. Urquhart (1986) has published new estimates of GNP for Canada for the years 1870–1926. These estimates, the product of nearly a decade of work, are based primarily on value-added methods by sector. Urquhart provides extensive details of his methods as well as his sources of data. His methods appear to be consistent throughout the period although extensive use was made of interpolation, by sector, between benchmark years. Urquhart's estimates are used for our earliest period; official Canadian statistics are used for the interwar and postwar period.

Figures 2.1–2.6 display growth rates in either GNP or GDP for the periods 1871–1914, 1922–38 and 1951–84. The data, except for Canada, are from the European Historical Statistics and the periods were chosen to maintain comparability between series and to avoid the war years. The data for Norway and Sweden are for GDP; the data for the United Kingdom, Italy, Denmark, and Canada are for GNP.

The figures show a reasonably consistent pattern. For all countries except Sweden and perhaps Canada the variance of real GNP growth appears roughly similar for the periods 1871–1914 and 1951–84. The period 1922–38, however, exhibits considerably more variability.

The data in table 2.4 confirm the impressions from the figures. Except for Sweden and possibly Canada, there is only a mild decrease in the standard deviation of GNP or GDP growth in the post World War II era compared to the pre World War I period. As benchmarks, the Kuznets–Gallman series were twice as volatile in the earlier period while Romer's series exhibited 40 percent more volatility. For Sweden, the standard deviation is nearly 2.5 times as large in the earlier period

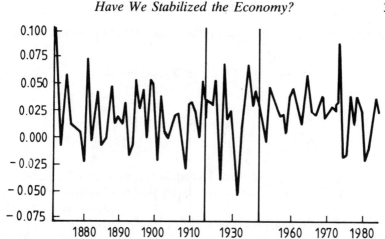

Figure 2.1   Real GNP growth for the United Kingdom. The three segments of the graph correspond to the periods 1871–1914, 1922–38, 1951–84

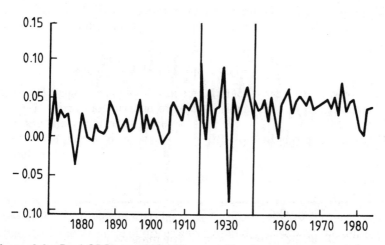

Figure 2.2   Real GDP growth for Norway. The three segments of the graph correspond to the periods 1871–1914, 1922–38, 1951–84

as compared to the postwar era. Canada exhibits 70 percent more volatility in the earlier period. The remainder of the countries are below 25 percent by this measure. Data on industrial production, as reported by Sheffrin (1988a), exhibit even less of a decrease in volatility. Thus, every country except Sweden exhibited a smaller decrease in volatility than the Kuznets–Gallman data indicated for the United

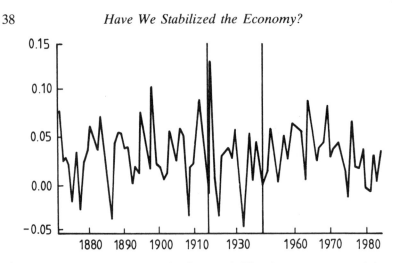

Figure 2.3   Real GNP growth for Denmark. The three segments of the graph correspond to the periods 1871–1914, 1922–38, 1951–84

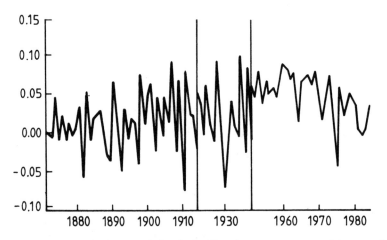

Figure 2.4   Real GNP growth for Italy. The three segments of the graph correspond to the periods 1871–1914, 1922–38, 1951–84

States. Only Canada and Sweden exhibit more dampening of the business cycle than Romer's adjusted series for the United States.

Because the data for Sweden exhibit such a dramatic decrease in the severity of business fluctuations in the postwar era, it is worthwhile to examine the data a bit more closely. As noted above, the standard reference for historical Swedish statistics on gross domestic product is

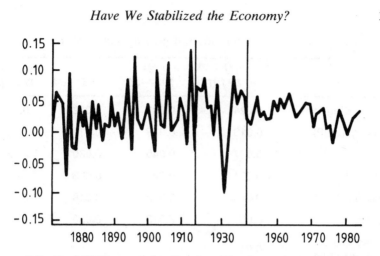

Figure 2.5   Real GDP growth for Sweden. The three segments of the graph correspond to the periods 1871–1914, 1922–38, 1951–84

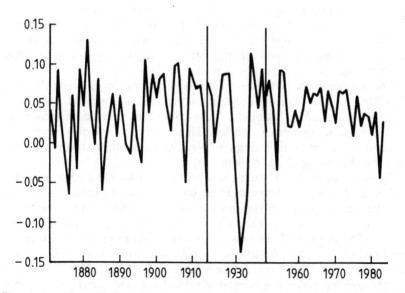

Figure 2.6   Real GNP growth for Canada. The three segments of the graph correspond to the periods 1871–1914, 1922–38, 1951–84

Table 2.4   Standard deviation of growth rates GNP or GDP

	(1) *1871–1914*	*(2)* *1922–39*	*(3)* *1951–84*	*Ratio of (1) to (3)*
United Kingdom	0.024	0.031	0.022	1.09
Norway (GDP)	0.018	0.038	0.015	1.20
Italy	0.037	0.045	0.030	1.23
Denmark	0.031	0.041	0.025	1.24
Sweden (GDP)	0.044	0.052	0.018	2.44
Canada	0.051	0.073	0.030	1.70
United States Romer (1986b)	0.040			
Commerce	—	0.085	0.028	1.42

Johansson (1967), who provided estimates for the period 1861–1955. Johansson, in fact, warns against the naive use of his estimates for the analysis of cyclical experience: "The statistical series presented here are not suitable for an analysis of short-run changes, such as, for instance, business cycle fluctuations. The main reason for this is that the year-to-year changes are too often concealed by linear or other kinds of interpolations and extrapolations" (p. 13).

The estimates for GDP are calculated as the sum of the contributions by different sectors in the economy which are for the most part calculated by value-added methods. Data limitations preclude estimates of the change in inventory stocks. This is the principal reason that Johannson felt that his estimates "were unsuitable for studies of year-to-year changes in the economy" (p. 21).

Does the neglect of changes in inventory stocks and a heavy reliance on methods of interpolation bias the data in favor of excessive volatility for the earlier periods? The answer to this question is probably "no" with perhaps a presumption of too little volatility in the historical series. The neglect of changes in inventory stocks may understate the fluctuations in GDP. As Blinder (1981) and others have pointed out, the variance of GNP exceeds the variance of final sales for the United States and this pattern has been observed for other countries as well. Interpolations, by their very nature, also tend to understate fluctuations.

Comparing sectoral data for the earlier period to similar data in Sweden for the modern period may be useful in detecting any unusual pattern in the earlier data. In particular, it may detect the type of biases identified by Romer for the United States. Using the sectoral data from Johannson for the period 1871–1914 and from the OECD *National Account Statistics* for the period 1961–82, we construct comparable data for five sectors of the economy: agriculture, manufacturing, construction, transportation, and service (including government). Table 2.5 contains the correlations of the growth rates of these sectors with the overall growth rate in GDP along with sectoral shares for the years 1890 and 1976.

Several points emerge from the table. First, the growth rate in agriculture is much more highly correlated with the growth rate in GDP in the earlier period whereas manufacturing is much more highly correlated in the latter period. These findings are not particularly surprising because agriculture's share in GDP fell from over 30 percent to under 4 percent whereas manufacturing's share rose from 15 percent to 25 percent. The correlation of the growth rate of services remained roughly the same over the two periods. The transportation sector did exhibit a sharply different pattern in the two periods. In the early period, it was highly procyclical whereas in the most recent periods its growth rate was actually countercyclical. Although this type of finding could be indicative of artificial volatility in the data of the sort noted by Romer, the fact that transportation is only 6 percent of gross domestic product sharply reduces the economic significance of this finding. Thus, the data on the correlation of sectoral growth rates do not, with the aforementioned exception, provided any evidence of artificial volatility.

Table 2.5 Correlations in growth rates and sectoral shares

Sector	1871–1914		1961–1982	
	Correlation of growth rate with growth rate of GNP	Sectoral share 1890	Correlation of growth rate with growth rate of GDP	Sectoral share 1976
Agriculture	0.58	0.32	0.17	0.03
Manufacturing	0.69	0.15	0.90	0.25
Construction	0.28	0.07	0.40	0.07
Transportation	0.48	0.06	−0.10	0.05
Services (including government)	0.68	0.37	0.56	0.46

Except for the case of Sweden, the data from other countries do not exhibit the dramatic decrease in the volatility of real economic activity that is present in the original data for the United States. This provides some indirect support for the arguments by Romer that the data for the United States may overstate the change in the severity of economic fluctuations. All these countries experienced similar structural changes to the United States and also had governmental policies which could, in principle, have created expectations of stability in the private sector.

The data for Sweden suggest that the possibility that explicit and particular stabilization policies succeeded in reducing economic fluctuations. Sweden's efforts in this regard are discussed in detail by Lindbeck (1974). Particular note should be given to their programs designed to reduce fluctuations in investment spending. Taylor (1982) provides some evidence that these "fund release" programs succeeded in reducing fluctuations in investment spending on structures. Other aspects of Swedish stabilization policy, including credit rationing, may have had an important influence on the behavior of these aggregates.

Diversity

The diversity in the volatility of GNP growth across countries in the period 1871–1914 as depicted in table 2.4 is perhaps even more intriguing than the reduction in volatility within countries. At one extreme we have Norway, which exhibits as little volatility in the early period as Sweden does in the later period. On the other hand, we have the extremely volatile record for Canada, which is nearly three times as volatile as Norway.

Among all the countries, Canada, Sweden, and the United States exhibit the most volatility in the earlier period even using Romer's figures for the United States. In Europe, Sweden and Norway bracket the extremes of volatility with Denmark falling between the extremes.

Before turning to possible explanations for this diversity, it is instructive to take a closer look at Norway, the country with the least volatility. Norway is not exactly a model country from the perspective of economic development during the earlier period. Its growth rate of real GNP was only 2.1 percent compared to rates of 2.8 percent for Sweden and Denmark and much higher rates of 3.8 percent and 3.5 percent for the United States and Canada. As Lieberman (1970) describes, there was net emigration, limited railroad construction, laggard agricultural development, and export led growth with few backwards linkages. Norway during this period is a good reminder that lack of volatility should not be the only criterion by which to judge economic progress.[3]

Simon Kuznets once argued that rapid GNP growth should be positively correlated with volatility. This hypothesis does not work particularly well with data for the earlier period. Two sets of neighbors cast doubt on this hypothesis. The United States grew more rapidly than Canada but Canada exhibited substantially more volatility. Sweden and Denmark grew at precisely the same rate but Sweden's growth was considerably more volatile. With an anemic growth rate of 1.3 percent, Italy's growth was considerably more volatile than that of Norway or Denmark. As Alexander Field (1980) stressed, even Kuznets noted a counterexample in that Germany grew extremely rapidly but had very stable growth.

Field suggested that the different pattern of railroad investment between the United States and Germany could explain the difference in volatility experienced by these countries in the later part of the nineteenth century. While the United States was engaging in a rapid railroad building phase during this period, Germany had largely completed its railroad investment by 1870. Field argued that railroad investment was inherently volatile and explained the different volatility in Keynesian terms.

Railroad investment does appear to be an important factor in accounting for the different patterns of volatility across countries. Largely because of its forbidding terrain, Norway added few railroad miles during this period. Denmark, another low volatility country, also built few railroads. On the other hand, as Lieberman (1970) pointed out, Sweden's efforts were immense and dwarfed the railroad investment of its Scandinavian neighbors. Again, Sweden had much more volatile growth than Norway and Denmark.

Canada, the most volatile country in our sample, embarked on a massive railroad building program starting about 1870. This program was part of the effort to open the western plains and received government subsidies and support. As the western plains were opened, wheat became a dominant crop and the volatility of wheat prices and yields also played an important role in explaining the volatility of the Canadian economy.

The railroad—volatility linkage can perhaps also account for the finding by Backus and Kehoe (1988) that economic growth in pre World War I Australia exhibited extreme volatility compared to the postwar period and, by some measures, even exceeding that of Canada. Butlin (1964) emphasizes the importance of railroads in Australian economic growth. From 1861−89, investment in railways grew at an annual rate of 13.9 percent. This investment reached a peak of 6.4 percent of GDP in 1885−6 and remained between 4.6−6.4 percent through the 1880−90 period. Only residential and pastoral capital investments were of equal size. Moreover, there is evidence that railroad investment was also highly volatile. Describing the slump of the 1890s, Butlin wrote, "It was, at all events, railways which were most severely affected, capital outlays falling further and longer than those of other components" (1964, p. 444). From 1891−94, investment fell by 7.5 million Australian pounds; railway investment fell by 5 million pounds, nearly two-thirds of the total.

Thus, railroad investment appears to separate Sweden from the other Scandinavian countries, differentiates the fast-growing US economy from Germany, played an important role in Canadian development, and can account for the Australian data. While Field adopted a Keynesian perspective and suggested that railroad investment caused fluctuations in aggregate demand, it is possible that the railroad investment caused spurts in aggregate supply. Without a careful analysis of price movements and monetary factors, it is difficult to separate the two hypotheses.

What perhaps is most interesting about this discussion is the type of factors included in possible explanations and those excluded. Variable growth rates and railroad investment appear to be important in accounting for volatility while government policies, except perhaps the promotion of railroads, do not appear to be a factor. Structural factors play the important differentiating role, not policy.

Time series properties

There is a general presumption that business cycles in the postwar have become more protracted or more persistent. DeLong and Summers (1986b), in fact, argued that the increased persistence of business cycles was evidence against the hypothesis that stabilization policy had been actively employed in the United States. Romer (1986d), on the other hand, argued that her data show little change in the stochastic properties of output fluctuations.

Before turning to examine the data from a wide range of countries, a word of caution is required. Time series properties of economic series can be very sensitive to the methods used to create the data. Although the data from the European countries may be accurate enough to obtain reliable estimates of volatility, the pre World War I data is certainly less reliable than post World War II data. Only if there is strong and clear evidence concerning changes in the stochastic structure of economic fluctuations should we accept the hypothesis of a change.

Table 2.6 presents the first four autocorrelations of GNP growth for all our countries for the period 1875−1914 and 1955−83. If a general pattern does emerge from the table it is that, for the most part,

Table 2.6 Sample autocorrelations of growth rates

Country	Period	Lag: 1	Autocorrelations 2	3	4
United Kingdom	1875–1914	−0.24	−0.13	0.10	0.02
United Kingdom	1955–1983	0.06	−0.24	0.04	−0.01
Norway	1875–1914	0.40	0.01	−0.01	0.19
Norway	1955–1983	0.18	−0.05	−0.00	0.14
Sweden	1875–1914	−0.50	0.05	0.18	−0.05
Sweden	1955–1983	0.50	0.20	0.15	0.35
Italy	1875–1914	−0.45	0.25	−0.16	0.11
Italy	1955–1983	0.35	0.17	0.23	0.23
Denmark	1895–1914	0.12	−0.14	−0.26	−0.29
Denmark	1955–1983	0.09	0.15	0.28	0.05
Canada	1875–1914	0.00	0.03	0.00	−0.03
Canada	1955–1983	0.19	0.10	0.09	−0.09
United States (Romer data)	1875–1919	0.02	−0.06	0.04	0.07
United States	1955–1983	0.16	−0.07	−0.17	−0.04

economic fluctuations have changed from becoming negatively correlated over time to positive or zero correlation; or, in other words, fluctuations have shown a tendency to become more persistent. However, the pattern is only very strong for a few countries.

Sweden and Italy exhibit the most dramatic patterns. For both these countries, there is strong negative first-order autocorrelation of growth rates in the early period and strong positive first order autocorrelation in the postwar era. Table 2.7 contains estimates of time series models for both countries for both periods. For Sweden, first-order moving average models were estimated and the moving average coefficient changed from negative to positive as anticipated and coefficients in both periods were statistically significant. For Italy, first-order autoregressive models fit the data best and the lagged coefficient again changed from negative in the early period to positive in the later period as expected and the coefficients were again significant.

The United States and Canada move from virtually no first-order

Table 2.7   Growth rate regressions for Sweden and Italy

Sweden				
1875–1914	gswede	= 0.026	−	0.062 e(−1)
		(0.006)		(0.15)
	$\overline{R^2}$	= 0.268		d.w. = 1.80
	s.e.	= 0.039		
1955–1983	gswede	= 0.029	+	0.52 e(−1)
		(0.003)		(0.19)
	$\overline{R^2}$	= 0.187		d.w. = 1.99
	s.e.	= 0.016		
Italy				
1875–1914	gitaly	= 0.020	−	0.46 gitaly(−1)
		(0.005)		(0.14)
	$\overline{R^2}$	= 0.192		d.w. = 1.92
	s.e.	= 0.034		
1955–1983	gitaly	= 0.028	+	0.38 gitaly(−1)
		(0.010)		(0.18)
	$\overline{R^2}$	= 0.096		d.w. = 2.00
	s.e.	= 0.029		

Standard errors in parentheses.
Regressions for Sweden are first-order moving averages on gswede –
the growth rate of Sweden.
Regressions for Italy are first-order autoregressive on gitaly – the growth
rate of Italy.

serial correlation in the early period to mildly positive first-order correlation in the postwar period. First-order moving average models
estimated over the postwar era led to moving average coefficients of
0.19 for both countries but the coefficient had *t*-statistics in the neighborhood of 1 and thus were not significant.

Turning to the other countries, the United Kingdom moved from
negative first-order autocorrelation to roughly no correlation. Denmark
exhibited little change in first-order correlations but the higher order
correlations which were negative in the earlier period became slightly
positive in the later period. Norway is a clear outlier. For the early
period, the data exhibit strong positive serial correlation but this is
reduced to the order of the correlations for the United States and
Canada for the later period.[4]

While the data do indicate a trend towards more persistence, the
evidence is only fully persuasive for Italy and Sweden. More detailed
studies of the stabilization process for these countries must take these

facts into account. The next chapter will discuss a potential interpretation of the increase in persistence which suggests the efficacy of
stabilization policy.

2.6   An Accounting

It is time now to take stock of our review of Romer's arguments and
her critics and the international evidence and come to some conclusion
concerning the accuracy of Romer's new estimates compared to the
original estimates. But before taking a definitive position, it is worthwhile to review several key points.

First, if nothing else, this debate has provided extensive evidence of
the *fragility* of estimates of annual GNP and unemployment for the
earlier periods in the United States. Extrapolating an extremely large
component of GNP from the narrow base of commodity output is
fraught with potential errors. Interpolating employment on the basis
of output indices is also a fragile procedure. Hopefully the days of
unreflective use of nineteenth-and early twentieth-century GNP and
unemployment data are over.

Second, even using Romer's GNP estimates, the cross-country comparisons place the United States in the group of most volatile countries
for the pre World War II era. Regardless of any corrections to Kuznets's
procedures, the basic fact is that commodity output in the United
States was very volatile in itself. Field's (1980) comparisons of the
United States, Germany, and the United Kingdom using narrowly
defined commodity series illustrates this point. The volatility of commodity output translates into relatively volatile GNP by any account.
However, the data that Kuznets had available already included this
volatile sector. What is at issue in Romer's challenge is whether the
remainder of GNP was equally volatile.

Third, once more using Romer's estimates, the cross-country comparisons indicate that the United States again experienced more reduction in volatility of GNP as measured by the ratio of standard
deviations than most of the other countries. Only Sweden, Australia,
and perhaps Canada exhibited a greater fall in the volatility of GNP. It
is fair to group the United States with those countries that experienced
the most reduction of volatility. By any reasonable account, the pre
World War I era was more volatile than the post World War II era.
The business cycle has been dampened in the United States.

With these perspectives in mind, let us re-examine the controversy
for the United States. Is Romer guilty, as Lebergott argues, of using
pseudo-laws to impose her will on the data? Or, is it more accurate to
follow Romer's characterization that Kuznets and Lebergott were at

times just psuedo-Hempelians, not recognizing that they were implicitly imposing their own laws, albeit implicit ones, upon the data?

As we discussed in our review of the methods, one defense of the procedures of Lebergott and Kuznets was that they were actually working within a different paradigm of historical research, weaving their assorted facts from a variety of different sources into a convincing whole. Indeed, in some cases, this was true: Lebergott's own discussions revealed a sensitivity to proper choices for series used for interpolation as well as the importance of reconciling diverse facts.

Unfortunately, this picture is too idealized for the estimates of Kuznets and Lebergott as a whole. Kuznets, at the end, was forced to assume fixed distribution margins within decades to convert commodity output to GNP while Lebergott did, at times, interpolate employment one-for-one on the basis for output. Both writers would have preferred to have the additional data to pursue their task along the lines of the traditional historian, piecing together a consistent whole. But the data limitations forced both investigators to rely on less satisfactory procedures.

The critics of Romer who accepted her methods, Weir and Balke and Gordon, arrive at estimates not too dissimilar from her own. This partly arises because of an iterative process by which ideas of the critics are embodied in refined estimates. Romer's final GNP estimates are actually more volatile than some of the measures advocated by Balke and Gordon. When the unemployment data are extended to the 1890s, and it is hard to see why we would want to exclude a decade with serious unemployment problems in our comparisons, Weir's estimates are roughly as volatile as Romer's. Finally, if the rhetoric is swept away and all parties admit that the pre World War I economy was more volatile than the post World War II economy (although perhaps by not so much as was previously thought), the differences between Romer and her critics appears to be second-order.

Concentrate now on the numbers. From table 2.1, the standard deviation of GNP growth according to Romer is 4.0 percent in the early period and 2.7 percent in the postwar period. The prewar period was 50 percent more volatile than the later period or, alternatively, volatility fell roughly one-third. We have seen that by comparative standards, this was a relatively large fall. But what about absolute standards? Do we need a host of detailed explanations to account for this change or is this the type of change we might expect based on changes that are familiar to us within the postwar economy?

Recall that Arthur Burns placed great weight on the host of institutional features that led to the stabilization of income to the private sector — dividend smoothing by large corporations and automatic stabilizers. How large might these factors be?

The only way possibly to arrive at an estimate of these stabilizing features of the economy is by means of a familiar econometric model. The objections to this approach are well known. All large models are susceptible to the Lucas critique, which implies that they may give misleading answers to fundamental simulations. In addition, if households have access to perfect capital markets then institutions which smooth disposable income may have no effect. The counter-objections are also well known. No one has yet nor perhaps ever will produce a large, calibrated econometric model which meets the Lucas critique. The evidence on liquidity constraints is not conclusive but a wide range of studies find evidence of binding constraints especially during business cycles. Objections aside, there is still no alternative to an econometric model.

What do simulations with an econometric model show? The most comprehensive study was performed for the Joint Economic Committee by Donald Kiefer (1980) using the DRI model. He essentially compared the results of two simulations. In the first simulation, he shocked the consumption and investment equations to produce a base case with a business cycle. In the alternative simulation, he kept all the key taxes in the DRI model (personal, corporate, social security, and excise) at a constant percent of full employment or potential output.

Before presenting the results, it is important to raise a few cautions. Major changes in econometric models often make them unstable and it appears that this became a problem in the simulations. For example, the model failed to converge for an alternative simulation in which all taxes but personal income taxes were held at constant proportions of nominal GNP. In addition, the DRI model emphasizes the financial market consequences and their effects on interest rates more than many other models. Finally, monetary policy was kept constant through all the simulations.

With these cautions in mind, the results of his simulations showed that the alternative economy without automatic stabilizers experienced 50 percent more volatility compared to the base case where volatility is measured by the standard deviation of output from potential output. Or expressed another way, automatic stabilizers reduced the variability of output by one-third.

This reduction is almost identical to the percentage reduction in Romer's revised data and the data for the postwar era. Although this is certainly not definitive, it does suggest that automatic stabilizers could be the principal factor explaining the change in the volatility of the economy over time.

Of course, there are other possibilities. The severity of shocks may have changed over time. Changes in wage and price flexibility have also been cited as important explanatory factors. We will discuss these issues in later chapters. Nonetheless, the approximate size of the dampening of business cycles for the United States appears consistent with the effect of automatic stabilizers. But there *is* something to explain – despite historical revisionism, the postwar business cycle has been dampened relative to the prewar cycle.

Notes

1 This observation and several others in the chapter are due to Paul Rhode.
2 Backus and Kehoe (1988) demonstrate that the results presented below are not just artifacts of growth rates. Alternative detrending methods produce similar results.
3 Although this chapter focuses on volatility, another important issue is the degree to which actual output remains near potential output. DeLong and Summers (1988) consider this criterion explicitly.
4 Using deviations from linear trends rather than growth rates changes the magnitude of the autocorrelations (increases them) but not their relationship between periods. For the United States, there is some increase in persistence in the postwar era.

3

The Challenge of Real Business Cycle Theory

3.1 Introduction

The idea that real factors in the economy (as opposed to monetary factors) are responsible for business fluctuations has deep historical roots. One old explanation of the Great Depression was that it began with population growth in the 1920s leading to first a housing boom and associated speculative fever and then eventually the collapse of asset markets. The hoary belief that business fluctuations were caused by sunspots is also a "real" theory. However, the term "real business cycle" as applied to macroeconomics in the 1980s is a term of art. It refers to the body of work based on the premise that it is possible to explain macroeconomic fluctuations based on models that (1) rely on complete optimization and market clearing methods of analysis and (2) rely on real factors, particularly changes in the level of technology, to account entirely for macroeconomic time series.

Looking back to the early 1970s, it would have been nearly impossible to envisage this development in macroeconomic theory. The late 1960s and the early 1970s was the time the profession was coming to grips with Milton Friedman's 1968 Presidential Address and its implications for the Phillips curve, inflation, and unemployment. The primary issues of the day were the interactions between real and monetary phenomena and issues of technology and growth were the focus of microeconomic, not macroeconomic research. The pathbreaking paper by Robert Lucas in the 1972 *Journal of Economic Theory* focused entirely on real and monetary interactions and deliberately abstracted from complications to the real side of the economy.

Several factors, some external to the profession but most internal, led some researchers from the preoccupations of the 1970s to real business cycles. Fluctuations in prices of agricultural goods and especially oil led to the term "supply shocks" and a resurgence of research in real factors that could cause economic fluctuations. The term supply "shock" itself, however, indicated that these phenomena were to be viewed as important but isolated episodes and not the central concern of business cycle theory. The main impetus for the development of real business cycle theory came from the lessons gained from the empirical implementation and testing of rational expectation models of the business cycle that featured monetary shocks.

From the very beginning, the issue of "persistence" of business cycles became an important topic for debate. The original versions of the rational expectation models of fluctuations featured monetary shocks as the source of unanticipated inflation and resultant confusion between absolute and relative price movements. These models, however, featured rational agents who would learn about their mistakes after they had made them. This implied that their mistakes in predicting inflation should be uncorrelated over time and thus serve as "white noise" shocks to the economy. But to turn white noise into the appropriate colors to match the frequencies of business cycles required a real sector that translated one-period mistakes into longer movements of output and employment. In other words, models had to exhibit "persistence" in order to account for the features of business cycles.

It did not take long to see a proliferation of models featuring persistence. One approach was to allow agents to learn only gradually about their mistakes. However, most of the mechanisms that were formulated focused on the real side of the economy. Capital, inventories, and costs of adjusting the labor force were the principal channels that were highlighted. Sargent's book (1979) provided the analytical tools to analyze such models in a linear-quadratic framework. Indeed, chapter 16 of his book provided a complete equilibrium account of the labor market based on optimizing models of demand and supply for labor which featured persistence mechanisms, costly labor demand and substitution of leisure, on both sides of the market. Shocks to either demand or supply could cause persistent movements in real wages and employment. The "persistence" problem, at least in principle, was fully solved.

The other problem that confronted rational expectation models of the business cycle featuring monetary shocks was that they required that monetary variables were not fully observable. If they were, the models would predict no relation between money and output because money was fundamentally neutral in these market-clearing models. Critics of these models quickly pointed out that in most advanced economies there is a proliferation of information about monetary aggregates and that models which rested on unobservable money were tenuous.

There were several responses to this basic criticism. Lucas (1987) defended unobservability of money as a proxy for the practical costs of information in a world with a vast multitude of price information. As perhaps an indication of the seriousness with which supporters of these models took these criticisms, Barro and Hercowitz (1980) took the observation that the basic monetary data were revised after they were initially published and tried to salvage the theory by defining unperceived money as the difference between the final figures and the initial figures for the money stock. This attempt did not work.

One can interpret real business cycle theory as an attempt to maintain the equilibrium approach to business cycle theory by jettisoning monetary shocks and putting the persistence mechanisms in the forefront. Or to put the research program in another light, to what degree is it possible to explain business cycle fluctuations with models based on perfect competition and feature persistence mechanisms but no monetary shocks?

This ambitious research project has built its very foundation on two controversial components. First, to the extent it is possible to explain fluctuation based on real models in which agents optimize without any externalities, then the first theorem of welfare economics dictates that the solution will be Pareto-efficient. Perhaps at some later date researchers will find it necessary to add externalities in order to match business cycle features. But at the present time the work is viewed as supporting propositions such as "economic fluctuations are optimal responses to uncertainty in the rate of technological change" (Prescott, 1986a, p. 21). Optimality, of course, is a much stronger claim than Pareto-efficiency but in the context of the typical representative individual model used in the analysis, there is no difference.

The other contentious feature is the lack of monetary institutions or monetary policy. Prescott (1986b) does not claim that monetary institutions never matter; he admits that periods of financial breakdown such as the Great Depression are not accounted for by his model. Nonetheless, he argues that postwar macro time series can be represented without explicit attention to monetary institutions. Of course, "explaining" a phenomenon with one variable that may be highly correlated with other variables is not definitive proof that the other variables do not matter. However, a successful accounting for the cyclical behavior of economic time series that relies solely on technological factors would be impressive.

The next section presents a prototype real business cycle model and discusses the manner in which these models are "calibrated" in order to model economic fluctuations. In this section we will also discuss what could be termed "internal criticisms" of the model, that is, those that would be debated by proponents of this class of model and which would be seen as the source of legitimate debate within the paradigm.

We then turn to three issues which bear directly on real business cycle models. The first concerns the time series properties of real GNP and other economic time series. There has been an extensive debate about whether real GNP should be modeled as a series in which there are deviations from a deterministic time trend or rather as a series in which shocks have a permanent effect on the trend in output. If shocks to GNP tend to be permanent, the plausibility of technological factors in accounting for GNP movements is enhanced. I shall survey the recent debate over the statistical properties of economic time series, present new evidence concerning our ability to interpret long-run properties of data from the time series that we have available to us, and provide a reinterpretation of some findings in the literature.

The second issue concerns the ability of real business cycle models to account for unemployment. On the surface these models appear to have nothing to say about unemployment because they focus on labor supply issues in cleared labor markets. However, an extension of the real business cycle model by Gary Hansen (1985) enriches the model to allow for unemployment, although unemployment for which there is full insurance. However, his model and other similar models of implicit contracts which feature insurance have implications for the behavior of consumption of employed and unemployed workers. Some recent evidence of the consumption of employed and unemployed workers will be examined to determine if it is consistent with models that feature insurance.

Finally, the last part of the chapter turns to monetary issues. One strong implication of real business cycle models is that changes in monetary regimes should have no effect on the stochastic behavior of real variables. Even apart from the Great Depression, this century has witnessed a number of significant changes in monetary regimes. Inflation was purged from the economy in the early 1920s and early 1980s. The Fed–Treasury Accord and the actions of the Eisenhower administration in the early 1950s ended the pegging of bond prices that persisted from World War II. The world moved off a fixed exchange rate system in the early 1970s and the late 1970s witnessed a dramatic change in the actual operating system of the Federal Reserve. If the time series behavior of real variables appears to shift at these junctures, this is evidence against the real business cycle approach.

3.2 The Real Business Cycle Model

The structure of the prototype real business cycle is quite straightforward. Preferences for the representative individual are given by the time-separable utility functional:

$$E_0 \sum_{t=0}^{\infty} \beta^t \, u[c_t, \, 1 - h_t] \tag{3.1}$$

where $0 < \beta < 1$ is the rate of time preference, c_t is consumption, h_t is hours of work from a total of one unit of available time, and E_0 is the conditional expectation operator. A convenient specialization for the instantaneous utility function is:

$$u[c_t, \, 1 - h_t] = \log c_t + A \log (1 - h_t) \tag{3.2}$$

Production is given by a Cobb–Douglas technology:

$$y_t = Z_t k_t^a \, h_t^{1-a} \tag{3.3}$$

where k_t is the capital stock and Z_t is technological parameter. This parameter is the sole source of randomness in the model and follows the stochastic process:

$$Z_{t+1} = \rho Z_t + \bar{\varepsilon}_{t+1} \tag{3.4}$$

where the $\bar{\varepsilon}_t$'s are independent and identically distributed and bounded away from zero. The mean of the $\bar{\varepsilon}_t$'s is $1\!-\!\rho$ which yields an unconditional mean of one for the Z_t's.

Two more constraints complete the description of the problem. Output can either be consumed or invested (x_t):

$$y_t = c_t + x_t \tag{3.5}$$

and the capital stock in period $t+1$ depend on the net effect from depreciation and investment:

$$k_{t+1} = (1 - \delta) \, k_t + x_t \tag{3.6}$$

A social planner would maximize equation (3.1) subject to (3.2)–(3.6). An identical solution would arise if the representative individual maximized (3.1) subject to constraint (3.2) and (3.6) and the budget constraint:

$$c_t + x_t = w_t \, h_t + r_t \, k_t \tag{3.7}$$

where w_t and r_t are the wage and rental rates and equal to the marginal products of labor and capital respectively. The theorems of welfare economics in this case ensure that a decentralized competitive solution will be equivalent to the social planning problem of maximizing the expected utility of the representative worker. This would not be true in the presence of externalities.

Although it is reassuring to an economist studying this problem that it has two equivalent solutions, there remain computational difficulties in actually calculating explicit solutions. The problem as stated is a nonlinear dynamic optimization problem whose solution generally involves complicated and expensive numerical methods. However, with judicious quadratic approximations, solutions to the problem are straightforward.

The solution method is described in the appendix to this chapter. Once the solution is found, the model can be simulated by picking initial values for the capital stock and technology parameter and then drawing realizations of $\bar{\varepsilon}_t$'s from its distribution.

Before any simulations can be performed, it is necessary to calibrate the model by specifying values for the parameter in the utility function, the depreciation rate, capital's share, and the parameters of the process driving technical change. Estimates of the depreciation rate and capital's share are relatively noncontroversial but the precise specification of the utility function and parameters of technological change are not.

The coefficient on the logarithm of leisure in the utility function, A, will determine the sensitivity of labor supply to the real wage. This determines the degree of *intertemporal substitution* in the model and is critical to its performance. A positive productivity shock in the model shifts out the production possibility frontier for the economy. However, since the shocks eventually dampen, there are incentives to both work more and accumulate more capital during good times. The higher the degree of intertemporal substitution, the larger will be the response of labor supply (employment) in the model.

As Prescott (1986a) discusses, early versions of real business cycle models, similar to this prototype, did not exhibit enough fluctuations in employment to match actual time series for data for the United States. Kydland and Prescott (1982) modified the model by replacing the leisure term in the utility function with a distributed lag on leisure. This was justified by the notion that a household builds up a stock of "leisure capital" which is also an input to the production of composite household goods in the tradition of Gary Becker's work. This has the effect of increasing intertemporal substitution. Prescott cites some evidence from micro panel studies supporting the idea that a distributed lag of leisure, not just leisure itself, belongs in the utility function. Another alternative to increased intertemporal substitution is to adopt Hansen's (1985) unemployment version of the model with insurance. As we will see later in the chapter, this has the effect of increasing the economy's employment response to shocks even if the individual utility functions themselves exhibit little intertemporal substitution. Both these approaches are controversial but a high degree of intertemporal substitution is critical for performance of the model.

Even more controversial are the procedures to model technical change. Real business cycle models follow our prototype model in that technical change follows a first-order autoregressive process with an autoregressive parameter close to but less than 1. The key parameter to be determined is the variance of the shock to technology. As Lucas (1987) pointed out, early versions of these models chose the variance of shocks to technology to generate the same output variance as for the US economy. However, this was not intellectually very satisfying because one of the claims of real business cycle models is that the macro phenomena they generate are based on specific parameters gleaned from micro studies − a rigorous, thoroughgoing microfoundation. Picking a convenient number for the variance of technical shocks does not fulfill the claims of this program.

In later work, Prescott took an alternative approach and calibrated the variance of technical shocks from the variance of the "Solow residual" in US time series. Under perfect competition, a Cobb−Douglas production function with a multiplicative parameter can be transformed into an equation which decomposes the growth in output into the growth of technical progress plus the growth of labor and capital inputs weighted by their factor shares. Thus, subtracting the weighted growth of inputs from the growth of output will yield an estimate of the growth of technical progress. Prescott computes these residuals and finds that the time series pattern for the residuals matches the hypothesized autoregressive pattern and has a variance which will produce "sufficient" variance for real output in simulations.

There have been two important criticisms leveled at this approach. The first focuses on the lack of specificity of the technical shocks. What precisely are the shocks that caused say, the boom in the 1960s or the deep recession of the early 1980s? Is there any independent way to identify them other than by noting that there was a boom in the early period and a recession in the later one? Moreover, what is the nature of technological know-how that allows output actually to fall in a recession?

Prescott defends his model not by pinpointing the origin of the shocks but by appealing to our modeling strategies in other areas of economics. We are quite comfortable in talking about "demand shocks" or "consumption shocks" even when they are nothing more than residuals in our estimated equations. Why should we treat technology shocks any differently? Moreover, we have also become accustomed to the notion that small random shocks may accumulate in ways to generate stochastic cycles and this may be the process generating macro technology shocks.

A second, and perhaps more serious charge, is that the Solow residual fails to measure technical change. Robert Hall (1986), in fact, attributes all cyclical variation in the Solow residual to monopoly power and none to technology shocks. Hall's argument is that using the Solow residual to measure technical change presumes perfect competition. Suppose that producers operate under conditions of monopoly with prices exceeding marginal cost by a constant mark-up factor, μ, related to the elasticity of demand. With capital fixed in the short run, marginal cost is the change in labor costs divided by the change in output adjusted for any technical change. If wages are constant, this relation becomes:

$$\frac{\text{marginal}}{\text{revenue}} = \frac{P}{\mu} = \frac{w\Delta h}{\Delta y - \left(\frac{\Delta Z}{Z}\right)y} = \text{marginal cost} \qquad (3.8)$$

where the last term in the denominator reflects the growth in output that would have occurred in the absence of any change in labor inputs and is the product of growth of technical progress and the output level.

Solving (3.8) for the growth rate of output yields:

$$\frac{\Delta y}{y} = \mu\left(\frac{wh}{Py}\right)\left(\frac{\Delta h}{h}\right) + \frac{\Delta Z}{Z} \qquad (3.9)$$

This expression decomposes the growth of output into two components. The first is the growth of labor input times labor's share (wh/Py) times the mark-up factor. The second is the rate of technical change or the Solow residual. If the mark-up coefficient is one, indicating perfect competition, then subtracting the growth of labor input weighted by labor's share will give an estimate of the Solow residual. But with $u > 1$, this procedure fails.

$$\frac{\Delta y}{y} - \left(\frac{wh}{Py}\right)\frac{\Delta h}{h} = (u - 1)\left[\frac{\Delta h}{h}\right] + \frac{\Delta Z}{Z} \qquad (3.10)$$

With monopoly power, the right-hand side becomes the sum of the Solow residual and the product of $(u - 1)$ and the growth of labor input. If $\Delta Z/Z$ were constant but an investigator incorrectly assumed perfect competition and measured the conventional Solow residual, he would find a procyclical "Solow residual," corresponding to the procyclical movement of labor input, but the procyclicality would be due solely to the presence of monopoly power.

The presence of monopoly power also can account for another important phenomenon. If one regresses the growth rate of output on the growth rate of labor input, the coefficient is usually close to one. As equation (3.9) indicates, under perfect competition, this number should be equal to labor's share which is roughly in the neighborhood of 0.75. The fact that a regression yields "too high" a value used to be termed the "short-run increasing returns to labor."

Real business cycle models have a ready explanation for this result. The error term in the regression with capital fixed is, as indicated in equation (3.9), the Solow residual. Since labor input is positively correlated with technology shocks in real business cycle models, the coefficient in the regression will be upwardly biased. In fact, one problem with real business cycle models is that they find too high a correlation between employment and output. Prescott attributes this primarily to measurement error in labor inputs and believes that "theory is ahead of measurement" in this area.

Monopoly power, however, can also explain the regression findings because with monopoly, the coefficient in the regression is the product of labor's share and the mark-up factor which exceeds one. Thus, the presence of monopoly also makes it difficult to distinguish between the presence of technology shocks and the cyclical implications of monopoly power.

Turning to issues of empirical implementation, Prescott detrends the United States data before comparing his model to the data. His method removes all components of the data that have frequencies greater than about eight years.[1] Although the purpose of this exercise is to highlight the cyclical properties of the real business cycle models, it is a bit odd that models which are based on integrating growth and trend considerations should abstract from trend growth.

The project of matching characteristics of the data with the simulations of the model has progressed within the research program of real business cycles and has improved as the underlying models have become more complex. There is no reason to expect this process not to continue. However, two troublesome areas remain.

The first problem concerns the method of matching simulated output with actual data. In most economic models that we want to take seriously, we specify the structure and try to estimate the parameters and then test the restrictions implied by the model. Real business cycle models fail this test and would clearly be rejected by conventional econometric methods.

The other problem stems from the fact that only one shock, the technology shock, drives the entire system. Data for the United States, show that lagged output has predictive power for investment behavior or "Granger-causes" investment. This is the empirical basis for the accelerator model of investment. With one shock driving both investment and output in real business cycle models, neither series will Granger-cause the other. How can these models account for the observed output–investment link? Sargent (1986) argued that capital is more poorly measured than output, and with these assumptions on measurement error it is possible to obtain the Granger-causal ordering observed in the data. Saving the model by appealing to asymmetries in measurement error is an ingenious but not fully persuasive approach.

3.3 Trends and Cycles

A typical econometric practice in the 1970s was to fit a regression of the log of real GNP on a time trend and then use the residuals as a measure of the business cycle. The justification for this practice was that potential output followed a path closely approximated by an exponential time trend and cyclical fluctuations were simply deviations from this trend.

In the 1970s economists began to become more seriously interested in the statistical properties of economic time series. Partly this was a function of the apparent success of Box−Jenkins methods or ARIMA models (autoregressive integrated moving-average models) in outpredicting large econometric models. Box−Jenkins methods for analyzing real GNP departed from the practice of linear detrending the log of GNP. Instead their recommended procedure (Box and Jenkins, 1976) was to take first-differences of the log of GNP and then proceed to analyze the autoregressive and moving average part of the resulting time series.

This may seem to be simply a technical issue but Nelson and Plosser (1982) forcefully argued that potentially much more was at stake than mere econometric practice. They argued that what underlied each practice was a different view of the economy with regard to the ultimate impact that shocks would have on the economy. Formally, Nelson and Plosser drew a contrast between *trend-stationary* models and *difference-stationary* models and argued that most familiar economic time series fell into the latter category. They also contended that this distinction had strong implications for the type of theories that could plausibly account for cyclical fluctuations.

To present these ideas, it is useful to develop a bit of notation. Let L be the lag-operator, that is, $L^n X_t = X_{t-n}$. $A(L)$ will indicate a polynomial in L of the form $A(L) = 1 - \theta_1 L - \theta_2 L^2 -- \theta_n L^n$.

Trend-stationary models represent a vision of the world with a smoothly growing trend with stochastic deviations from that trend. Equation (3.11) represents a variable Z that (e.g. log GNP) grows smoothly over time

$$Z_t = \underbrace{a + bt}_{\text{trend}} + \underbrace{A(L)\bar{\varepsilon}_t}_{\text{cycle}} \qquad \bar{\varepsilon}_t \text{ white noise} \qquad (3.11)$$

but is also subject to shocks $\bar{\varepsilon}_t$ which persist through time but eventually die out after a period corresponding to the highest power of the lag operator. Shocks, therefore, temporarily affect the deviation of Z_t from trend but have no effect on the long-run trend itself. If one wished to forecast Z far into the future, only the trend term would be relevant because the cyclical effects would have disappeared by that time. Detrending Z_t by a linear time trend is appropriate in this model.

Difference-stationary models allow the *change* in Z_t ($\Delta Z_t = (1-L)Z_t = Z_t - Z_{t-1}$) to be buffeted by shocks:

$$(1-L)Z_t = \Delta Z_t = \mu + B(L)\,\tilde{\eta}_t \qquad \tilde{\eta}_t \text{ white noise} \qquad (3.12)$$

In this model, Z increases by μ each period in the absence of any shocks. A shock η_t will eventually have no long-run effect on the change in Z_t (or growth rate if the variable is in logs) but will have a *permanent* effect on the *level* of Z_t. Consider a simple version of (3.12), a random walk without drift:

$$Z_t - Z_{t-1} = \eta_t \qquad (3.13)$$

A shock η_t will raise Z_t this period but in the absence of any future shocks, Z will be at this permanently higher level. Or, in other words, the "trend" level of GNP is now stochastic and permanently affected by shocks. If the log of real GNP followed the simple random walk, then a recession in which GNP fell by 2 percent would lead to a "permanent" fall in GNP by 2 percent − or at least until new disturbances changed the trend level.

A stochastic process is termed "stationary" if it has a constant mean (p) and constant variance and autocovariances, that is, $E(Z_t-p)(Z_{t+k}-p) = \gamma_k$, independent of t. The trend-stationary process is stationary once the time trend is removed. The difference-stationary process is stationary in the first differences but will be nonstationary in the levels. Conditional on an initial value for Z_{t-1} (say Z_0) the variance of Z_t for a random walk, for example, grows over time according to the formula $t\,\sigma_\eta^2$ and thus is not independent of time. Finally, because we can write difference-stationary processes as $(1-1{\cdot}L)Z_t$, we say that they have a "unit root" in their representation.

Simply writing a stochastic process in the form of (3.12) does not guarantee that it is difference-stationary. If the lag polynomial $B(L)$ can be factored into $(1-L)C(L)$, that is, it has a "unit root" itself, then the unit root terms will cancel and the process will be trend-stationary. As an example, consider the process:

$$(1-L)Z_t = \tilde{\varepsilon}_t - \theta\,\tilde{\varepsilon}_{t-1} = (1-\theta L)\varepsilon_t \qquad (3.14)$$

For $|\theta|<1$, this process is difference-stationary. But at $\theta=1$ the $(1-L)$ terms cancel and we have that $Z_t = \tilde{\varepsilon}_t$ which is a trend-stationary process. This example also shows that if θ is close to 1, a long-run impact from a shock $[(1-\theta)]$ will exist but it will be small. Thus, it is also important to know how "significant" is the unit root representation.

Nelson and Plosser argued that there are radical implications for business cycle theory if most economic series exhibit significant difference-stationary behavior. Apart from non-neutralities of money (which are generally ignored for cyclical analysis), we do not expect monetary shocks to permanently affect the trend level of output. Thus, if most economic series are difference-stationary, it would be difficult to justify monetary theories of the business cycle. This would leave the door open for real business cycle theory or any theories which would allow for the possibility of permanent effects from shocks to output.

Real business cycle theories with permanent productivity shocks would not be the only story consistent with difference-stationary data. Another example is the model of hystersis of unemployment developed by Blanchard and Summers (1986). In their model, employed workers belonged to unions whose sole objective was to maximize the well-being of their current members. If a negative monetary shock reduced output and employment, the reduced number of workers would set a higher wage to increase their income and ignore the plight of the laid-off worker. In the absence of any further shocks, the unemployment rate would remain at a higher level with a corresponding lower output level. The monetary shock would be permanent. However, this is a model which abandons the notion of a "natural rate" of unemployment in order to account for difference-stationary behavior. Traditional natural rate models with monetary shocks would not be consistent with the difference-stationary processes.

Nelson and Plosser presented three arguments in favor of a difference-stationary specification for real GNP and other variables. First, they noted that the autocorrelation function of the level of GNP dampened very slowly – the correlation between current log real GNP and the level six years prior was 0.69. This slow dampening is characteristic of nonstationary processes such as random walks.

They also noted that the autocorrelation function of the first difference of log real GNP had a significant positive autocorrelation at lag 1 but was not significant for higher lags. They argued that if the true specification was trend-stationary, then the first difference of the trend-stationary specification would be:

$$(1-L)Z_t = b + (1-L)A(L) \, \bar{\varepsilon}_t \qquad (3.15)$$

The last term would have powers in L higher than 1 unless $A(L) \equiv 1$. In that case, the model would reduce to

$$Z_t = b + \varepsilon_t - \varepsilon_{t-1}$$

which has an autocorrelation at lag 1 of -0.5. However, the data indicated that the autocorrelation at lag 1 was positive, not negative. This casts doubt on a trend-stationary specification.

Finally, they conducted formal statistical tests to test for unit roots. Consider the regression:

$$\Delta Z_t = c \, Z_{t-1} + \sum_{i=1}^{n} a_i \, \Delta Z_{t-i} + \varepsilon_t \qquad (3.16)$$

If the coefficient c is negative, then the process will be stationary. If $c = -0.1$, for example, equation (3.16) can be written as $Z_t = 0.9 Z_{t-1} + \ldots$ which is trend-stationary. Test statistics, however, differ from usual least squares rules but have been tabulated by Dickey and Fuller and thus are called "Dickey–Fuller" tests. Nelson and Plosser could not reject the null hypothesis that $c = 0$, or, in other words, could not reject the difference-stationary process. They were careful to note that this test does not have much statistical power against near non-stationarity in levels. Nonetheless, all three diagnostic methods pointed in the same direction.

Dickey–Fuller tests are not fully adequate when the representation of ΔZ_t has moving average components under the null hypothesis. Stock and Watson (1986) and Peron and Phillips (1987) perform alternative tests. Peron and Phillips can reject the null hypothesis of unit roots for log GNP for the periods 1869–1975, 1869–1919, and 1869–1940 but not for the postwar era. These results could arise either if the tests had low power in small samples or the stochastic process for GNP changed in the postwar era.

Finding unit roots, however, does not mean that they are economically significant. Campbell and Mankiw (1986) proposed a simple way to assess their significance. Suppose we estimate the equation:

$$\Delta Z_t = A(L) \bar{\varepsilon}_t \qquad (3.17)$$

then the *sum* of the coefficients in $A(L)$ will indicate how much a shock will permanently change the level of Z_t. For trend-stationary processes the sum will be zero, while for a random walk, the sum will be 1. On quarterly postwar data, Campbell and Mankiw find a sum approximately equal to 1.6. This means than a 1 percent fall in GNP will eventually led to a 1.6 percent fall in the level of GNP! The process they find for postwar GNP is more persistent than a random walk.

Another approach taken by Watson (1986), Clark (1986) and Nelson and Plosser is to consider "unobserved component" models. A series Z_t is decomposed into a trend component, Y_t, which follows a random walk and a stationary cyclical component $C_t = C(L)\eta_t$.

$$\begin{aligned}
Z_t &= Y_t + C_t \\
Y_t &= Y_{t-1} + \bar{\varepsilon}_t \qquad (3.18) \\
C_t &= C(L) \, \tilde{\eta}_t
\end{aligned}$$

We observe only the sum of the two components but, with additional assumptions (necessary to ensure identification) it is possible to estimate the variance of the permanent component and the variance of the cyclical component. While Nelson and Plosser tried to argue on a priori grounds that $\sigma_\varepsilon^2 > \sigma_\eta^2$, Watson and Clark both found much less persistence of shocks in estimated unobserved component models for postwar data than implied by the results of Campbell and Mankiw. In contrast to a long-run estimate of 1.6 percent from a 1 percent shock, Watson finds the long-run effect is 0.6 percent in quarterly postwar data, a substantially lower effect.

Cochrane (1988a) developed another measure of the significance of the unit root but, even more importantly, put the debate with its conflicting estimates into some perspective. Cochrane suggested that we look at the variance of what he termed "long differences" or $\frac{1}{k} \text{var}\ (y_{t+k} - y_t)$ as k grows large. Recall that for a random walk, the variance grows with the time interval k. Dividing by k would give precisely the variance of the one period shock. For trend-stationary processes, the variance of long differences (with the trend substracted out) will converge to a constant; hence, dividing by k will drive this statistic towards zero. Moreover, Cochrane goes on to show that as $k \to \infty$, this measure equals the variance of the permanent component ($\bar{\varepsilon}_t$) in the unobserved component model.

Cochrane also calculates the ratio $\dfrac{1/k\ \text{var}\ (y_{t+k} - y_t)}{\text{var}\ (\Delta y_t)}$ which he terms the "variance ratio." As k grows large, this equals the variance of the permanent component divided by the overall variance of the first difference. This is a natural measure of the significance of the permanent component. For 1869–1984, he estimates the variance ratio to be about 0.4, close to the spirit of Watson's results. Using Monte-Carlo methods, he also calculates confidence intervals and concludes he cannot reject trend-stationary specifications for the entire sample.

To gain some additional perspective on these questions, it is valuable to think, as Cochrane did, in terms of the frequency domain. Any stationary time series has a spectral representation which essentially gives the variance of the time series at different frequencies. Low frequencies correspond to trend-like or long period movements in the data. Higher frequencies correspond to shorter period or more cyclical movements in the data. Since we are interested in the long-term properties of stochastic processes, the frequency domain has a natural appeal. The spectrum of stochastic process for yearly data plots the variance by frequency, v, where frequencies range from 0 to $\frac{1}{2}$ cycles per year. The period T of a cycle is $1/v$ so that a frequency of 1/16 cycles per year, for example, corresponds to a cycle of 16 years.

Cochrane proves that as $k \to \infty$ his statistic converges to the spectral density of Δy_t evaluated at a frequency of zero, that is, for very long (infinite) cycles. By comparing the spectral density near zero with its values for higher frequencies it is possible to evaluate the importance of long-run components in a time series.[2]

A simple example can illustrate this method. Consider the process from equation (3.14):

$$(1-L)y_t = \varepsilon_t - \theta\varepsilon_{t-1} \qquad \begin{array}{l} \varepsilon_t \text{ white noise} \\ \text{var } (\varepsilon_t) = 1 \end{array} \qquad (3.19)$$

For this series, the autocovariance function (which gives the auto-correlations as a function of the lag) is

$$R(m) = E(\Delta y_{t+m} \cdot \Delta y_t) \qquad \text{which equals:}$$

$$R(m) = \begin{cases} 1+\theta^2 & m=0 \\ -\theta & m=1, -1 \\ 0 & m\neq 0, 1, -1 \end{cases}$$

The spectrum for process, which gives the variance by frequency, is related to the autocovariance function by the following formula:

$$f(v) = \sum_{m=-\infty}^{\infty} R(m)\, e^{-2\pi ivm} \qquad (3.20)$$

which in this case reduces to:

$$\begin{aligned} f(v) &= (1+\theta^2) - \theta[e^{2\pi iv} + e^{-2\pi iv}] \\ &= (1+\theta^2) - 2\theta \cos (2\pi v) \end{aligned} \qquad (3.21)$$

Figure 3.1 plots the spectrum for four values of θ:

$$\begin{array}{ll} \theta = 0 & \text{random walk} \\ \theta = 1 & \text{stationary white noise} \\ \theta = \tfrac{1}{2} & \text{"Watson"} \\ \theta = -\tfrac{1}{2} & \text{"Campbell–Mankiw"} \end{array}$$

For the random walk case, the spectrum is flat. This means that the short-run effects are the same as the long-run effects as is true for a random walk. For $\theta=1$, the unit roots cancel and we have a stationary process which has *no* variance at zero since the long-run effects are zero.

The two other cases are designed to correspond to Watson's and Campbell and Mankiw's results. For $\theta=\tfrac{1}{2}$, the long-run effect is smaller than the short-run effects; for $\theta=-\tfrac{1}{2}$, the long-run effects exceed the short-run effects. Using the sum of the coefficients in the moving average representation gives a similar qualitative account of the time series.[3]

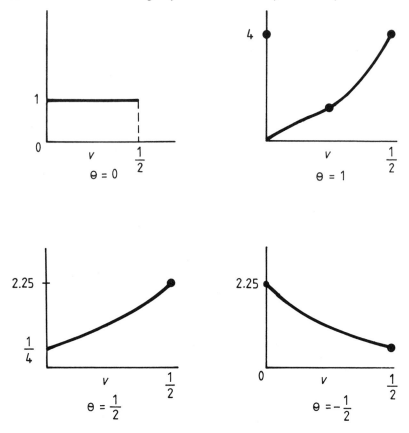

Stochastic process : $\Delta y_t = \varepsilon_t - \theta \, \varepsilon_{t-1}$

Figure 3.1   Spectrum for alternative processes

While all statistical techniques have potential problems, the problems with the variance ratio measure are actually illuminating. With
finite data, we can never estimate the spectrum precisely at zero or for
"infinite" cycles. Analogously, the variance of long differences equals
zero when k equals the sample size because there is only one observation. But this tells us precisely that it is very difficult to estimate very
long-run effects for relatively short periods of data. In practical applications, we have to assume that the spectrum is smooth at frequencies
near zero.

Figure 3.2 contains a plot of the spectrum of the growth of real

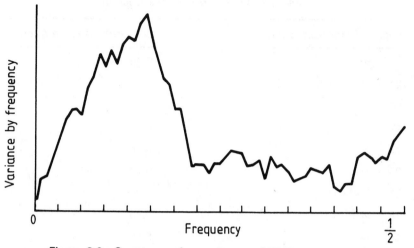

Figure 3.2   Spectrum of growth rate of GNP, 1870–1983

GNP (Δlog GNP) from 1870 to 1983 or for 114 years. We smoothed the spectrum with a relatively wide window or bandwidth of 11/114= 0.096 which assumes the spectrum is smooth in the neighborhood $\left[v - \dfrac{0.096}{2}, v + \dfrac{0.096}{2} \right]$. There is a peak at about 6.4 years indicating a possible cycle at that period. More importantly for our purposes is the average value of the spectrum "near zero" as compared to the overall variability of the series. Table 3.1 gives the average value "near zero" divided by the total variance of the series Δy for different portions of the spectrum "near zero" or for differing notions of the long run.

The estimate of the spectrum at a zero frequency is 0.4 when the overall variance Δy is normalized to 1, precisely what Cochrane estimated. As the interval near zero widens, the percentage increases. In a sense, as we widen the interval, we are double-averaging to obtain an estimate near zero because we are already using a wise bandwidth to smooth the spectrum. As the graph indicates, as we widen the interval we begin to include variance from the cyclical peak.

Although these estimates are below those offered by Campbell and Mankiw, they do indicate a permanent component in the long GNP series. But is this surprising? Figure 3.3 plots the residuals from a regression of log GNP on a time trend. The picture resembles what one would obtain by detrending a random walk − long pseudo-cycles artificially induced by the detrending. It does stretch plausibility to

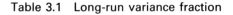

Table 3.1   Long-run variance fraction

Length of long run (years)	Long-run variance fraction
∞	0.40
127 − ∞	0.50
64 − ∞	0.54
42 − ∞	0.60
32 − ∞	0.66
25 − ∞	0.73
21 − ∞	0.8
18 − ∞	0.85
16 − ∞	0.88

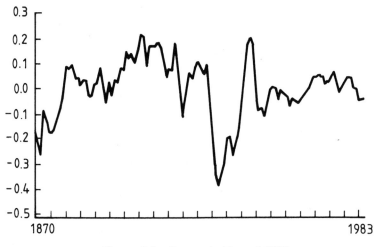

Figure 3.3   Detrended log of GNP

believe that potential output grew smoothly through two world wars, several major depressions, the growth of the welfare state, and the radical shift from an agricultural based economy to one based on services and manufacturing.

For shorter time periods, the possibility for trend-stationary series is more plausible. But the message from Cochrane's analysis is that we must look at very long frequencies and this requires long time series. Changing the sampling interval to quarterly data does not help.

Why do Campbell and Mankiw using ARIMA models find stronger long-run effects than do Watson, Clark, and Cochrane? As Cochrane pointed out, ARIMA models do a very good job of capturing the cyclical movements in time series but are not very helpful in measuring long-run effects. Maximum likelihood methods will fit models that do well over frequencies in the spectrum − not just the low frequencies that are critical for assessing the long run effects of shocks. Unobserved component models are essentially restricted ARIMA models that can be restricted in such a way as to capture long-run frequencies. This can explain why unobserved component models and spectral methods give similar results. Still, there is a large degree of uncertainty. Applying the spectral methods used above to quarterly postwar data (1948:1−1984:4) produced estimates close to one for the variance at zero divided by the overall variance.

Not all the analysis has concentrated on a single time series. Evans (1986) considered the possibility that the bivariate relationship between unemployment and output could illuminate the long-run behavior of output. Evans found that when unemployment was high, output grew faster than normal and, in addition, that unemployment was a stationary series. Thus, a negative shock that precipitated a recession would, through the increase in unemployment, generate a process returning the economy through trend. Evans's overall results were quite similar to those of Watson and Clark for postwar data.

Two propositions can perhaps summarize these diverse empirical findings:

1 It is inherently difficult to pin down the long-run effects of shocks to the level of GNP. Different statistical methods often yield conflicting results.
2 Postwar economic data exhibit more persistence than earlier years. Statistical tests can never reject difference-stationary specifications in the postwar era but can for earlier periods.

Can conventional Keynesian or classical monetary models explain these results?

With regard to the first point, it is possible that conventional monetary models can produce near non-stationary behavior and thus make definitive statistical testing impossible. West (1988) has shown how monetary policy can produce near nonstationary behavior for real variables in John Taylor's overlapping contract model extended to include real interest rates − a model analyzed in the next chapter. If the Fed smoothes interest rates and makes them follow processes close to random walks, then shocks to interest rate will cause output to also approximate a random walk. The Taylor model already generates persistence through the structure of its wage contracts. This persistence is increased when interest rate shocks tend to persist. Since prices are sticky, nominal interest rate movements tend to lead to corresponding real rate movements. Since output depends on real rates, persistent behavior in interest rates is translated into persistent output movements.

West's finding suggests it will be difficult to assess definitely whether series are generated from stationary or nonstationary models since plausible stationary models produce near nonstationary behavior. Moreover, the uncertainties in this debate raise the larger issue of whether our econometric methods coupled with our relatively limited data are powerful enough to detect long-run relationships between economic variables. McNamara and Sheffrin (1989) simulated a modified Solow growth model with a fixed saving rate to address this question. The growth model included government spending. Changes in government spending stimulated output (though Keynesian mechanisms) in the short run but crowded out investment and led to lower output in the long run. They examined whether commonly advocated econometric methods could detect the negative long-run relationship between government spending and GNP in data artificially generated by this model.

Their results were largely negative. Co-integration methods, advocated by Engle and Granger (1987), always suggested a positive long-run link between government spending and output. Data filtered to remove short-run fluctuations did suggest negative relationships but ones which were much smaller than the true relationship. A method related to unobserved components also failed to detect the true relationship. These results suggest that the inconclusiveness of the trend-cycle debate could be endemic to *all* attempts to discover long-run properties in economic data.

West also offered an explanation for the increase in persistence in the later time series for the United States. Mankiw et al. (1987) argue that the behavior of interest rates changes around the period surrounding the foundation of the Federal Reserve. In particular, interest rate movements became smoother at this time. According to West's model, this should lead to more persistence in output movements after the founding of the Fed.

The European and Canadian evidence is roughly consistent with this story. Campbell and Mankiw (1987) argue in favor of random walk behavior for a wide variety of European countries in the postwar period. For the early period, the results suggest less persistence. Except for Denmark, simple Dickey–Fuller tests cannot reject the null hypothesis of nonstationarity. However, the evidence reviewed in the last chapter suggests that autocorrelations were higher in the postwar era for most European countries. These results were particularly pronounced for Sweden and Italy. For example, the estimated moving average regressions for the growth rate of GNP Sweden from table 2.7 were:

$$1875-1914 \qquad gswede = 0.026 + \varepsilon_t - 0.62\varepsilon_{t-1}$$
$$1955-1983 \qquad gswede = 0.029 + \varepsilon_t + 0.52\varepsilon_{t-1}$$

In the postwar era, the sum of the moving average coefficients is 1.52, close to the long-run effect estimates of Campbell and Mankiw for the United States. But for the earlier period, the sum is only 0.38.

DeLong and Summers (1988) offer a complementary explanation of the increase in persistence in output that appears to have occurred in a variety of countries. Suppose we consider decomposing actual output into potential output and deviations of output from potential. Potential output is likely to follow a nonstationary process as the result of changes in technology and permanent shifts in labor force participation. Deviations of output from potential, on the other hand, are likely to be stationary series. If stabilization policy has been successful in the postwar era, either from discretionary policy or automatic stabilizers, the variance of the stationary component of the time series should decrease. This, however, would make the overall time series for output more persistent. It is precisely the success of stabilization efforts that makes the postwar time series appear more persistent!

Delong and Summers (1988) show that if potential output follows a random walk and the deviation of output from potential is white noise, then the first-difference of output will follow a moving average process with a negative coefficient, just as in the case of prewar Sweden. The coefficient of the moving average component will be a function of the relative variances of potential output and the white noise deviation of output from potential. As the variance of this white noise term decreases, that is, as stabilization becomes more effective, the absolute value of the moving average term decreases. The "unit root" in the output representation increases and output becomes more persistent.

In the last chapter we documented that there was some dampening of economic fluctuations in many countries, particularly in the United States, despite recent revisionism. According to the DeLong and Summers interpretation of the trend-cycle debate, effective stabilization of GNP should lead to more persistence in time series as the forces determining potential output become more visible. This is observed quite clearly for the United States and Sweden, two countries in which the economy has been effectively stabilized. Ironically, the trend-cycle debate which initially began as an attack on conventional macro, may actually support conventional conclusions about the historical effectiveness of stabilization policy.

A final irony. Before Prescott examines US data to compare it to the predictions of his model, he uses a detrending procedure which allows only a very minor permanent component. This practice came under attack by Nelson and Plosser whose purpose was to widen the scope for real business cycle theories. Econometrics respects no one.

3.4 Consumption and Unemployment

All competitive equilibrium models of economic fluctuations, including the early real business cycle models, have been criticized for ignoring unemployment. In his Yrjo Jahnsson Lectures, Lucas is quite blunt in confronting this claim. "The work of 'equilibrium' macroeconomists is often criticized as though it was a failed attempt to explain unemployment (which it surely fails to do) instead of as an attempt to explain something else" (1987, p. 48).

Lucas argues that in some instances we do want to understand the phenomenon of unemployment *per se*, for example, if we wished to analyze the consequences of alternative unemployment compensation schemes. Search theory, job matching, models of implicit contracts, and models of incomplete information may enable us to understand the creation and destruction of employer−employee relations and the various forms that they take. But for analyzing fluctuations, Lucas believes the best research strategy for economic fluctuations is to focus on the employment−nonemployment margin and leave as second-order questions the precise allocation of time for nonemployed individuals. "If the hours people work − *choose* to work − are fluctuating it is because they are substituting into some other activity ... but such a finer breakdown need not substantially alter the problem Kydland−Prescott have tried to face of finding a parameterization of preferences over goods and hours that is consistent with observed employment movements" (pp. 67−8).

This is a bold and honest statement of a research strategy. But not all macroeconomists will want to have unemployment become an applied topic in labor theory courses and removed from the macro curriculum. Nor is it evident that there are no crucial feedbacks from workers who term themselves "unemployed" to the aggregate fluctuations in the economy. Nor has it been the view of proponents of real business cycle theory who have tried to incorporate unemployment into real business cycle models.

Gary Hansen (1985) developed an implementable real business cycle model with unemployment which has become the real business cycle school's answer to the unemployment challenge. The model was motivated by the observation that most changes in aggregate hours worked in the economy arise because of changes in the number of employees, not the number of hours per employee. Another motivation was the controversy concerning whether there was sufficient inter-temporal substitution in leisure across time to generate sufficient fluc-tuations in hours worked over the cycle.

In Hansen's model, workers can either work a full day or remain at home. Fixed costs will generally lead to some lumpiness in labor supply and the all-or-none labor supply decision is a useful approxi-mation of this phenomenon. However, this all-or-none decision creates a nonconvexity in the general equilibrium problem and this means that not all Pareto-efficient allocations can be supported by competitive equilibrium. Since the solution method for real business cycle models, as outlined in the first part of this chapter, relies on the equivalence of competitive equilibrium and the planning solution, this creates a prob-lem for the solution method.

The problem is "solved" by convexifying the economy by allowing individuals to trade lotteries in employment in which the winners of the lotteries work but all individuals receive the expected amount from working.[4] This is equivalent to having complete insurance against unemployment. *Ex ante* all workers are identical. *Ex post* some work and some do not but all are fully insured against unemployment.

Hansen develops the model for the case in which consumption and leisure are separable in the utility function and the results for this case are striking. The utility function is the same as in equation (3.2), namely:

$$u(c_t, 1-h_t) = \log c_t + A \log (1-h_t) \tag{3.22}$$

Workers either work h_0 hours with probability α_t (the probability of winning the lottery) or 0 hours with probability $1-\alpha_t$. Their expected utility is thus:

$$E(U) = \log c_t + \alpha_t A \log (1-h_0) \tag{3.23}$$

For the economy as a whole $h_t = \alpha_t h_0$. Substituting into (3.23) expected utility becomes:

$$E(U) = \log c_t + B(1-h_t) - B$$
$$B = \frac{-A\log(1-h_0)}{h_0} \tag{3.24}$$

Two points emerge from equation (3.24). First, consumption is independent of employment status. This follows from the availability of unemployment insurance and, as we will discuss below, the separ-ability of labor and leisure. Second, the utility function is now *linear* in leisure implying an infinite elasticity of substitution of leisure between different periods regardless of the elasticity in the original function.

This provides a high degree of responsiveness of labor supply to movements in the real wage which is derived from aggregation considerations — not properties of individual preferences.

The model has the striking properties that consumption is independent of labor market status and that the unemployed are better off than the employed! Unemployed workers both enjoy leisure and receive the same income (consumption) as employed workers. Are these unintuitive and unappealing properties inherent to the model? It is possible for employed workers to be better-off if consumption and leisure are nonseparable but the conditions essentially require leisure to be an inferior good. Rogerson and Wright (1986) study these issues in detail but the essence of their argument can be more easily seen in an example of insurance but with continuous values for labor supply.

Let the concave utility function over consumption and leisure be given by $U[c, l]$. If there is perfect insurance, then the marginal utility of consumption will be constant regardless of the amount of leisure:

$$U_c\,[c,\ l] = k \text{ all } l \qquad (3.25)$$

This result is easy to derive. An insurance firm can offer a payment in state i of "a" which occurs with probability π as long as it takes an amount "b" where $b = \dfrac{\pi}{1 - \pi}\,a$ in state j for any two states i, j. This will be a fair bet of expected value zero for the risk-neutral insurance company. The worker can maximize expected utility across the two states by choosing "a" or:

$$\max_{a}\ \ \pi U[w^i + a,\ l^i] + (1 - \pi)\,U[w^j - b,\ l^j]$$

The first-order condition for an optimum yields equation (3.25); the marginal utility of consumption is constant across states.

With insurance, the relationship between consumption and leisure can be found by totally differentiating (3.25) or:

$$\frac{dc}{dl} = -\frac{U_{cl}}{U_{cc}} \qquad (3.26)$$

Since U_{cc} is negative by concavity, the sign of dc/dl depends on the sign of U_{cl}. For workers with more leisure to have less utility than workers with less leisure (the employed), we require $dc/dl < 0$ which implies $U_{cl} < 0$. However, this is only a necessary condition for the employed to be better off.

Total utility between workers can be compared by differentiating the utility function with respect to leisure taking into account the effects from the provision of insurance (equation 3.26):

$$\frac{dU}{dl} = U_c \frac{dc}{dl} + U_l$$

$$\frac{dU}{dl} = U_c \left(\frac{-U_{cl}}{U_{cc}} \right) + U_l$$

(3.27)

For total utility to increase with more employment, the right-hand side must be negative. However, the right-hand side of (3.27) is the expression which determines the sign of the income effect in a standard labor—leisure problem (see Rosen, 1985). A negative value of this expression means that leisure must be an inferior good. This is not the traditional wisdom in labor economics.

Allowing for complete insurance thus leads to an unsatisfactory theory of unemployment. Lucas (1987) stresses that analyzing incomplete insurance markets leads to the development of interesting economic models and he is certainly correct on this point. But the equivalent of complete insurance markets is essential for both the traditional computational methods and policy conclusions of real business cycle models. Without these markets, the economy cannot be modeled as a maximizing representative agent and the outcomes are not necessarily Pareto-efficient. Perhaps more important is that there are an unlimited number of ways in which markets may be incomplete. The externalities and spillovers that can result from incomplete markets can entirely change the character of the underlying models.

Dynarski and Sheffrin (1987) provide evidence that the effects of unemployment on the consumption of workers are very large and difficult to reconcile with a view of substantial insurance. They first developed a model of workers who had access to capital markets but no insurance and faced different stochastic environments. Workers in jobs with high layoff rates but also high recall rates would not be expected to have substantial drops in consumption upon becoming unemployed because their consumption decision takes into account the significant possibility of becoming unemployed. Workers in jobs with low layoff and low recall probabilities would decrease consumption substantially upon unemployment both because the unemployment was largely unexpected and prospects for recall poor.

In their empirical analysis, Dynarski and Sheffrin found that blue-collar workers and white-collar workers fit the typology of the high layoff—high recall and low layoff—low recall groups respectively. Using the food consumption measure from the Panel Study on Income Dynamics, they found that, as anticipated, white-collar workers exhibited substantially more significant drops in consumption upon becoming unemployed.

The magnitudes of the decreases in consumption following unemployment were so large, however, that they cast doubt on plausibility of the permanent income hypothesis for unemployed workers as well as demonstrating the lack of insurance. Using cross-sectional grouping measures familiar from the permanent income literature, Dynarski and Sheffrin had estimated the marginal propensity to consume food out of permanent income. They could then calculate from the decrease in food consumption an estimate of the decrease in permanent income implied by the behavior of food consumption following unemployment.

Table 3.2 compares the decrease in permanent income and disposable income for blue- and white-collar workers per week of unemployment. The ratio of the change in permanent income to the change in disposable income is a rough indicator of the discount rate necessary to rationalize the data with the permanent income hypothesis. (For an infinitely lived worker, a $1 temporary fall in disposable income would lead to a drop in permanent income of $1 times the interest rate.) For blue-collar workers, the implicit interest rate is 65 percent per year. This is very high but perhaps not inconsistent with the estimates in Hall and Mishkin (1982), particularly if the blue-collar group contains a high percentage of liquidity-constrained workers. For white-collar workers, the implied interest rate is 229 percent per year! Dynarski and Sheffrin offer alternative conjectures to explain this number but it is abundantly clear that white-collar workers do not have access to good markets to insure against labor risk.[5]

These findings do not preclude the development of alternative real business cycle models that include employment. But they do indicate that the current models fail to come to grips with the phenomenon of unemployment. A serious macroeconomic account of unemployment must account for the lack of insurance and its possible repercussions in equilibrium theory.

Table 3.2   Unemployment and consumption

	Decrease per week of unemployment		
	(1) Disposable income	(2) Permanent income	Ratio (2)/(1)
Blue-collar workers	$43	$28	0.65
White-collar workers	$51	$114	2.29

Source: Dynarski and Sheffrin (1987)

3.5 Monetary Regimes

Most real business cycle models do not include money or financial assets and therefore cannot explain financial phenomena. Since their purpose is the analysis of real fluctuations, the neglect of monetary features is important only if this prevents an account of real cyclical features of the economy. Prescott (1986b) admitted that these models could not account for periods of financial breakdown, such as the Great Depression, but argued that monetary factors appeared superfluous in less dramatic times.

Financial and real variables interact in all economies. For real business cycle theory, money and finance are epiphenomena, not central to the underlying real factors governing the economy. This view would not be tenable if shocks or disturbances, initiating in the financial sector, had important effects on real variables. One way to test this idea would be to determine whether exogenous monetary disturbances influenced real variables using conventional econometric methods. The difficulty with this strategy rests in assuring the exogeneity of monetary shocks.

An alternative method is to study the behavior of real variables around periods of monetary regime shifts. Although institutional changes can also be endogenous, there is more consensus that particular regime changes can be viewed as exogenous to the real sector. This strategy has been followed by Huizinga and Mishkin (1986), Walsh (1987b), and Driskill and Mark (1988).

Huizinga and Mishkin regress the *ex post* real interest rate on a series of variables in order to obtain consistent estimates of the *ex ante* real rate process. They then explore for shifts or breaks in the process by estimating separate regressions about the hypothesized shift point. In the postwar era, they found significant regime changes near October 1979 corresponding to the well-publicized change in operating procedures by the Federal Reserve. They also found another shift in 1982, again corresponding to a shift in Fed policy.

Huizinga and Mishkin also examined the early 1920s when the Fed departed from prior policy and raised the discount rate twice and also found a shift in the real rate process at that time. The early 1920s and the late 1970s were quite similar with regard to the behavior of real interest rates. Changes in Federal Reserve policy were accompanied by sharp reductions in the inflation rate and a significant rise in *ex post* and *ex ante* real rates of interest. In fact, Huizinga and Mishkin found that inflation variables had more explanatory power for real rates than traditional monetary variables.

Schwert (1986) and Walsh (1987b) questioned whether Huizinga and Mishkin were finding shifts in the real rate process stemming from changes in monetary policy or rather shifts occuring from changes in the inflation rate. Walsh showed that Huizinga and Mishkin's procedures could, in some circumstances, mistakenly find regime shifts in real rates when there were only shifts in the process driving inflation. Walsh argued that this probably was true in 1982 but that the October 1979 period was a legitimate regime shift.

Driskill and Mark (1988) tested a wide variety of real variables for monetary regime shifts. They examined the founding of the Federal Reserve, the Fed–Treasury Accord, and the two episodes identified by Huizinga and Mishkin. Their procedure was to estimate time series models for real variables including GNP, interest rates, durable and nondurable consumption as well as the GNP deflator and look for shifts in the time series processes for these variables at the regime shift points. They found that 60 percent of their potential break points were significant and that the processes for real interest rates and durable consumption always shifted with the regime.

The evidence on monetary regimes is even more dramatic when evidence from exchange rate regimes is considered. In a comprehensive study, Mussa (1986) examined the behavior of real exchange rates (the nominal exchange rate adjusted by the consumer price indices (CPIs) of the relevant countries) under both fixed and flexible exchange rate regimes. If monetary regimes did not matter, the behavior of real exchange rates should not vary systematically across regimes. Real exchange rates are relative prices of nation's output which affect real variables and, if real business cycle theory is correct, these relative prices should not depend on whether governments fix nominal exchange rates.

Mussa, however, found that the exchange rate regime had a profound effect on the behavior of real exchange rates. In particular, the variance of real exchange rates under flexible exchange rate regimes was substantially greater than under fixed rate regimes. This finding is consistent with the observed volatility of nominal exchange rates under flexible exchange rates coupled with relatively sticky domestic prices of goods and services.

Mussa's study was particularly impressive in the range of evidence he brought to bear on the question. One problem with comparisons of fixed versus flexible exchange rate regimes is that most countries departed from fixed rates at the time of the demise of the Bretton Woods agreements in the early 1970s. However, Mussa also considered evidence from the 1920s, from the Canadian experience of floating during the 1950s, and from the countries that participated in the European Monetary System (EMS), which pegged exchange rates among its members. One instructive case was Ireland. Ireland's currency was at one time pegged to the British pound but Ireland later joined the EMS. Mussa found that the behavior of Ireland's real exchange rate depended heavily on monetary regime. When it was pegged to the British pound, it was closely tied to movements in the British real exchange rate; after it joined the EMS, it was closely correlated with West Germany, the dominant member of the EMS.

These results indicate at a minimum that real business cycle models will have to be extended if they are eventually to match US time series. This will require sacrificing some of their simplicity and policy recommendations. It also will suggest to those not sympathetic to these models that regime shifts are not atypical and that monetary shocks have profound effects on real variables.

3.6 Conclusion

Real factors certainly do play an important role in economic development and economic fluctuations. The previous chapter suggested that railroad investment played an important role in the volatility of economic growth in several countries in the nineteenth century. The oil shocks of the 1970s had profound macro and sectoral effects throughout the Western world.

But it is a long distance from documenting the effects of real shocks on the economy to real business cycles. This chapter has raised several deep issues with models of real business cycles that have been developed to date. First, it is difficult to detect movements in technical change. Existing attempts to isolate movements in technical change are based on models of perfect competition and would give inconsistent results in the presence of monopoly power.

Second, the statistical literature on trends and cycles does not, as commonly believed, provide complete support for real business cycles. Conventional monetary models can generate near nonstationary time series which are difficult to distinguish from nonstationary models. Models that do not feature a natural rate (such as the unemployment hysteresis models) could also account for the time series properties that are observed. Moreover, the increase in the persistence of output apparent in a variety of countries can be construed as evidence in favor of successful stabilization policy. While real factors do affect potential output, stabilization policy may have reduced the gap between actual and potential output for a variety of economies.

Third, the behavior of consumption of individuals suggests that insurance against economic fluctuations is far from complete. Without full insurance, however, the economy is likely to behave quite differently from the manner predicted by real business cycle theory. These issues are considered in some detail in chapter 5.

Finally, real business cycle theory allows no role for monetary factors. Yet domestic and international evidence on changes in monetary regimes suggest that real variables are significantly affected by regime shifts. This is most evident in the behavior of real exchange rates in floating versus fixed exchange rate regimes. The evidence from these historical experiments is inconsistent with the basic thrust of real business cycle models.

It is important to develop models which integrate growth and fluctuations. It is also an old macroeconomic theme. Solow's growth theory (which ignored fluctuations) was a partial response to Harrod's worries about investment, cycles, and growth. Modern real business cycle theory, however, cannot dispense with either monetary factors or consideration of incomplete markets if it hopes to explain growth and cycles. Including these two phenomena will, however, change the character and policy conclusions of the current theory.

Notes

1 See Prescott (1986a) for a precise description of his detrending method.
2 Shumway (1988) provides a clear introduction to spectral methods.
3 For the precise relation between Cochrane's variance ratio and the sum of the coefficients, see Campbell and Mankiw (1987).
4 Rogerson (1988) develops this idea in more detail.
5 Cochrane (1988b) presents a related test of consumption insurance.

Appendix

Following Hansen and Sargent (1988), here are the steps necessary to solve an approximate version of the basic real business cycle model, equations (3.1)–(3.6).

1 Set $Z_t=1$ (its unconditional mean) and study the deterministic analog to the real business cycle model.
2 Calculate the steady-state values $k_t=k^*$, $h_t=h^*$ for the deterministic model. These can be derived from the steady state of the Euler conditions as (a) the marginal rate of substitution between consumption and leisure equals the real wage or marginal product of labor and (b) the rental rate or marginal product of capital equals the sum of the depreciation rate plus the rate of time preference.
3 Substitute $Z_t k_t^\alpha h_t^{1-\alpha} - x_t$ for consumption in equation (3.2) and take a second-order Taylor expansion in Z_t, k_t, h_t around the steady-state values calculated above.

The instantaneous utility function can then be written as

$$X_t' q X_t + u_t' \, r \, u_t + 2 \, u_t' \, w \, X_t$$

where

$$X_t = \begin{bmatrix} Z_t \\ k_t \\ 1 \end{bmatrix} \qquad u_t = \begin{bmatrix} h_t \\ x_t \end{bmatrix}$$

and q, r, and w are matrices given by the Taylor expansion.
The full problem then can be written as:

$$\max_{(X_t, \, h_t)} E_0 \sum_{t=0}^{\infty} \beta^t \, [X_t' \, q \, X_t + u_t' \, r \, u_t + 2 \, u_t' \, w \, X_t]$$

subject to:

$$X_{t+1} = \begin{bmatrix} \rho & 0 \\ 0 & (1-\delta) \\ 0 & 0 \end{bmatrix} X_t + \begin{bmatrix} 0 & 0 \\ 0 & 1 \\ 0 & 0 \end{bmatrix} u_t + \begin{bmatrix} 1 \\ 0 \\ 0 \end{bmatrix} \bar{\varepsilon}_{t+1}$$

or

$$X_{t+1} = a \, X_t + b u_t + g \, \bar{\varepsilon}_{t+1} \tag{A1}$$

The problem has now been transformed into a standard linear-quadratic optimal control problem with additive uncertainty. The solution to this problem is well known (Sargent, 1987 chapter 1) and has the form that the control vector $u_t = (h_t, x_t)'$ is a time-invariant function of the current state vector X_t or

$$u_t = -f x_t \tag{A2}$$

where: $f = \beta \, (\beta b' P b + r)^{-1} \, (a' P b + w)$ and P is the limit as $t \to \infty$ of the Ricatti equation:

$$P_{t+1} = q + \beta a' P_t a - \beta^2 \, (a' P_t b + w') \, (r + \beta b' P_t b)^{-1} \, (b P_t a + w)$$

starting at $P_0 = [0]$.

Equation (A2) gives the current values for labor input and investment as a function of the current state vector. The dynamics of the state vector itself can be found by substituting (A2) to (A1)

$$X_{t+1} = (a - bf) X_t + g \bar{\varepsilon}_{t+1} \tag{A3}$$

The matrices a and b were part of the data of the problem and f was calculated in the solution. To simulate the economy, simply pick initial values for k_0 and Z_0 and then draw realizations of the $\bar{\varepsilon}_t$'s from its distribution. Once the time paths for X and u have been determined it is possible to calculate any desired statistic in the model.

4

Is Price Flexibility Destabilizing?

4.1 Introduction

The past several years have witnessed a reconsideration of the issue of whether too much wage and price flexibility could be destabilizing. The question itself seems a bit odd in the postwar macroeconomic debate. Most of the challenges to conventional Keynesian postwar macro have come from equilibrium theorists. For these theorists, market clearing and therefore perfect price flexibility is the preferred mode of analysis and the question of "too much" price flexibility is not easily addressed in this framework. Moreover, the traditional Keynesian models are predicated on wage and price inflexibility as a source of output fluctuations. Remove wage and price inflexibilities and the models quickly become variants of classical models.

All the recent papers on the possibilities of wage and price inflexibilities stem directly from Tobin's "Keynesian Models of Recessions and Depression" (1975). In this paper, Tobin observed that a low price level had different effects on the economy than a falling price level. Lower prices would increase real balances and through both the Pigou and Keynes effects would tend to stimulate output and restore the economy towards full employment. Falling prices, however, to the extent that they created expectations of deflation, could lead the economy away from full employment. Expectations of deflation would lead to a shift away from capital and into money thereby raising real rates of interest — the so-called "Mundell effect." Higher real interest rates could deter interest-sensitive spending and thus counteract the effects of a lower price level. Thus, to the extent that lower prices led to a belief in continuing falling prices, the overall impact of lower prices could be contractionary and destabilizing.

Although the idea that deflation could be destabilizing is foreign to the postwar macroeconomic tradition, Tobin and others recognized that similar ideas have an illustrious macroeconomic past. Indeed, chapter 19 of the *General Theory* has been rediscovered in which

Keynes argued that downward wage flexibility would not only be insufficient to restore the economy back to full employment but could, in fact, further destabilize the economy. DeLong and Summers (1986a) also cite Irving Fisher as another example of a prominent macro theorist who warned of the dangers of price flexibility.

But, in fact, Fisher and Keynes had very different views concerning price flexibility and stability. Keynes was much more interested in dispelling the claim that wage flexibility would be sufficient to restore the economy to full employment than he was in demonstrating that wage flexibility would necessarily be destabilizing. Fisher, on the other hand, had a much more pessimistic and profound view of the dangers of deflationary price movements and stressed a different transmission mechanism from Keynes. Yet, as we will see, the recent literature has focused almost exclusively on the part of Keynes's writings that stressed the perversities that could arise from expectations of deflation and ignored Fisher's analysis. It is worthwhile to examine both Keynes's and Fisher's rich treatments in more detail.

Keynes treated wage flexibility in depth in chapter 19 of the *General Theory*. He started the chapter by noting that the issue of wage flexibility was crucial to the development of his theory but that his remarks could not have been understood without the material in the previous chapters of the *General Theory*. Specifically, changes in money wages would only have a lasting effect on output and employment if they led to a change in aggregate demand. "Thus the reduction in money-wages will have no lasting tendency to increase employment except by virtue of its repercussions either on the propensity to consume for the community as a whole, or on the schedule of marginal efficiencies of capital, or on the rate of interest" (p. 262).

Following this plan, Keynes spends the bulk of the chapter outlining and discussing the various ways that a fall in money wages would affect aggregate demand. Keynes itemized seven explicit channels by which changes in money wages would influence aggregate demand. First, a fall in money wages would reduce prices and shift the distribution of income away from workers and also away from entrepreneurs to *rentiers*. This would most likely lower the marginal propensity to consume and reduce aggregate demand. The second and third channels applied to open economies under fixed exchange rate systems. A fall in money wages would tend to decrease the relative price of domestically produced goods and thereby stimulate net exports and aggregate demand. On the other hand, the reduction of the standard of living implied by the changing relative prices would decrease real income and could lead to a fall in consumption spending.

The fourth channel can best be described today as an intertemporal substitution mechanism as described in chapter 3 above. According to

Keynes, a fall in money wages relative to money wages in the future would stimulate investment because it would increase the marginal efficiency of investment. On the other hand, if the fall of money led to anticipations of a further fall, this would lead to postponement of investment plans.

The fifth mechanism worked through the financial system. A fall in money wages and prices would reduce the demand for money and lead to declines in interest rates. The primary effects would be felt on short-term rates not long-term rates. Moreover, if the fall in money wages disturbed political confidence, this could lead to an increase in liquidity preference and an increase in interest rates.

The sixth channel anticipates modern discussions of informational limitations and the non-neutrality of money. To the extent that entrepreneurs mistake a general fall in money wages for a specific fall in money wages, this may stimulate confidence and break a cycle of pessimistic expectations. However, to the extent that workers make the same mistake they will strongly resist this decline and labor unrest could result.

Finally, the last factor Keynes highlights concerns the effects of indebtedness. "On the other hand, the depressing influence on entrepreneurs of their greater burden of debt may partly offset any cheerful reactions from the reductions of wages. Indeed, if the fall of wages and prices goes far, the embarrassment of those entrepreneurs who are heavily indebted may soon reach the point of insolvency − with severely adverse effects on investment" (p. 264).

Which factors did Keynes believe were most important? Interestingly, he ignored distributional and insolvency issues and focused on the intertemporal substitution channels and effect on interest rates. He discussed in detail the possibility that wage deflation could raise *ex ante* real rates of interest:

> The most unfavorable contingency is that in which money-wages are slowly sagging downwards and each reduction in wages serves to diminish confidence in the prospective maintenance in wages ... On the other hand, it would be much better that wages should be rigidly fixed and deemed incapable of material changes, than that depressions should be accompanied by a gradual downward tendency of money-wages, a further moderate wage reduction being expected to signalize each increase of, say, 1 percent in the amount of unemployment. For example, the effect of an expectation that wages are going to sag by say, 2 percent in the coming year will be roughly equivalent to the effect of a rise of 2 percent in the amount of interest payable for the same period. (p. 265)

We will call this the *Keynes ex ante effect* and show below that it is the basis for almost all the models discussing the effects of wage and price flexibility. The effect can be illustrated in the context of a simple IS–LM model treating expected inflation (π^ε) as an exogenous variable. The IS curve depends on the real interest, r, while the LM curve depends on the nominal rate $r+\pi^\varepsilon$. In standard form:

$$\text{IS:} \quad \underline{y} = c(y) + I(r) + \overline{G}$$
$$\text{LM:} \quad \overline{M/p} = L(r+\pi^\varepsilon, y)$$

We plot these equations in $r-y$ space in figure 4.1. Decreasing expected inflation shifts the LM curve to the left increasing real interest rates and decreasing output. This is the Keynes *ex ante* effect. Note that it requires some price inflexibility to operate. If the price level was free to adjust to maintain output at full employment, the IS curve would then determine a unique real interest rate independent of the rate of inflation. Price inflexibility coupled with variations in expected inflation are the two keys to the Keynes *ex ante* effect.

To complete the story, Keynes also thought that effects through interest rates would be weak. Moderate falls in money wages and prices would only effect short-term interest rates and not long-term

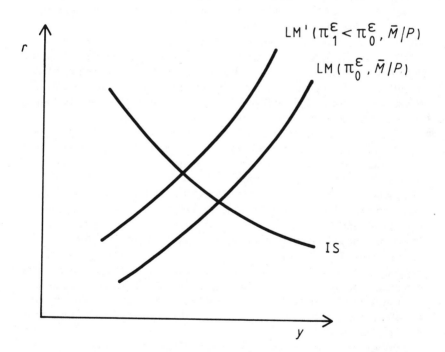

Figure 4.1 The Keynes *ex ante* effect. A decrease in expected inflation shifts the LM curve to the left leading to an increase in real interest rates and a fall in real output

rates. More dramatic falls would most likely increase uncertainty and probably raise long-term interest rates. Deflation runs into the same pitfalls as does monetary policy in a depression. Small increases in the supply of money will only affect short-term interest rates but large changes are likely to disturb investor confidence and fail to lower long-term rates. Neither deflation nor monetary policy can cure a depression.

Reading through Keynes's entire chapter, one is left with the impression that he was much more interested in arguing that deflation could not cure a depression rather than the proposition that deflation or wage flexibility was the *source* of depressions. This approach was taken partly to prevent the rest of his arguments in the *General Theory* from being undercut, but it also seems that deflation was more an abstract, theoretical evil rather than a familiar devil.

Irving Fisher's views on depressions detailed in *Booms and Depressions* and his 1933 *Econometrica* article "The Debt–Deflation Theory of Great Depressions" were quite different from Keynes. As the title of the *Econometrica* article suggests, in Fisher's view debt and deflation were the two chief ingredients of business cycles.

There were essentially nine factors that Fisher stressed in his accounts of depressions. Starting from a situation of overindebtedness (1), some event causes a change in confidence and distress selling. As bank loans are paid off and not extended, the money supply falls (2). This leads to a fall in prices (3) which Fisher terms "a swelling of the dollar" and a decline in both net worth (4) and profits (5). These lead to a reduction in output and employment (6) followed by increased pessimism (7), hoarding of money (8), and finally decreases in nominal interest rates coupled with increases in real rates (9).

Of course, Fisher recognized that these events would not occur precisely in this order. Hoarding or decreases in the velocity of money and pessimism, for example, would accompany the deflation and distress selling. Moreover, overindebtedness does not simply appear out of nowhere. In his book, Fisher discusses in detail how overindebtedness can arise. In a typical sequence, technological breakthroughs fuel legitimate demands for borrowing in order to earn excess returns. However, these legitimate demands for credit lead to typical speculative enthusiasms. Finally come the charlatans and crooks. "Probably no great crash has ever happened without shady transactions. Indeed, the disclosure of these is often the last straw which breaks the camel's back and precipitates the calamitous liquidation" (1932, p. 40). Periods of inflation can also lead to overindebtedness as it breeds illusions of easy profits.

Neither debt nor deflation by themselves are sufficient to trigger major depressions but the combination can be deadly. Fisher believed he unlocked the deep secret of depressions and describes the key secret with the enthusiasm of a religious convert: *"The very effort of individuals to lessen their burden of debts increases it, because of the mass effect of the stampede to liquidate in swelling each dollar owed.* Then we have the great paradox which, I submit, is the chief secret of most, if not all, great depressions: *The more debtors pay, the more they owe"* (italics in the original; 1933, p. 344). The very process of liquidating the debt leads through the banking system to a decline in deposits and eventually prices. The fall in prices outstrips the attempts to liquidate debts and real indebtedness rises. Thus, even the "good risks" are exposed to increased real debt burdens and potential problems even if they do not attempt to liquidate assets themselves.

Although both Fisher and Keynes discussed increases in real interest rates that accompany deflation, Keynes primarily focused on *ex ante* real rates while Fisher stressed *ex post* real rates. This is clear from his discussion in *Booms and Depressions* of interest rate movements. Unlike Keynes, who stressed the deterring effects of high *ex ante* real rates on investment decisions, Fisher emphasized the catastrophic effects on debtors of high *ex post* real rates or increases in their real indebtedness. To distinguish Fisher's views from Keynes', we will call Fisher's the *ex post theory of deflation.*

Before examining the plausibility and explanatory power of more recent models of wage and price flexibility, it will be useful to take a closer look at the historical evidence. Have wages and prices in fact become much more flexible in the postwar era?

4.2 Historical Trends in Price Flexibility

There is a general belief that since World War II wages and prices have become less flexible. Except for a brief spell right after the war, broad indices of prices have risen throughout the period. This stands in sharp contrast to the sharp deflations that marked the pre World War II era. But the question of wage and price flexibility is more subtle than these observations suggest. In fact, a reasonable summary of the available evidence is that the short-run response of inflation to changes in real GNP has not changed dramatically since 1870!

There, of course, has been considerable debate over these issues. Cagan (1979) measured the changes in wholesale prices from peak to trough in business cycles and concluded that price flexibility decreased sharply after World War II. Schultze (1981), however, found that other wage and price indices did not exhibit these patterns. Using a method similar in spirit to Cagan, he computed the change in wage or price inflation divided by the change of nominal income over business cycles and called the ratio the "flexibility coefficient." Schultze found that the flexibility coefficient did indeed decline for wholesale prices but that the flexibility coefficients for the GNP private nonfarm deflator and the CPI excluding food did not fall in the postwar era. While he found that manufacturing wages did exhibit more cyclical flexibility in the postwar era, a result similar to one reported by Sachs (1980), broader measures of wages did not exhibit dramatic changes and even the flexibility of manufacturing wages was small to begin with in the pre World War II era.

A fair reading of the Schultze and Cagan studies is that broad indices of prices and wages did not exhibit changes in cyclical variability over time but narrow indices did respond differently. With food included, Schultze found that the flexibility coefficient for the CPI did decline and that some decline was evident in the overall GNP deflator (in contrast to an actual increase in the private nonfarm deflator).

Yet, the methods employed in these studies are not fully satisfactory in that they fail to deal seriously with the obvious differences in the stochastic processes for inflation over time. A closely related problem is the treatment of the "expected inflation" term in standard Phillips curves. Let p denote the inflation rate, p^e the expected inflation rate, and y an index of the deviation of real GNP from potential output. Then a standard Phillips curve can be written

$$p = p^e + c * y \qquad (4.1)$$

where c is the coefficient linking movements in output to inflation, holding expected inflation constant. It is clear that the type of analysis conducted by Cagan and Schultze, in which changes in inflation are directly compared to changes in output, are only appropriate if the expected inflation term does not change. These considerations suggest that it would be best to estimate equation (4.1) with proxies for expected inflation and thereby determine the coefficient for "c".

Schultze (1986) and Gordon (1980) followed essentially this procedure and concluded that the short-run responsiveness of inflation to output did not change dramatically over time. Gordon's specification was slightly different in that he emphasized effects from the rate of change of output but he still concluded that the responsiveness of inflation to output had not changed over time. Both Schultze and Gordon conducted their studies using the GNP deflator. While Sachs's (1980) Phillips curve regressions using money wages in manufacturing do show a decrease in cyclical responsiveness, he admits (1982) that this pattern is not evident with data for the GNP deflator.

There is an important difference, however, between regressions for the postwar period and earlier periods. If last period's inflation rate is used as a proxy for the expected inflation rate, the coefficient on the lagged inflation rate is close to 1 in the postwar data but much smaller for other periods.

Table 4.1 illustrates the differences in regression estimates for the periods 1873−1914 and 1953−82. In each model, the inflation rate is regressed on the lagged inflation and the percentage deviation of real GNP from detrended output. The detrended output series in these regressions are seven-year centered moving averages of real GNP. For the early period, both the standard Kuznets−Gallman series and Romer's series (1986b) are employed.

Comparing the regressions using the Kuznets−Gallman data to those using the postwar data, the coefficient of output deviations is actually higher in the postwar era. Since the Romer data are less volatile, we would expect a higher coefficient using her data. Indeed, the estimated coefficient using her data is slightly higher but the differences are slight and not statistically meaningful.

The regressions for the earlier period do not explain nearly as much variance in inflation as the postwar regressions. This is largely due to the difference in the contribution of the lagged inflation term. Holding output constant, inflation is much more persistent in the postwar era. The coefficient on the lagged inflation rate is 0.92 compared to 0.22 in the earlier era. Nonetheless, the short run effects of output movements are virtually identical in the two periods.

Evidence from other countries is somewhat mixed but, if anything, suggests that the responsiveness of inflation to real output has increased

Table 4.1 Inflation regressions

1873−1914	(Kuznets−Gallman data)
	$P = 0.22\,P(-1) \quad + \quad 0.34\,[\text{GNP gap}]$
	$\quad\quad(0.14) \quad\quad\quad\quad\quad (0.19)$
	$\overline{R}^2 = 0.14$
1873−1914	(Romer data)
	$P = 0.22\,P(-1) \quad + \quad 0.41\,[\text{GNP gap}]$
	$\quad\quad(0.14) \quad\quad\quad\quad\quad (0.19)$
	$\overline{R}^2 = 0.11$
1953−1982	
	$P = 0.92\,P(-1) \quad + \quad 0.37\,[\text{GNP gap}] + 0.005$
	$\quad\quad(0.07) \quad\quad\quad\quad\quad (0.003)$
	$\overline{R}^2 = 0.83$

P, inflation rate measured by GNP deflator.
GNP gap, percentage deviation of GNP from trend defined as a centered seven-year moving average.
Standard errors in parentheses.

in the postwar era. In regressions not reported here (see Sheffrin and Liu, 1988), there is clear evidence that Italy, Sweden, and the United Kingdom all exhibit *increased* responsiveness of inflation to output movements in the postwar era regardless of the method used to detrend the data. Results for the other countries (Canada, Norway, and Denmark) were highly sensitive to the methods of detrending the data but none exhibited a sharp decrease in sensitivity in the postwar era. For all the countries, the persistence of inflation, as measured by the coefficients or lagged inflation variables, was much higher in the postwar era.

How should we interpret this consistent evidence from the regressions reported in table 4.1? Should the similar coefficients on output deviations indicate that price flexibility has not changed or should the larger coefficients on lagged inflation in the postwar regressions indicate a decrease in price flexibility? There is disagreement on this issue even within what would be thought of as the Keynesian camp. Schultze (1986) argues that the lagged inflation terms should be conceived of as inflation norms built into wage and price decisions and that these norms are subject to change, not with momentary fluctuations in the inflation rate, but with the underlying policy mechanisms governing the inflation process. Within the context of a fixed policy regime, the response of inflation to output movements has therefore not changed over time in the United States.

In interpreting similar regressions, Taylor (1986) argued that they indicated a decrease in price flexibility because the lagged inflation terms were really a proxy for long-term nominal contracts. The growth of long-term contracts in the postwar era led, in his view, to increased persistence in the inflation rate and less price flexibility.

As it will turn out, the recent models of the dynamics of price flexibility focus primarily on the coefficient linking aggregate demand to inflation ("c" in equation 4.1). The evidence is reasonably clear that this coefficient simply has not changed very much in the postwar era, at least for broad measures of price movements.

The next section discusses in detail some recent models of destabilizing price expectations. This material is somewhat more technical than the remainder of the chapter and, depending on tastes, the reader may wish to skim quickly over this material at first. The two principal conclusions of the section are: (1) it is possible to construct models in which increased wage flexibility is destabilizing but the results are sensitive both to the types of shocks that impinge on the model and the definition of price flexibility; (2) the historical evidence on the relationship between output and inflation is not consistent with the notion that a decrease in wage flexibility in the postwar era led to more stable output.

4.3 Models of Price Flexibility

The recent flurry of models of the effects of price flexibility on output stability are all formulated within the context of rational expectations. Despite continuing debate on whether rational expectations is the most appropriate empirical assumption in economic situations, there are essentially three reasons for employing it in these models. First, it is too easy to concoct a scenario for expectations (specifically, highly extrapolative expectations) that would automatically cause deflation to be destabilizing. Imposing this from the onset would beg the theoretical question. Second, the key issue under investigation is the operating characteristics of systems with differing degrees of price flexibility. Rational expectations analysis was designed essentially for these applications.

The last reason for preferring rational expectations models to analyze these issues is a somewhat technical one. The concept of "stability" used in rational expectations models is different than in other classes of models. In most practical applications of rational expectations models, there are unstable characteristic roots. The solution concept employed in solving models with these roots is, whenever possible, to choose initial conditions to eliminate the effects of these roots and to concentrate on the set of convergent solutions. On the other hand, in models which feature, for example, adaptive expectations, increases in the coefficient of adaptation can often cause a model to become unstable. This has the unpleasant implication that as expectations adjust more quickly and become more "rational", the model is more likely to "blow-up." The rational expectation solution concept prevents this occurrence.

In choosing models to study the effects of increasing price flexibility, it is natural to begin with models of a Keynesian type which feature some rigidities. John Taylor's (1979, 1980) model of overlapping wage contracts is ideally suited for this task because it features both nominal rigidities as well as rational expectations. Many of the papers use a modified version of the Taylor model to study the question of price flexibility.

It is worthwhile to begin our review of alternative models with a brief examination of the original two-period Taylor model. This will permit an easier discussion of the more complex variants of his model. The original Taylor model has a rather simple aggregate demand structure along with a more complex specification of aggregate supply. All variables are expressed in logs and as deviations from trends.

Aggregate demand is given by the quantity equation with units chosen so that the log of velocity is constant and equal to zero.

$$y_t = m_t - P_t \qquad (4.2)$$

This is equivalent to the assumption of interest-inelastic money demand.

Monetary policy is endogenous and policy authorities are allowed to respond contemporaneously to current price movements.

$$m_t = gP_t \qquad (4.3)$$

The parameter "g" measures the degree to which monetary policy accommodates price movements. Combining (4.2) and (4.3) gives the final expression for aggregate demand:

$$y_t = -\beta P_t \qquad \beta = 1-g \qquad (4.4)$$

If $\beta=0$ ($g=1$), monetary policy fully accommodates price movements and aggregate demand does not fluctuate. Higher values for β allow trade-offs between output and price movements.

The specification of aggregate supply begins with the key contract-setting equation. Workers set contract wages, X_t, for two periods. Contracts are overlapping with exactly half of the workers setting new terms in each period. Workers are assumed to be concerned about both the wages of the other group (their current wage and the wage they will set in period $t+1$) as well as the state of the economy that will prevail during their contract period.

$$X_t = \frac{1}{2}X_{t-1} + \frac{1}{2}{}_{t-1}X^\varepsilon_{t+1} + \frac{\gamma}{2}[{}_{t-1}y^\varepsilon_{t+1} + {}_{t-1}y^\varepsilon_{t+1}] + u_t \qquad (4.5)$$

The notation ${}_{t-1}X^\varepsilon_{t+1}$ stands for the conditional expectation of X_{t+1} given information at time $t-1$. The first two terms of the right-hand side are the wages (prevailing and future) of the other group. The state of the economy is measured by ${}_{t-1}y^\varepsilon_t, {}_{t-1}y^\varepsilon_{t+1}$ which are the expectations at time $t-1$ of the deviations of output from trend for periods t and $t+1$. The parameter γ is the key parameter of interest. It measures the sensitivity of wages to the output movement.

Finally, the only source of uncertainty or fluctuations in the economy is u_t, the shock to the wage-setting process. This is a nominal, supply-side shock which captures unpredictable elements and our uncertainty in understanding the dynamics of money wages.

The price level is given by a mark-up formula. Specifically, the price level is the (geometric) average of the prevailing money wages in the economy:

$$P_t = 1/2[X_t + X_{t-1}] \qquad (4.6)$$

To solve the model, use the aggregate demand and pricing equations (4.4 and 4.6) to eliminate the expected output terms in the contract-setting equations. Taking expectations at $t-1$, the resulting contract equation can be rewritten as a difference equation in the expected contract wage:

$$_{t-1}X^{\varepsilon}_{t+1} - 2c_{t-1}X^{\varepsilon}_t + _{t-1}X^{\varepsilon}_{t-1} = 0 \text{ where}$$

$$c = \frac{1 + \dfrac{\beta\gamma}{2}}{1 - \dfrac{\beta\gamma}{2}}$$

The solution for the contract wage will have the form $X_t = \rho X_{t-1} + u_t$ where the parameter ρ will be the function of the underlying parameters of the model.

The stochastic behavior of prices and wages can also be derived. Combining the solution for the contract wage with the pricing equation leads to an equation for prices:

$$P_t = \rho P_{t-1} + \frac{1}{2}(u_t + u_{t-1}) \tag{4.8}$$

where "ρ" is the same solution to the contract wage equation. The asymptotic variance of prices can be shown to be:

$$\sigma^2_p = \frac{\sigma^2_u}{2(1-\rho)} \quad \frac{\partial \sigma^2_p}{\partial \rho} = \frac{\sigma^2_u}{2(1-\rho)^2} > 0 \tag{4.9}$$

As γ, the wage-sensitivity parameter, ranges from 0 to ∞, ρ goes from 1 to -1. Since the variance of prices is increasing in ρ, increases in γ decrease the variance of prices.

Since output is given by $y_t = -\beta P_t$, the asymptotic variance of output is:

$$\sigma^2_y = \beta^2 \sigma^2_p \tag{4.10}$$

which is also decreasing in γ, the wage sensitivity parameter. In this version of the Taylor model, increased wage flexibility is clearly stabilizing. Both the variance of prices and output decrease with the sensitivity of wages to fluctuations in output.

The possibilities of instability arising from rapidly adjusting wages and prices is limited, in this model, by the absence of real interest rate effects. To include these effects, it is necessary to modify the aggregate demand side of the model.

To study the possibility of instability, it is necessary to introduce the real interest rate into aggregate demand. First, let output depend on the expected real interest rate:

$$Yt = -a\{i_t - E_t P_{t+1} + P_t\}. \tag{4.11}$$

Nominal interest rates are determined in the money market:

$$m_t - P_t = -\beta i_t \qquad \beta > 0. \tag{4.12}$$

Finally, let the Fed follow a nominal interest rate rule (which includes as a special case a constant money supply):

$$m_t^s = \alpha i_t. \tag{4.13}$$

The interest rate is measured in natural units while all other variables are in logs. Combining (4.11)−(4.14) yields the expression for aggregate demand:

$$y_t = aE_t P_{t+1} - bP_t \tag{4.14}$$

where

$$b = a\left[1 + \frac{1}{\beta+\alpha}\right]$$

We assume $\beta + \alpha > 0$, a condition satisfied by a constant money stock, which implies $b > a$. The aggregate supply side of the model remains the same and consists of the contract equation (4.1) and the pricing equation (4.6).

The solution to this model is described in the appendix to this chapter. Driskill and Sheffrin (1986) prove two key results for the model. First, for any feasible values of γ, b, a, there exists a unique, stable autoregressive parameter ρ^* for the wage process. Second, increases in γ, the wage flexibility parameter, always decrease the autocorrelation parameter ρ^*.

We can now examine the lag patterns of prices and output and also the responsiveness of the asymptotic variances of prices and output to changes in the wage flexibility parameter. The incorporation of the real rate makes it possible that an increase in wages and prices arising from a positive realization of the shock u_t would lead to a contemporaneous increase in output, a result which is not possible without the real rate of interest.

With some manipulation, prices and output can be expressed as functions of current and all past shocks:

$$p_t = \frac{1}{2}\{u_t + (\rho + 1)u_{t-1} + \rho(\rho + 1)u_{t-2} + \rho^2(1 + \rho)u_{t-3} + \dots\} \tag{4.15a}$$

$$y_t = \omega_1 u_t + (\omega_2 + \rho\omega_1) \times \{u_{t-1} + \rho u_{t-2} + \rho^2 u_{t-3} + \dots\} \tag{4.15b}$$

where

$$\omega_1 = (a(1 + \rho) - b)/2; \tag{4.16a}$$

$$\omega_2 = -(b/2). \tag{4.16b}$$

From (4.15a), we see that the price level exhibits a "humped" lag pattern, a positive shock u_t pushes the price level up in the current period, then pushes it even higher in the next period, after which time the price level gradually decreases back to its long-run value. This means that a current positive shock increases both the current price level and also creates expected inflation from the current period to the next.

The increase in expected inflation associated with the positive realization of u_t means that the current-period real rate of interest can fall. Hence, output in the current period can increase. In terms of (4.16a), this means that ω_1 could be positive. This feature of our model is clearly a result of the incorporation of the real rate of interest in aggregate demand.

This "*ex ante* Keynes effect" of an increase in prices creating expected inflation which in turn creates a lower real interest rate can only last one period in our model. After that, the model predicts expected deflation, and the real rate must be above its long-run value. The quantity $\{\omega_2 + \rho\omega_1\}$ is negative, confirming that the effect of a positive wage shock reduces output in subsequent periods, regardless of the first period effect. Figure 4.2 sketches possible lag patterns for output and price.

The asymptotic variances of prices and outputs can be computed as:

$$\sigma_p^2 = \sigma_u^2/2(1-\rho) \tag{4.17a}$$

$$\sigma_y^2 = [\{(b-a)^2 + b^2 + \rho a(a-2b)\}] [\sigma_u^2/4(1-\rho).] \tag{4.17b}$$

The expression for the variance of prices is the same as before but the output expression is different.

Taking derivatives of the expressions with respect to ρ, it is easy to show that they are both increasing in ρ. Since increases in γ, the wage flexibility parameter, decrease ρ, this means that both the variance of output and prices decrease with increases in wage flexibility. Despite the possibility of an *ex ante* Keynes effect as depicted in figure 4.2, the overall variance of output still falls with an increase in wage flexibility. Moreover, as wage flexibility increases and γ falls, the coefficient on the hump in prices falls and so does the first lagged coefficient on output shocks, ω_1. Thus, the Taylor model extended to include real interest rates still exhibits the property that increases in wage flexibility are stabilizing.

DeLong and Summers (1986a) demonstrated that modifications of the Taylor model with real interest rate effects can lead to increased

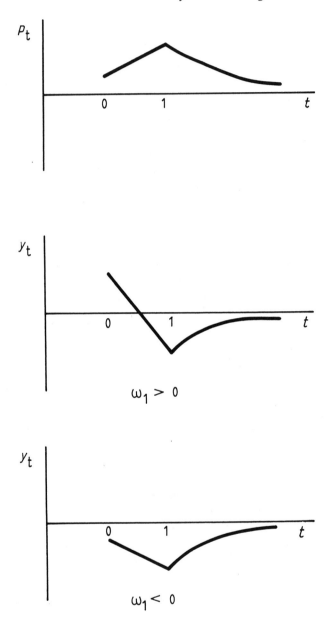

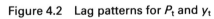

Figure 4.2   Lag patterns for P_t and y_t

wage flexibility being destabilizing. Their fundamental change over Driskill and Sheffrin's model was to replace the wage shock with a serially correlated demand shock. They follow Driskill and Sheffrin in considering alternative interest rate strategies by the monetary authorities. Their reduced form for aggregate demand then has the form:

$$y_t = aE_t(P_{t+1} - P_t) - bP_t + Z_t \qquad (4.18)$$

where

$$Z_t = \lambda Z_{t-1} + \bar{\varepsilon}_t$$

The only salient difference between this expression and equation (4.14) is the serially correlated demand shock Z_t. The supply side of the economy − the pricing and contract equations − remain unchanged.

Since the supply side is predetermined, an innovation to demand or a shock to Z_t will lead directly to an increase in y_t without any current movements in prices. However, as long as there is positive serial correlation in the demand shocks ($\lambda > 0$), prices must rise in the next period and for some time in the future. The initial effect on the price level is the largest, leading to a hump-shaped pattern for inflation. This leads to an increase in the expected inflation rate from zero to some positive number and a further rise in y_t through the *ex ante* Keynes effect.

Increasing the flexibility of wages to output (increasing γ) has two effects, one destabilizing, the other stabilizing. The faster wages and prices adjust, the greater will be the initial expectations of inflation and the significance of the potentially destabilizing *ex ante* Keynes effect. On the other hand, the more rapidly wages and prices adjust, the faster the economy will return to its long-run equilibrium following the shock. This stabilizes output.

In the Driskill−Sheffrin model, positive wage shocks would normally lead to a fall in output as the aggregate supply curve shifts to the left with the shock. The expected inflation induced by this shock partially offsets the effect of the initial shock but the overall effect is still to lower output. Increases in wage flexibility do not change these fundamental forces and the initial effect of the shock always dominates.

DeLong and Summers (1986a) simulate their model and find for some plausible parameters that increased wage flexibility can lead to increased output variability. They indicate that as wage flexibility increases, the persistence of output (as measured by the autocorrelation parameter ρ in the Driskill−Sheffrin model) falls but the variance of output nonetheless increases. Figure 4.3, adapted from DeLong and Summers's paper, illustrates this result. Following a demand shock the initial impact on output is larger with greater price flexibility but the effect of the shock dampens more quickly. On balance, this can lead to

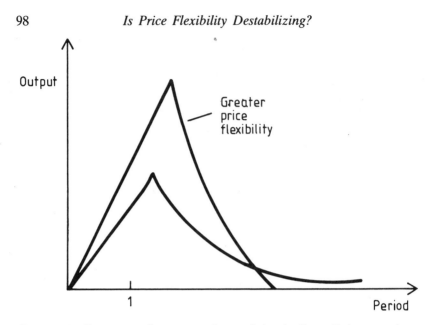

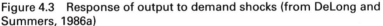

Figure 4.3   Response of output to demand shocks (from DeLong and Summers, 1986a)

increased variance but with less persistence. The sharp response of output again highlights the importance of the peak in the inflation rate following the shock and its impact on output through the *ex ante* Keynes effect.

DeLong and Summers experiment with other ways to model increased wage and price flexibility. They find that with two methods of modeling increased contract lengths the variance of output can decrease with increased contract lengths. The mechanisms are precisely the same as in the previous version of their model.

Before further analysis of these issues, it is worthwhile to clarify the nature of experiments conducted by DeLong and Summers and Driskill and Sheffrin. DeLong and Summers allow the monetary authorities to respond to current interest rate movements but do not allow them to gear their policy to past shocks. A more general monetary policy rule could eliminate or offset the serial correlation in their model which would have the effect of eliminating the possibility of instability through the *ex ante* Keynes effect. With no effective serial correlation in demand, there is no reason for expected inflation to increase and magnify the initial shock. Thus, the DeLong and Summers model is appropriate for analyzing an uninformed and untutored monetary authority that is unwilling to offset the effects of past shocks. The wage shocks which are the focus of the Taylor and Driskill—Sheffrin models persist even in the face of enlightened monetary authorities. Taylor (1979) has analyzed the trade-offs they pose between output and price stability. In other work (1986), he has documented their importance for business cycle activity.

King (1986) has suggested another definition of increased wage and price flexibility. In his view, the proportion of workers setting wages in auction markets as opposed to contract markets is a more appropriate measure of wage flexibility. King analyzes the effects of serially correlated demand shocks in a model with real interest rates, workers with contract wages set analogous to those in Taylor's model, and workers whose wages are set in auction markets. He finds through simulations that increases in wage flexibility, according to his definition, decrease the variability — the opposite result from DeLong and Summers. How do we reconcile the results from these models?

Cantor (1987) has developed a framework based on a simple model of imperfect competition that can illuminate the difference between the results of DeLong–Summers and King as well as highlight some testable implications of the models.

Let there be a continuum of firms, indexed i, producing homogeneous output y_t^i at price P_t^i. Average output, y_t is the average of the y_t^i's and the average price P_t is the average of the P_t^i's. Demand for any individual firm's output depends on total demand and its price relative to the average price:

$$y_t^i = y_t - \eta(P_t^i - P_t) \qquad (4.c1)$$

where $\eta > 0$ is the elasticity of demand for the firm's product.

Aggregate demand is the same as in DeLong–Summers, namely:

$$y_t = a[E_t\, P_{t+1} - P_t] - b\, P_t + Z_t \qquad Z_t = \lambda Z_{t-1} + \bar{\varepsilon}_t \qquad (4.c2)$$

and thus includes an *ex ante* Keynes effect, the traditional negative dependence of aggregate demand on price, as well as a serially correlated aggregate demand shock.

Substituting for y_t in (4.c1) and re-arranging yields:

$$y_t^i = (\eta - b - a)P_t + a\, E\, P_{t+1} - \eta\, P_t^i + Z_t \qquad (4.c3)$$

All firms desire to supply precisely one unit of output (zero in logs). There are three types of firms in the economy. A fraction q^* have perfectly flexible prices, a fraction $q1$ commit to their prices for one period, and a fraction $q2$ ($q2 \equiv 1 - q^* - q1$) commit to their prices for two periods. This model of price stickiness is the analog to the Fischer–Gray contract wage models and is an alternative to Taylor's model.

Let the prices set by the flexible firms be denoted by P_t^*. Using (4.c3) and the assumption that the log of desired output is zero yields the following expression for P_t^*:

$$P_t^* = [(\eta - b - a)P_t + a E_t P_{t+1} + Z_t]/\eta \qquad (4.c4)$$

The other firms set their prices to minimize the expected squared deviation of output from desired output. This implies $P_t^1 = E_{t-1} P_t^*$ and $P_t^2 = E_{t-1} P_t^*$. At any point in time, one-half of the two-period contract firms are in the first period of their contract so that the average price level is given by:

$$P_t = q^* P_t^* + (q_1 + 0.5q_2) E_{t-1}P_t^* + 0.5q_2 E_{t-2} P_t^* \qquad (4.c5)$$

Since all the variables are measured as deviations from zero, the price can be written as an infinite sum of current and lagged shocks:

$$P_t = \sum_{k=0}^{\infty} \pi_k \, \varepsilon_{t-k} \qquad (4.c6)$$

where the π_k are undetermined coefficients. Using the prior equations, we can derive expressions for the output of the two types of contract firms:

$$\begin{aligned}
y_t^1 &= (\eta - b - a)[P_t - E_{t-1}P_t] + a[E_t P_{t+1} - E_{t-1}P_{t+1}] + (Z_t - E_{t-1}Z_t) \\
&= [(\eta - b - a)\pi_0 + \theta\pi_1 + 1]\, \varepsilon_t \\
y_t^2 &= (\eta - b - a)[P_t - E_{t-2}P_t] + a[E_t P_{t+1} - E_{t-2}P_{t+1}] + (Z_t - E_{t-2}Z_t) \\
&= [(\eta - b - a)\pi_0 + \theta\pi_1 + 1]\, \varepsilon_t \\
&\quad + [(\eta - b - a)\pi_1 + \theta\pi_2 + \lambda]\, \varepsilon_{t-1} \qquad (4.c7)
\end{aligned}$$

The output for the purely flexible firms is, of course, always zero.

Cantor solves the model for two special cases that correspond to King's model of price flexibility and the DeLong–Summers model of price flexibility. For the King model, he assumes that there are only purely flexible firms and one-period firms, that is, $q2 = 0$ and $q^* = 1 - q1$. He then considers the behavior of output for y_t^1 as q^* increases, that is, as the flexible sector grows relative to the contract sector.

Using the standard methods of undetermined coefficients, Cantor solves the equation for prices and the expression for y_t^1 and total output. His results for the price equation indicate that an increase in the proportion of firms setting prices in the spot market will increase the contemporaneous response of prices to a shock (π_0) but will leave the coefficients on lagged terms (π_k) unchanged. This means that the extent of expected inflation precipitated by a demand shock *falls* as the proportion of firms with flexible prices falls. Thus there is less scope for the *ex ante* Keynes effect to operate.

Output becomes less variable as the proportion of flexible price firms increases for two reasons. First, flexible price firms exhibit no output volatility so increasing their proportion naturally leads to a reduction in volatility. Second, the lessening of the expected inflation effect reduces the volatility of output for the y_t^1 firms. Therefore, increases in price flexibility according to King's definition will lead to reduced output volatility and a decrease in the initial expected inflation precipitated by a demand shock.

To study the DeLong–Summers notion of flexibility, Cantor assumes that no firms are in the spot market ($q^*=0$) and firms are therefore divided between one- and two-period contracts. Increased price flexibility then translates into an increase in the proportion of firms (q_1) in one-period contractual relationships. This corresponds to decreasing average contract length in the economy. Using the method of underdetermined coefficients, Cantor derives the expression for the coefficients in the price equation.

$$\pi_0 = 0$$

$$\pi_1 = \frac{a\pi_2 + \lambda}{(\eta/0.5(1 + q1)) - (\eta - b - a)} \qquad (4.c8)$$

$$\pi_k = \frac{\lambda^k}{b + a(1 - \lambda)} \qquad k > 1$$

Demand shocks have no effect on prices in the current period since all firms are locked into some contracts. The price level rises in the next period and continues to rise in the following period ($\pi_2 > \pi_1$) creating a "humped-shaped" pattern. Increasing the proportion of firms in the first period of their contract ($q1$) decreases π_1 and thus increases the expected inflation in period $t+1$ induced by a shock at time t.

In this model, the effects of an increase in flexibility are ambiguous. An increase in $q1$ increases the hump in the price level and by inducing increased expectations of inflation tends to destabilize the economy through the *ex ante* Keynes effect. But as the proportion of one-period contract firms increases, they can adjust prices to eliminate a greater proportion of the serially correlated part of the demand shock. This, of course, tends to be a stabilizing force for the economy.

Table 4.2 summarizes the results of Cantor's (1987) analysis of the King and DeLong–Summers models of price flexibility. In King's version, increased price flexibility is defined by the fraction of firms setting prices in spot markets and is characterized by less volatility in output and less induced expected inflation. Cantor's interpretation of the DeLong–Summers version of increased flexibility is a decrease in average contract length. This leads to an increase in the hump in prices and thus higher induced expected inflation and ambiguous results for output volatility. This increased hump in prices is consistent with DeLong and Summers's own specification and accounts for the higher "spike" in output that accompanies a higher degree of price flexibility.

Table 4.2　Price flexibility and stabilization

Definition of Price flexibility	Effects of Increased flexibility on	
	Expected inflation	Output variability
King	Decrease	Decrease
DeLong−Summers	Increase	Ambiguous

Source: Based on Cantor (1987)

Delong and Summers (1986b) were partly responsible for the growth in this literature because of their provocative thesis that the decline in wage and price flexibility was responsible for the vastly greater stability of output in the postwar era. In the last chapter, we carefully reviewed the evidence concerning the diminution of the business cycle and concluded that there was a dampening of output fluctuations. Could the decrease in wage and price flexibility partly account for the fall in volatility?

Evidence presented in Taylor (1986) and King (1986) indicates that, in the postwar era, the "hump" in the inflation rate has increased dramatically over the postwar era. Specifically, this result emerged from analyzing moving-average representations of inflation stemming from output shocks. According to the model of DeLong and Summers, a decrease in price flexibility in the postwar era should have led to a *decrease* in the hump in inflation rate which in turn would reduce the significance of the *ex ante* Keynes effect. However, the data show that the hump has increased, not decreased. King's model predicts that a decrease in wage flexibility should lead to increased output volatility. It therefore cannot explain the decrease in postwar volatility by appealing to decreased wage flexibility. Neither of these models of the *ex ante* Keynes effect, it appears, contributes much to our understanding of historical changes in output dynamics.

Nor is the situation improved by examining the data from other countries. In related work, Sheffrin and Liu (1988) find that the "hump" in the inflation rate in the moving-average representations of inflation from output shocks increased in the postwar era for all the countries examined in chapter 2. This result was robust to choice of detrending method. The increase in the hump in postwar data leaves little scope for the *ex ante* Keynes effect as an explanation for postwar stability.

There have been several other models developed to study questions of increasing price flexibility but all essentially operate on the same principle. Flemming (1987) and Howitt (1986) study models with less complex wage-setting behavior than in Taylor's model. Unlike the Taylor or Howitt models, Flemming has price determined in an aggregate demand−supply framework rather than as a mark-up on wages. In Flemming's model, however, wages are predetermined but prices and employment always adjust so that the real wage equals the marginal product of labor on a firm's demand curve.

Nonetheless, the underlying economic mechanism is similar to the other models under review. Consider an adverse demand shock. Wages are predetermined but will be expected to fall. The greater the degree of wage flexibility, the larger will be the degree of expected deflation and this will lead to higher *ex ante* real interest rates depressing demand. Prices can fall in this model but given the money wage they only fall as employment and output fall. The result is that the impact effect from shocks is greater to prices, output, and employment the higher the degree of wage flexibility. In Flemming's own words, "Thus the greater the flexibility of a wage that does not jump the greater the impact effect of shocks on the price level, the real wage, and output" (1987, p. 169). This is precisely the hump-shaped inflation phenomenon of the previous models.

Greater wage flexibility also means that the economy returns to equilibrium faster following shocks. The overall impact of increased wage flexibility on output variability then depends on the relative strength of this stabilizing effect versus the destabilizing *ex ante* Keynes effect from the increased hump-shape for inflation. These are precisely the same considerations as in the prior models and thus Howitt's model as well runs afoul of the empirical evidence that the hump-shaped pattern seems to have increased in the postwar era.

Chada (1987) studied the issue of contract length and output stability in a continuous time version of the staggered contract model. Firms write contracts which expire stochastically according to a Poisson distribution. Thus, average contract length can be indexed by the probability that an existing contract will not expire in the next period. Increasing this probability increases the average contract length in the economy.

Chada's results reinforce the notion that the hump-shaped behavior of inflation is the key to these models. Increasing contract length increases the persistence of output but decreases the impact effect of shocks. This impact effect on output is diminished because the hump in the inflation rate becomes smaller. Again, this runs counter to the existing empirical evidence.

Finally, Hahn and Solow (1986) take a radically different approach to this question, abandoning the extended IS−LM framework for an overlapping generations model with fiat money and a payment system generating demand for this money. They stress the indeterminancy of paths towards a new equilibrium following a disturbance and the possible undesirable characteristics of some of these paths. However, the structure of the model is so far removed from any economy that it cannot be used to confront data and thus remains as an example within the catalog of pathologies of overlapping generations theory.

Our models of the *ex ante* Keynes effect have run into two empirical roadblocks. First, the historical evidence on the behavior of wages and prices does not suggest that there has been a dramatic change in the responsiveness of broad indices to output. Second, the hump-shaped pattern for inflation, which we have seen to be at the heart of the model, is primarily a phenomenon of the postwar era and is inconsistent with the notion that postwar wage flexibility has decreased. Thus, the models fail to be of use in illuminating differences between early and later periods of output behavior for the United States.

Perhaps the models might fare better in a different laboratory. Do the *ex ante* Keynes effect or the *ex post* Fisher effect appear to be important for the great deflation of the Great Depression?

4.4   Deflation and the Great Depression

From 1929 to 1933 the United States experienced a virulent deflation. Wholesale prices fell by 31 percent while the consumer price index and the GNP deflator each fell by 25 percent. If we believe that any of the theories of the perverse effects of deflation on real output are important, we would hope that they would have some relevance to the period to which everyone refers as an example of the evils of deflation.

In assessing the Keynes *ex ante* effect, there is an inherent difficulty. Without direct data on individuals' expectations, it is difficult to infer precise estimates of expected deflation and thereby an estimate of the effects of deflation on increasing real interest rates. Fortunately, how-ever, precision is not required to answer this question.

In a reassessment of the role of monetary factors in the Great Depression, James Hamilton (1987) carefully examined the extent to which the deflation during the period 1929 to 1933 was anticipated. Hamilton examined three types of evidence that suggested that the bulk of the deflation was *not* anticipated. First, statements in the 1930s by business leaders and other prominent individuals do not indicate a widespread belief in a coming deflation. Of course, this type of evidence is inherently difficult to substantiate. We can always find individuals who foresaw the problem. Quoting himself (gleefully) in a chapter entitled "Price Forecasts" in his book with Pearson (1935), George Warren writes: "August 22, 1930. 'My guess is that wholesale prices will fall below pre-war ... If my diagnosis is correct, the individual

American farmer should anticipate a still lower price level ... He should be careful about long-time debts.'"

Nonetheless, as Hamilton points out, it would be hard for the average individual to predict the chaos in policymaking at the Fed that was so well documented in Friedman and Schwartz (1963). With some members of the Federal Reserve system constantly worrying about the dangers of reflation, it would be hard for the average person to predict the policies of malign neglect which the Fed followed.

The second piece of evidence that Hamilton reviewed concerned the predictability of equations from time series models. If economic actors behaved as if they believed in the statistical equations that account for prices *ex post*, they would not have been able to account for much of the deflation. Neither were time series models for this period useful for forecasting far into the future with much accuracy.

The final and original piece of evidence that Hamilton presents is the most convincing. He looked at the prices quoted in futures markets for several commodities with detailed data on cotton. He calculated two series. The first was the difference between the one-month and seventh-month futures price and was his proxy for the expected inflation over six months for that commodity. The reason he used two futures prices rather than spot prices was to avoid complications concerning the timing and quality of delivery under the contract. The second series was his measure of the actual price change for the commodity and consisted of the difference of two one-month futures contracts, six months apart.

Hamilton first looked at the two series to see how closely the expected inflation series tracked the actual inflation series from 1922 to 1929. First, he could not reject the hypothesis that the expected inflation series was an unbiased although noisy predictor of the actual inflation series. Second, the variance of the expected inflation series was less than the variance of the actual inflation series as is required by the "volatility" tests for rational forecasts. Despite these properties, it was still difficult to predict actual price movements for cotton: futures markets could only account for about 20 percent of the variance.

The data for the period January 1930 to July 1932 for cotton are fascinating. On average, over each six-month period the market anticipated inflation of 9.4 percent on an annual basis. Actual inflation over the period averaged −39 percent! Moreover, these mistakes persisted throughout the whole period. For the six-month period ending in January 1932, the market anticipated a 13.4 percent increase in the price of cotton. The actual price of cotton fell by 95.9 percent for this period. The data for wheat, corn, and oats exhibited similar patterns.[1]

Clearly, the markets did not anticipate the deflation experienced in the commodity markets. Did this lack of foresight carry over to broader indices such as the CPI? Here Hamilton presents some indirect evidence. The value of actual commodity prices helps to predict the CPI based on its past value and the effect is economically and statistically significant. In fact, knowledge of the actual course of commodity prices would have reduced the forecast variance of the CPI by about 70 percent.[2] Thus, there is good reason to believe that the deflation in the broader indices was also unanticipated.

Hamilton's interest in these questions was twofold. First, he wanted to reinvestigate the role of monetary policy in causing and prolonging the Depression. Second, he also wanted to assess the explanatory power of the traditional Keynesian model for understanding the dynamics of the Depression. Nominal interest rates on all but the most risky securities were falling during this period. If there was tight monetary policy during this period causing high *ex ante* real interest rates, it would have to therefore show up in terms of expected deflation. Yet, the evidence is fairly persuasive that the markets were not anticipating deflation. Thus, if monetary factors were important in explaining the dynamics of the downturn, they were not operating in the traditional textbook Keynesian manner.

Our scope is narrower than Hamilton's in that we are only assessing the mechanisms by which the deflation itself could have contributed to the downturn. However, it is clear from his evidence that the deflation was not causing high *ex ante* real interest rates. This could only occur if the deflation was anticipated and the bulk of the evidence suggests strongly that it was not. There simply is no scope for the *ex ante* Keynes effect during this period. We had previously seen that the models featuring this effect did not fit the dynamics of the postwar era. Now we see they are irrelevant to the greatest deflation of the twentieth century.

The *ex post* Fisher effect survives much better due largely to Ben Bernanke's reinterpretation of the Great Depression. Bernanke (1983) pointed out that the decline of the money stock meant not just that liabilities of the banks fell but their assets did as well. For many businesses and farms, local financial institutions had developed specific capital in knowledge of particular borrowers who had no recourse when banks were closed. More generally, the distress of financial institutions during the period raised what he termed the "cost of financial intermediation" and therefore the implicit interest rates facing borrowers.

Irving Fisher echoed similar themes but put more emphasis on the sheer burden of debt which was increased by the deflation and its progressive deleterious effects on the economy. In his view, this situation deteriorated until precisely the time Roosevelt took action.

Those who imagine that Roosevelt's avowed reflation is not just the cause of our recovery but that we had "reached the bottom anyway" are very much mistaken. At any rate, they have given no evidence, so far as I have seen, that we had reached the bottom. And if they are right, my analysis must be woefully wrong. According to all the evidence, under that analysis, debt and deflation, which had wrought havoc up to March 4, 1933 were then stronger than ever and, if let alone, would have wreaked greater wreckage than ever after March 4. Had no "artificial respiration" been applied, we would soon have seen general bankruptcies of the mortgage guarantee companies, savings banks, life insurance companies, railway municipalities, and states ... For we would have insolvency of our national government itself, and probably some form of political revolution without waiting for the next legal election. (1933, pp. 346−7)

In modern language, this would have raised the cost of intermediation.

Fisher believed that reflating the price level was the key to recovery. In his view, "The fact that immediate reversal of deflation is easily achieved by the use, or even the prospect of use, of appropriate instrumentalities has just been demonstrated by President Roosevelt" (1933, p. 346). Fisher cited Sweden's efforts to control the price level in the early 1930s which, as Lars Jonung (1981) documents, was the explicit policy previously advocated by Wicksell and endorsed by the most prominent Swedish economists of the time.

Devaluation and abandonment of gold were the most immediate tools to achieve rapid reflation. Eichengreen and Sachs (1985) document the recovery of European countries following their devaluations. Since the immediate effect of the devaluations was an increase in wholesale prices, this supports Fisher's views about the positive effects of reflation.

Fisher's full prescription for recovery was to reflate the price level up to the average level at which debts were contracted. Although there was about a 7 percent increase in the GNP deflator from 1933 to 1934, by 1937 the deflator still stood at only 82 percent of its 1929 value. This leads directly to an interesting and unresolved question: was the extra inflation induced by Roosevelt's policies, particularly, those of the National Industries Recovery Act (NIRA), beneficial or deleterious to the recovery?

Friedman and Schwartz (1963) and Weinstein (1981) take the traditional position that the macroeconomic effects of the NIRA were adverse. Essentially Title I of the act suspended antitrust laws and allowed industries to adopt codes of competition. Wages and prices were increased through this process. Using dummy variables to capture the effects of the acts, Weinstein estimated that these led to increases in prices during the period 1933—5 of about 14 percent which was sufficient to eliminate any real increase in the money supply because the nominal money supply increased only 14 percent during this period. Since increases in the real money supply were negated by the NIRA induced inflation, the economy was without the stimulus from monetary policy which, using conventional multiplier estimates, Weinstein estimates would have led to average increases in real output of over 8 percent per year for the period.

Friedman and Schwartz offer a similar analysis. Given the common perceptions of their views, it is somewhat surprising that they explain the behavior of wages and prices from 1933 to 1937 by a wage—price spiral. Indeed, it is the only period in their book for which they felt this explanation was justified. In their view, *increasingly* strong unions and monopoly power over this period led to *increasing* price levels. Gold inflows from abroad led to increases in the monetary base and thus accommodated the government generated wage and price inflation.

The effects from this inflation were to reduce the growth of real income. "If this analysis is right, it suggests that, in the absence of the wage and price push, the period 1933—37 would have been characterized by a smaller rise in prices and a larger rise in output than actually occurred." (Friedman and Schwartz, 1963, p. 499) This follows from assuming that nominal income is unchanged. However, there would be one additional effect. Without the exogenous inflation, the balance of trade would be more favorable for the United States and gold inflows would be higher. Assuming no sterilization, this would lead to a higher money supply and higher nominal income.

Both these views totally ignore the possibility of the beneficial effects that reflation may have had on existing debtors and financial institutions. By Fisher's norm, the price level had probably not been

Table 4.3   The effects of inflation and deflation

Doubling the price level by inflation	Halving the price level by deflation
1 Commodity prices double	1 Commodities fall 50 percent
2 Commodity prices overshoot the 200 mark but return to it	2 Prices decline below the 100 mark but return to it
3 Debts are easy to pay	3 Debts are difficult of payment
4 Bondholders and other creditors lose, but even poor debts are collectable	4 Creditors gain if they can collect, but often lose everything
5 Life insurance earnings rise	5 Life insurance earnings fall
6 The buying power of the	6 Universities suffer because

Table 4.3   (*continued*)

Doubling the price level by inflation	Halving the price level by deflation
income of universities declines but new funds are available	income is reduced and new funds do not appear
7 Buying on credit is popular and is commended.	7 All debts are abhorrent
8 Taxes are easy to pay	8 Taxes are difficult to pay
9 Public services expand	9 Taxpayers' leagues are formed but accomplish little
10 Tramps disappear	10 Many self-repecting persons are fed at public expense
11 "New rich" appear	11 "New poor" appear
12 Labor union membership rises	12 Labor union membership falls
13 Wages lag but there is work for everyone	13 Wages lag but jobs disappear
14 Promotions to higher class of labor are easy to obtain	14 Promotions are slow. Demotions are common
15 Farmers prosper	15 Farm depression is long and severe
16 The standard of living of the southern mule improves	16 The mule's standard of living is reduced
17 Building of city residences is checked	17 Building in cities is overdone and then stopped
18 Fire insurance losses are small	18 Fire insurance losses are large
19 Goods are hoarded	19 Cash is hoarded
20 The laundry business increases	20 Sales of washing machines increase
21 Doctor's fees lag, but business increases and debts can be collected	21 Doctor's fees lag, but business decreases and many debts are uncollectible
22 Hospital fees lag, but hospitals are filled and gifts are large	22 Hospital fees lag, but hospitals are not filled and gifts decline so that higher fees are needed
23 Suicides decrease	23 Suicides increase
24 Stealing decreases	24 Stealing increases
25 Interest rates rise	25 Interest rates decline on safe paper
26 The size of life and fire insurance policies increases	26 The size of life and fire insurances policies decreases
27 Marriage increases	27 Marriage decreases
28 Expansion of production	28 Contraction of production
29 Full employment with rising wages	29 Decreasing employment with falling wages

Source: Warren and Pearson (1935)

restored fully. The traditional story fails to account for the effect that the reflation could have had on preventing further deterioration of the intermediation system. If Hamilton is right that Keynesian (or monetarist) models with their emphasis on real balances cannot account for the peculiar characteristics of the downturn, why should we rely on them to account for the recovery?

Clearly the financial system was still in great difficulties even after Roosevelt's actions in 1933. Friedman and Schwartz document carefully the shift in banks' portfolios towards government bonds and other safe investments and away from more traditional lending activities. Bernanke discusses several contemporary surveys ranging from those sponsored by banking associations to small business organizations and all found evidence of credit difficulties, particularly for small businesses. Home mortgages would have virtually disappeared without direct government intervention in the market as some traditional lenders, such as life insurance companies, virtually curtailed their activities.

What further damage to the credit system would have been done without the partial reflation of the NIRA? Critics of the macro effects of the program, such as Weinstein and Friedman and Schwartz, would have to address this question seriously before reporting sanguine calculations based simply on hypothetical measures of real money balances for the economy.

But Fisher's prescription for full reflation to previous levels is not fully correct. Once the damage to financial institutions and other intermediaries (such as bank closings and bankruptcies) has been done, a policy of reflation will not be enough. It will not in itself restore the previous channels of intermediaries or revive insolvent debtors. The economy exhibits hysteresis (or path dependent outcomes) and a policy that simply restores the previous price level is not enough.[3] The interesting historical question is how the reflation generated by the NIRA matched up to the ideal reflation strategy – one sufficient to rescue marginal debtors and financial institutions but not too great to damage the economy through the excessive reduction of real balances.

Is increased price flexibility destabilizing? Our review of the models and evidence suggests that the question is too sweeping and needs to be broken down. Yes, models exist in which too rapid adjustment of wages and prices to output could destabilize output. But, no, those based on *ex ante* real interest rate effects are not consistent with the historical data. Unanticipated deflation, however, can and did cause severe difficulties. It is the latter type of price flexibility, or better yet, price collapse which should cause us concern.

Finally, observers during the Great Depression had a keen appreciation of the effects of inflation and deflation. Table 4.3 contains the musings of Warren and Pearson (1935, p. 434), which should be read along with more modern accounts of the "costs of inflation."

Notes

1 Mishkin (1987) argues that Hamilton's method may be misleading in other contexts, particularly in interpreting shifts in Federal Reserve policy in the late 1970s.
2 The predictive power of commodity prices for the CPI would not be as strong in the postwar era.
3 This is an example of how financial factors, as well as real shocks, can give rise to nonstationary movements in output.

Appendix

This appendix outlines the solution method for the Taylor model with real interest rate. The structural model consisting of equations (4.5), (4.6) and (4.14) involves expectations of variables at time t and $t-1$, current stochastic shocks, current endogenous variables and only one state variable, lagged wages. Leon Wegge (1982) has shown that such a rational expectations structural model has the following solution form for the contract wage:

$$X_t = \rho X_{t-1} + \pi u_t, \qquad (A1)$$

where ρ and π are, in general, functions of structural parameters. Combining (A1) with the pricing equation (4.6), we can write prices as the following ARMA (1,1) process:

$$P_t = \rho P_{t-1} + k(u_t + u_{t-1}) \qquad k = \pi/2. \qquad (A2)$$

Taking expectations of P_{t+1} at time t, we have

$$E_t P_{t+1} = \rho P_t + k u_t. \qquad (A3)$$

Substituting (A3) into the expression for aggregate demand and simplifying yields

$$y_t = -\hat{\theta} P_t + a k u_t \qquad \hat{\theta} = b - \rho a. \qquad (A4)$$

Aside from the error term, this expression for aggregate demand is the same as Taylor's basic model which has aggregate demand solely as a function of the real money supply and a money supply equation linking the nominal money supply to prices. In this model, however, $\hat{\theta}$

now depends on the (unknown) value of ρ. The final step in the solution is to exploit the similarities between the real rate case and the standard Taylor model to determine the value of ρ.

Treating $\hat{\theta}$ as predetermined for the moment allows us to calculate ρ and π by the standard method of undetermined coefficients:

$$\rho = \frac{\phi}{\hat{c} - \rho(1-\phi)}; \; \pi = 1 \qquad (A5)$$

where

$$\hat{c} = \left(1 + \frac{\hat{\theta}\gamma}{2}\right) \Big/ \left(1 - \frac{\hat{\theta}\gamma}{2}\right).$$

However, since $\hat{\theta} = b - \rho a$, there is a second relationship between ρ, and $\hat{c}$, namely:

$$\hat{c} = \left(1 + \frac{\gamma(b-\rho a)}{2}\right) \Big/ \left(1 - \frac{\gamma(b-\rho a)}{2}\right) \qquad (A6)$$

Equations (A5) and (A6) determine ρ and $\hat{c}$, for any given values of γ, b and a. Driskill and Sheffrin (1986) prove that a unique value of ρ^* exists and increases in γ always decrease ρ^*.

5

A New Keynesian Economics?

5.1 Introduction

The previous two chapters have taken critical positions against two important challenges to the conception of modern stabilization policy. Real business cycle theory reminds us that fluctuations in potential output can be important but has not provided the type of evidence that would suggest that stabilization efforts be halted. Increasing price flexibility still appears to lead to greater stability in output, not less stability.

In recent years a new brand of economics has developed which, for the most part, views its task as providing microfoundations for Keynesian economics. According to adherents of this approach, there was not a dramatic *empirical* failure in Keynesian economics, but there was a theoretical crisis. If we allow the Keynesian empirical tradition to include the notion of an expectations-augmented Phillips curve and excuse it from not recognizing in advance the strong effects possible from supply shocks, then a reasonable case can be made for the empirical accuracy of Keynesian models. If we freeze the Keynesian tradition in the mid-1960s with a conventional Phillips curve, then there are both empirical and theoretical failures. These fundamental differences in the empirical tradition divide protagonists such as Alan Blinder (1987) and Robert E. Lucas on this issue.

But include, for the moment, supply shocks and expectational elements into the wage–price process. As Blinder (1987) argued, there is certainly room for debate over the extent of empirically relevant propositions that emerged from the development of "New Classical Economics." Business cycles based solely on imperfect information and associated neutrality of either anticipated or perceived money were controversial from the beginning and have passed out of empirical favor. While the Lucas critique, the idea that changes in policy rules will change the underlying behavioral relations in the economy, has been accepted as a theoretical principle by most economists, there has been little evidence that it has been important for interpreting experience in the United States.[1]

Proponents of the new Keynesian microfoundations, however, stress that the true lessons of modern Keynesian economics have themselves been under attack because of the lack of persuasiveness of the theories rationalizing Keynesian phenomena. Sticky money wages, even coupled with rational expectations, such as in the now famous models of Fischer (1977) and Taylor (1980), do not satisfy the increased demands for theoretical purity. Following Barro (1977), economists ask themselves why rational people should write fixed money wage contracts that will lead to apparently inefficient outcomes *ex post* depending on the vagaries of monetary shocks. Hall's (1980) challenge also echoes in the debates: how do we know that labor allocation decisions are not made according to some optimal rules and that nominal contracts are simply convenient mechanisms to make installment payments on a long-term contractual basis?

There have been at two important strands in the literature on new Keynesian microfoundations. The first aims to provide a rigorous foundation for price inflexibility based on the idea that there are real costs involved in actually changing prices. The second emphasizes the consequences of incomplete markets for macroeconomic phenomena with particular emphasis on the consequences for credit and monetary phenomena.

The literature on the new Keynesian microfoundations, particularly the sticky price part, has grown immensely in the past several years and includes surveys by Rotemberg (1987) and Blanchard (1987b). These surveys are primarily written from a theoretical vantage point and explore the nuances of alternative models of sticky prices.

The purpose of this chapter is somewhat different. It addresses the question of whether the new Keynesian microfoundations has delivered or can deliver new insights into practical stabilization issues. The first part of the chapter explores the foundations of the sticky price models. It first highlights several of the key theoretical contributions in order to demonstrate their straightforward logic. It then turns to some recent empirical work which can shed some light on the potential practical contributions of this literature.

The second part of the chapter reviews recent work in the incomplete market approach which has not received as much attention and surveys a variety of contributions. Insights from this literature, interestingly enough, have found their way both into Keynesian and new classical treatments of the business cycle.

The last part of the chapter documents a shift in perspective away from faithful adherence to an efficient markets view of financial markets. Both new evidence and new theoretical pespectives have contributed to this shift. Although not directly related to the new Keynesian economics, this attack on efficient markets naturally opens the scope for potential policy prescriptions.

5.2 Sticky Price and Business Cycles

The new Keynesian microfoundations concentrates, for the most part, on sticky prices rather than sticky wages. This represents a clear change in fashion in the Keynesian tradition although "administered prices" and kinked demand curves were part of an active Keynesian tradition at an earlier time.

Is there any theoretical advantage to emphasizing sticky prices over sticky wages? Perhaps the most important point is that it is much more difficult to explain away sticky prices as purely an economic epiphenomenon. As we discussed above, some economists have argued that sticky wages do not have any allocative significance but are merely installment payments on long-term relationships. Allocative decisions, according to this viewpoint, are made independently of the actual wage payments that occur in any particular time period.

This position is much more difficult to sustain for sticky prices. Although it is certainly possible that long-term customer relations are important in the trade of intermediate products between firms, it is not possible to make this claim for ordinary retail products. Some evidence, described below, indicates that magazine prices are quite sticky in nominal terms. While the stickiness of long-term prices can be rationalized by long-term contracts, it is difficult to explain away retail price stickiness.[2]

Price stickiness also allows theorists to entertain a wider variety of explanations for business cycle phenomena. Real wages do not apparently vary much over the business cycle, contrary to the predictions of a variety of theories ranging from Friedman's money illusion (1968) to Fischer's contract stories (1977). Traditionally, this fact has been explained in the Keynesian tradition by arguing that firms maintain a fixed markup of wages over prices. The state of unemployment determines labor's bargaining power and the change in money wages but real wage changes are limited by firm's pricing behavior. Nominal stickiness flows from labor markets while real stickiness flows from product markets.

If prices are sticky then these types of stickiness can be reversed. A number of labor market theories predict that firms and workers will want to have sticky real wages. The implicit contract models developed in the 1970s were based on the assumption that firms provided insurance against income fluctuations to workers in a form which resulted in sticky real wages. Efficiency wage theories, reviewed in more detail below, argue that firms need to pay real wages above market clearing levels in order to either maintain employee morale or ensure discipline. If there is independent nominal price stickiness, then product markets can be the source of nominal stickiness while labor markets become the source of real wage stickiness.

What is the evidence for nominal price stickiness? Using aggregate data, Blanchard (1986) attempted to disentangle wage and price stickiness and found that price stickiness was even more important than wage stickiness. However, these efforts are naturally limited by the limited aggregate behavior in real wages. More persuasive evidence comes from looking at individual retail transactions. Cecchetti (1986) looked at price changes for thirty-eight magazines from 1953 to 1979. Some data from his study appear in table 5.1. The first column indicates the number of magazines that changed their newsstand price in any year and the second column shows the average cumulative inflation since the magazines last changed their prices. In the 1970s, more than 20 percent of the real value of magazine price had been inflated away before the magazines adjusted their prices. The other noticeable fact from the table is that the frequency of price changes increases when average inflation increases — in other words, there is not a fixed "contract period" for prices and their frequency of changes depends on the inflation rate.

There are two fundamental concepts in the new Keynesian microfoundations for price stickiness: menu costs and near-rationality. Menu costs are simply the costs of changing prices. The literature presents arguments to suggest that even if costs of changing prices are small, the social consequences from small menu costs can be large. Near rationality models are based on the idea that the private consequences of following "near rational" (but not fully rational) decision rules may be small to the individual, but the social consequences from these near rational decisions may be large. A closer look at each of these notions is warranted.

Mankiw (1985) developed a very simple but illuminating treatment of menu costs in the context of a monopolist. The literature on the microfoundations of price stickiness has been developed in the context of either monopoly or oligopoly because there is no room for purely competitive economic factors to set prices. Imperfect competition does, however, itself have implications which will become evident.

Mankiw's model is illustrated in figure 5.1. Given the aggregate price level, the monopolists sets a profit-maximizing price at p^*. Now suppose that the aggregate price level increases and the monopolist does not change his price so that the real price falls to $p1$. How does the monopolist and society fare? Since the monopolist by assumption

Table 5.1 Evidence of price stickiness

Year	Number of magazines changing price (from total of 38)	Average inflation since last change
1953	1	15.7
54	2	17.9
55	4	16.4
56	8	18.3
57	12	22.6
58	4	23.1
59	2	5.7
60	1	37.1
61	3	4.3
62	5	17.8
63	12	14.3
64	7	10.2
65	5	10.8
66	9	10.8
67	11	9.8
68	8	18.3
69	9	17.2
70	8	23.6
71	4	22.2
72	4	19.4
73	8	22.9
74	19	28.0
75	11	24.3
76	17	18.0
77	13	20.3
78	12	12.7
79	12	22.2

Adapted from Cecchetti (1986), p. 258

initially set a profit-maximizing price, profits must fall. In figure 5.1 the change in profits is the difference between ADFE and FGHC. However, this change will generally be small if the fall in the price is small. The gain to society will be the increase in the sum of consumer and producer surplus, which is the trapezoid DCHG.

Suppose now that there is real cost of changing prices which is greater than the loss in profits but smaller than the gain in social welfare. Then, in the face of the increased price level, the monopolist will not change his price and output increases. Social welfare also increases with the increase in output because society was originally in a

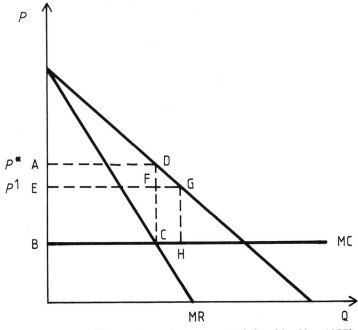

Figure 5.1   Monopoly and menu costs (after Mankiw, 1985)

position where price exceeded marginal cost. A boom (at least one in which price still remains above marginal cost) is good for society and the good feeling associated with a high-pressure economy is not simply an illusion as would be implied by models featuring imperfect information.

If the aggregate price level increased far enough, the loss in potential monopoly profits would be greater than the menu cost and the firm would change its price to the original profit-maximizing point. Small decreases in the aggregate price level (or decreases relative to what was anticipated when prices were set) will not decrease profits enough to incur the menu costs and the real price will increase with a loss in social welfare and lower output. Large decreases in the aggregate price level will cause the firm to reset its price. Thus, if we imagine aggregating across firms, there should be a nonlinear and decreasing relation between movements in the aggregate price level (or some appropriate proxy) and output. This is a testable implication of the model which we will explore below.

Akerlof and Yellen (1985) developed the concept of near rationality and have applied it in a wide variety of contexts, including business cycles. The basic idea is simple and is portrayed in figure 5.2. Suppose an economic decision-maker is choosing a variable x to maximize a smooth differentiable objective function. Denote the optimal choice as x^*. Now consider the consequences of small deviations from x^*. Since the objective function is flat at the top (as required by x^* truly being the maximum), the effects on realized value of the objective function will be small if the decision-maker deviates slightly from x^*. Losses from near rationality will be "second-order."

This point also can be made simply by an algebraic argument. Consider a second-order Taylor expansion around the optimal choice x^*:

$$\Pi(x) = \Pi(x^*) + \Pi'(x^*)(x-x^*) + \Pi''(x^*)(x-x^*)^2/2$$

The first term on the right hand side is just the profit at the optimal x^*. The second term, which represents the first-order effects from deviating from the optimal x^*, *vanishes* because the derivative of Π at the optimum must be zero. As portrayed in figure 5.2, the objective function is flat at the optimum. Thus, only second- and higher-order terms separate actual profit from potential profits if we deviate from the optimum level.

Although losses to an individual may be second-order from not following an optimal rule, the effects on society can be large. To see this point, consider a simple example. Suppose individuals are holding precisely the level of real balances they desire and the nominal money

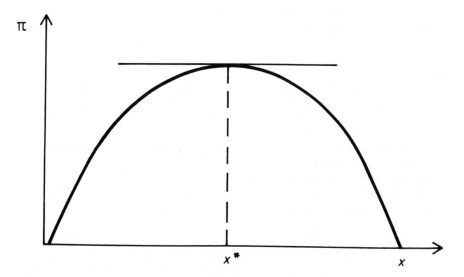

Figure 5.2   Near rationality

supply suddenly increases. If individuals do not change their prices, they will be holding too high a level of money balances but their loss will be second-order. The societal effects, however, can be large. If no one changes their prices, real balances will increase by the full amount of the nominal increase in the money supply. Akerlof and Yellen make these arguments precise by considering the differences in welfare between fully rational and near rational individuals, which they show to be second-order, and the effects on equilibrium which they show to be first-order in a wide variety of models.

These arguments require objective functions to be differentiable in the arguments that agents choose, which in the macro context, are usually wages and prices. In perfectly competitive models, this condition will not be satisfied. If a perfect competitor raises his price, profits will plummet to zero as customers desert the firm. Models with monopoly or monopolistic competition will satisfy this requirement for prices since the demand curves facing these firms will not be perfectly elastic.

Akerlof and Yellen also emphasize that if firms pay efficiency wages, then their objective functions will be differentiable in the wage level. Efficiency wages arise when the wage paid to workers affects their performance level in some way. Some evidence on the importance of efficiency wages is provided by Krueger and Summers (1988). They find persistent inter-industry wage differentials that cannot be explained by working conditions, quality of workers, or the usual human-capital variables. The most persuasive evidence concerns workers who switch to the industries that pay wage premia and apparently receive higher wages. This cannot be explained by unmeasured ability. Thus, if efficiency wages are important, this suggests that firms' profit functions are differentiable in wages.

Upon closer reflection, there is one very troublesome aspect of near rationality theory. Suppose a firm had initially chosen x^* and economic conditions changed so that a lower value of x was now optimal. By near rationality considerations, the firm does not suffer much since losses are second-order. However, suppose economic conditions change again and the optimal x falls further. Now the near rationality argument does not work because the firm was not at the optimal level or on top of the objective function prior to the second shock. In terms of the Taylor expansion, the derivative of profit at the new original position is not zero so the loss from not optimizing is now first-order.

Near rationality does not seem to work as a dynamic theory. In the face of continued shocks, not changing one's decisions will eventually hurt. If one is lucky enough to be at the optimum to begin with, then the initial loss will be small but continued intransigence must cost the firm or individual. Dynamic considerations severely limit the scope of near rationality arguments. More surprising, however, is that dynamic arguments also raise near fatal doubts about the menu cost view.

Caplin and Spulber (1987) present an ingenious argument that shows that menu cost effects may be significant for individual firms but can entirely disappear in the aggregate. They assume that firms face a fixed menu cost every time they change their price. Firms are assumed to follow Ss policies in changing their prices. Whenever the firms adjust their price they set the log of their real price equal to S. Inflation then erodes the real value of their prices. When the log of their real price hits $s < S$, they than change the price to S. Thus, all firms have their prices in the range $s - S$ and only change their prices when they hit the lower boundary.

Caplin and Spulber make two key assumptions in their analysis. First, they assume that the money supply (which drives the nominal variables in the model) is continuous and always increasing. This rules out the possibility that firms will want to optimally decrease their price which would not be compatible with the Ss format. For moderate inflation rates, however, this assumption does not seem too strong. The other key assumption is that at the beginning of time, prices are distributed evenly across the Ss interval. This assumption is meant to capture asynchronous price adjustment and also seems innocuous.

Caplin and Spulber then prove that as long as firms anticipate that aggregate real balances (M/P where P is an aggregate price index) will be constant, then indeed real balances will be constant and movements in money will have no effects on the economy! This occurs despite the fact that, in the face of an increase in the money supply, most firms will not change their price because of menu costs.

The logic of their argument can be seen with the aid of figure 5.3, which is adapted from their paper. The circle represents the range of real prices (Ss) with the high and low prices at the top of the circle. As inflation procedes, real prices are eroded and move counterclockwise along the circle. Relative prices r_1 and r_2 erode the same amount because of the inflation and are not adjusted. However, relative price r_3 first erodes far enough to hit the lower boundary, is adjusted immediately upwards to S, and then continues to erode. Note the amount that each relative price moves along the circle is the same and is independent of its initial position. Thus, if the distribution of relative prices is initially uniform, it will remain uniform after any period of monetary expansion. This ensures monetary neutrality.

Another way to understand their result is to recognize that although only a few prices will change with a monetary expansion, each price that does change will change by a large amount. Moreover, the greater the monetary expansion, the greater will be the number of prices that will change. Thus, on the surface, the Caplin and Spulber model seems

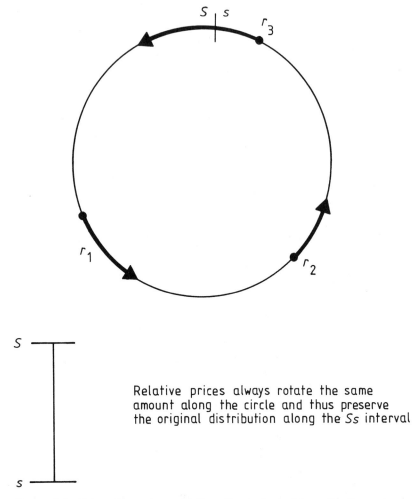

Figure 5.3   Price dispersion and *Ss* policy (adapted from Caplin and Spulber, 1987)

consistent with the magazine evidence in table 5.1. Real prices are eroded by inflation but the number of price changes is greater the higher the inflation rate. Yet, as the Caplin–Spulber model illustrates, this is potentially compatible with monetary neutrality.

In some sense, the menu costs models were too clever by half. By having agents decide to change prices based on optimizing strategies, these models were susceptible to having their basic points undone through aggregation. The older wage or price inflexibility stories, although not as intellectually satisfying, would not be susceptible to destruction through similar aggregation.

There have naturally been a number of criticisms of the Caplin—Spulber model but, on the whole, they fail to deflate its rather devastating message. First, as noted above, prices could fall in some industries, particularly at low average inflation rates. While this may be true for primary commodities, it is not likely to be serious for moderate inflation rates. Second, *Ss* policies may not themselves be fully optimal even in the framework of Caplin and Spulber. *Ss* policies have a long history in the inventory literature where it is well known that *Ss* policies are only optimal in some stochastic settings. Nonetheless, they operate as rough rules of thumb that allow endogenous price changes which would occur in fully optimal models.

Rotemberg (1987) suggests that these models miss the idea of a monetary "shock" in the sense that some prices always adjust to the money supply. Yet, to introduce a monetary shock requires some notion of imperfect information at least in the short run. While this is plausible, it would make the models harder to distinguish from other models of imperfect information that were developed in the 1970s. Others have criticized the assumption that the initial distribution of prices is uniform over the *Ss* interval. Caplin and Spulber defend this assumption as an approximate outcome if firms follow *Ss* strategies. Finally, one last criticism of the model is that the *Ss* bounds themselves should be functions of at least the mean inflation rate. Abrupt changes in the average inflation rate could then cause monetary non-neutralities.

While these criticisms all make legitimate points concerning the complete and full optimality of the rules followed in the Caplin—Spulber model, they do seem second-order. An analogy may be helpful here. Every student of monetary theory can recite an entire list of reasons why perfectly anticipated inflation can still have non-neutral effects (taxes, real balance effects etc.). Yet, very few economists ever took these effects seriously to explain business cycle fluctuations arising from money. Given the rationality assumed in the menu cost literature, the aggregation results from Caplin and Spulber are the most natural. If the result is not satisfactory, perhaps it is the theory itself which is misleading.

Despite the problems raised by Caplin and Spulber's criticism, two other theoretical aspects of the microfoundations of price stickiness may be important in future theoretical or empirical work. First, small menu costs can lead to externalities in the aggregate, a possibility which opens the door for conventional microeconomic analysis. Second, real rigidities and nominal rigidities interact to heighten the effects of nominal rigidities. Thus, if the endogenous timing of price changes, highlighted by Caplin and Spulber, is not sufficient to remove all aggregate price stickiness then a combination of nominal and real stickiness can lead to prolonged business fluctuations.

Externalities, first identified by Blanchard and Kiyotaki (1987), arise because individual decision-makers do not take into account the effects of their decisions on changing prices on the aggregate price level. In a typical model of monopolistic competition, demand for an individual firm's product depends on total aggregate demand and firm's relative price. Menu costs arguments suggest that the firm may not find the loss in profits to be greater than the cost of changing its price. However, if all firms make the same decision in the face of a monetary shock, the aggregate price level will not change which leads to changes in real balances and aggregate demand. Thus, individual micro decisions not to change prices lead to large first-order effects on aggregate demand.

Thus, in a recession, all firms would be better off if they incurred the menu cost and changed their price. This would not increase their own market share but would increase aggregate demand. Just as in conventional models of externalities, firms do not take into account the full social effects of their actions. Private and social incentives diverge and firms will not find it in their private interest to cut prices and incur the menu cost. Reinflating demand through a monetary expansion solves this particular coordination problem.

In a general equilibrium model with menu costs, these nominal rigidities are not a sufficient propagating mechanism for business cycles. Keynesian economists attacked the new classical models for the central role that intertemporal substitution of leisure over time played in new classical models of the business cycles. As a general rule, Keynesian economists generally downplayed any significant short- or long-run elasticity in labor supply except, perhaps, for some groups in the economy. Yet, with inelastic labor supply it is difficult to produce models of business cycles with menu costs.

Suppose there is a monetary shock in a model in which monopolistically competitive firms face menu costs. If they do not change their prices, aggregate demand will increase. However, as long as labor is inelastically supplied to the market, the increase in aggregate demand cannot increase total output. Only if the supply of labor exhibited significant short-run elasticity could output possibly increase in the face of a demand shock.

Combining nominal rigidities with real rigidities, however, widens the potential empirical scope of menu cost models. There are several reasons why real wages may be "rigid." The two most prominent are insurance through implicit contracts and efficiency wages. Suppose that firms do pay efficiency wages to ensure morale or reduce shirking. In this case, the real wage will be set above market clearing levels and labor will not be on its supply curve. In other words, there is involuntary unemployment. In equilibrium the wage level will be set for efficiency reasons while the quantity of labor employed will be such that the marginal product of labor (measured in efficiency units) will equal the real wage. The supply of labor to the firm does not affect its pricing or output decisions. Thus, a fall in labor demand, engendered by a decrease in aggregate demand, will lead to decreased employment regardless of the labor supply elasticity.

This is just one example of how real and nominal rigidities interact. Ball and Romer (1987) provide a more general argument that the presence of real rigidities opens the scope for nominal rigidities to be important in propagating business cycles. Consider a Nash equilibrium with menu costs where firms experience a nominal shock. As each firm contemplates the gain to changing its nominal price, it realizes that if it changes its price and other firms fail to change their prices then its real price will change. However, if the benefits of changing real prices are small, that is, if there is *real* price rigidity, then the incentive for a firm to change its price decreases. The scope for nominal shocks to affect the equilibrium is naturally increased if firms have less incentive to change their prices. Thus, real rigidities widen the scope for nominal rigidities.

The new Keynesian microfoundations abound with interesting arguments such as those based on externalities and the interaction of real and nominal rigidities. But there are also interesting counterarguments such as the basic neutrality results of Caplin and Spulber resulting from the endogenous timing of price changes. When theories collide empirical work generally flourishes. But there is surprisingly little empirical work in support of the aggregate implications of the microfoundations of price stickiness. The lack of empirical work is partly due to the aim of the research program which was to provide theoretical foundation for Keynesian principles. However, there are several testable propositions that do emerge from this literature.

A first, and very simple test of the menu cost model is to explore the implications of Mankiw's model that large monetary shocks should not matter because firms will want to incur the menu cost. A simple way to test this idea is to adapt the literature on the effects of monetary shocks. The strategy is to estimate a simple model relating business fluctuations to monetary shocks and then to test whether "large shocks" are neutral. The literature on testing for the effects of unanticipated and anticipated money is a good source for a basic framework. Although the literature failed to settle the controversy whether only unanticipated shocks matter and raised many subtle econometric issues, all investigators found that monetary shocks, regardless of how they were defined, seemed to affect output.

Table 5.2   Testing menu cost models

Basic regression: 1948–78

$$\log [U_t/(1-U_t)] = -2.21 \quad -5.8 \text{ DMR}$$
$$(+20.2) \quad (2.9)$$

$$-10.4 \quad \text{DMR } (-1) \ -6.8 \text{ G/Y}$$
$$(5.3) \quad (7.3)$$

$\bar{R}^2 = 0.759$
$dw = 1.67$

DMR = unanticipated money growth
G/Y = ratio of government spending to output
U_t = unemployment rate

Second regression (additional variables)

		coefficient	t-statistic
squared	DMR	−48.9	−0.46
squared	DMR(−1)	91.2	0.87

$\bar{R}^2 = 0.750$

Data from Barro (1981), pp. 144–53

Table 5.2 contains regressions testing for the effects of large shocks based on a standard model developed by Barro (1981). The first regression explains a nonlinear function of unemployment in terms of current and lagged monetary shocks (his DMR variable) and the ratio of government spending to output. Both current and lagged monetary shocks reduce unemployment and an increase in the ratio of government spending to output also decreases unemployment.

The second equation adds quadratic terms in current and lagged monetary shocks. If large shocks do not matter, then these coefficients should be significant and the combination of the linear and quadratic effects should be small for large shocks. Unfortunately, these coefficients are estimated imprecisely and are not statistically significant. Thus, there is no evidence that "large" monetary shocks have any different effects than "small" monetary shocks in annual US time series, contrary to the predictions of menu cost theory.

Ball, Mankiw, and Romer (1988) test menu cost models using cross-country comparisons. Their basic idea is straightforward. Price setters in countries with high average inflation rates change their prices more frequently than in countries with low average inflation rates. Thus, monetary shocks should have less effect in countries with high average inflation rates. In other words, the slope of the Phillips curve or output–inflation tradeoff should be flatter in high inflation countries.

This idea should sound very familiar to macroeconomists. Indeed, Lucas's famous paper (1973) on the slope of the Phillips curve introduced much of the profession to rational expectations models. Lucas's model, however, was slightly different. In his model, agents tried to disentangle movements in their real prices from movements in their nominal prices. In countries with high *variability* in nominal prices, agents would tend to interpret most price changes as nominal rather than real. The Phillips curve should be steeper in countries with highly variable aggregate prices. The countries, however, with the most variable aggregate prices were precisely those with higher average inflation rates. Thus, the Phillips curve in Argentina was steeper than the Phillips curve in the United States.

Ball, Mankiw, and Romer point out that in Lucas's model the average or mean inflation rate does not matter, only the variance of aggregate prices. However, menu cost models suggest that the mean inflation rate should also matter. They test their theory against Lucas's by examining regressions relating the slope of the Phillips curve across countries to the mean and variance of inflation rates.

There are a number of difficulties that will naturally plague this approach. First, the correlation between the mean and variance of inflation is very high (0.92) which implies that a premium must be placed on identifying the correct econometric equation to differentiate the effects of the two variables. Second, the slope of the Phillips curve is taken to be a constant for each country but according to either theory should vary across the sample as economic conditions change. Finally, it is hard to identify a constant mean and variance for inflation in unstable environments such as those which characterize most of the sample.

Ball, Mankiw, and Romer provide a variety of regressions which show that both the mean inflation rate and the variance of nominal income are correlated with the slope of the Phillips curve but that the effects from the mean are stronger when both variables are included. Akerlof, Rose, and Yellen (1988) take a careful look at the robustness of these econometric results and suggest that it is not possible to separate the effects. As an example, using the inverse of the slope of the Phillips curve as the dependent variable suggests the variance of aggregate demand may be more important than the mean inflation rate. This suggests that the basic results are not robust and too highly sensitive to functional forms.

At this juncture, the new Keynesian microfoundations for price stickiness are elegant stories but have produced few empirical insights or testable propositions. While they have added to the richness of the Keynesian tradition, they have not produced the evidence to dissuade either older Keynesians, content to live with the unexplained existence of nominal contracts, or non-Keynesians from changing their intellectual positions.

5.3   Keynesian Models of Incomplete Markets and Imperfect Information

Another strand in the new Keynesian microfoundation literature is predicated on deriving "Keynesian" features from models based on imperfect information. In a series of papers, Greenwald and Stiglitz (1986a, 1986b, 1987) have sketched their view of a new Keynesian microfoundation. While they do not present one complete model to feature all their ideas, they do provide an overview based on a variety of models to illustrate their points.

Greenwald and Stiglitz argue that any modern model that incorporates Keynes's valid insights must have several properties. First, a model or theory must account for fluctuations in unemployment and the persistence of unemployment. Motives for savings and investment must be carefully distinguished. Finally, disturbances in demand, not supply, must be the driving force for the economy.

Four theoretical ingredients form the foundation of what Greenwald and Stiglitz (1987) call the "New Keynesian Economics." These ingredients are efficiency wage theories, credit market imperfections, credit rationing, and a new view of monetary policy. All share a similar origin as theories based on incomplete information and incomplete markets, in contrast to the complete market vision of real business cycle theory.[3]

We have already reviewed the basic idea of efficiency wage theories. From Greenwald and Stiglitz's perspective, efficiency wage theories provide a rationale for why firms will not cut wages in the face of an excess supply of labor. Simply put, they do not cut wages because this would increase, not decrease their total costs.

Similar arguments, previously developed by Stiglitz and Weiss (1981), also apply to credit markets and can explain why interest rates do not always adjust to clear the market for loans. If a bank raises the interest rate it may change the customer mix and the behavior of customers in ways which will lower its total expected proceeds. Higher interest rates may attract less desirable borrowers who could not obtain funds from other sources and also cause existing borrowers to take undesirable risks. If banks limit the extent to which they raise interest rates, credit rationing may result in equilibrium.

Perhaps the most novel and important feature of arguments developed by Greenwald and Stiglitz is their notion of "equity rationing." Because of asymmetries between managers and investors, firms can only obtain a limited amount of funds directly through external equity financing. Further external funds can only be obtained through borrowing.

One current view of corporate financing suggests that managers of firms prefer equity to debt financing. With diffuse equity ownership, managers have more latitude than they do with debt financing which subjects the firm to both restrictive debt convenants and extensive scrutiny from banks and other large lenders. However, the market understands this and therefore limits external equity finance to corporations. Those corporations which must resort to raising funds through new issues of equity are generally penalized by the market.

With a reluctance to finance projects through new equity issues, firms must either rely on retained earnings, or external debt. Extensive debt financing, however, exposes a firm to the risk of bankruptcy. Although the conventional wisdom is that explicit costs of bankruptcy proceedings are small, the actions that a firm near bankruptcy are often forced to take can be very costly. The combination of explicit and implicit bankruptcy costs can therefore be significant.

Greenwald and Stiglitz argue that managers of firms are risk-averse. The fear of bankruptcy or near bankruptcy is exacerbated by the lack of future markets for firms' products. Production decisions must be taken in advance of knowledge of market conditions and firms must gamble with their limited equity capital anytime they make commitments to produce. In a simplified model, Greenwald and Stiglitz (1986a) stress the importance of working capital. Working capital consists of the gross proceeds from the prior sale of a firms' product less any required debt repayments. This scarce working capital must be committed in advance to any new undertakings of the firm. Scarce working capital (or generally equity capital) combined with the risks implicit in any decision to produce can explain several aspects of business cycles.

First, equity rationing with risk-averse behavior provides the foundation for Greenwald and Stiglitz's theory of business cycles:

> The theory of business fluctuations it provides is simple: in broad outlines, certain shocks to the economy affect the stock of working capital of firms. Even if firms had perfect access to the credit markets ... the amount they would be willing to borrow is limited by their willingness to bear risk; the fixed commitments associated with loan contracts implies that, as the working capital which is available is reduced, the risk (bankruptcy probability) associated with any level of borrowing increases. Thus, if their working capital is reduced, their desired production level is lowered; and it takes time to restore working capital. (1987, pp. 126–7)

Monetary shocks or other aggregate shocks reduce the working capital of firms and thus lead to decreased production through risk effects. In recessions, the bankruptcy probability of firm's purchasers or suppliers increases thereby exposing the firm to additional risk. Multiplier effects can arise from these interactions.

Second, the combination of equity rationing and risk aversion can also explain why "sectoral shocks" can be important. An increase in the price of oil or the relative price of any commodity will redistribute working capital among firms. This redistribution will not, in general, be neutral. With identical risk-averse firms facing increasing marginal costs, Greenwald and Stiglitz (1986a) show that aggregate output is a concave function of working capital among firms which implies that increased dispersion of working capital will reduce aggregate output. An oil price increase which transferred equity capital abroad to oil suppliers would increase the risk of domestic firms and decrease production.

Finally, several other features of business cycles can be explained by equity rationing and risk aversion. Firms are reluctant to produce for inventories during recessions when labor costs may be low because of the risk associated with accumulating a relatively illiquid asset, inventories, during a period of aggregate risk. Although interest rates fall during recessions, stock prices also fall, and the increased required yield on equities can raise a firm's effective discount rate. With a higher discount rate, the firm will be less reluctant to cut prices, sacrificing current profits for future customers, and less likely to hold inventories or related capital. Thus, price−cost markups may be countercyclical and desired inventories reduced even though market interest rates fall. Market interest rates provide a poor guide to the true shadow cost of funds for equity-rationed firms.

The theory of equity rationing and firm risk aversion produces a number of interesting implications but there are two difficulties with this theory as a foundation of a new Keynesian economics. The first difficulty and perhaps the most difficult is that the theory does not make direct contact with empirical macroeconomics or suggest how this contact should be made. One of the reasons that the rational expectations movement and even new classical economics influenced a wide range of economists was that they suggested a program for empirical research. Thomas Sargent and others developed new empirical methods for rational expectations models and new tests of theories were suggested by the new classical economics.

The empirical problems of the Greenwald−Stiglitz theory are compounded by the fact that the key empirical entity in their theory, the implicit cost of equity capital, is unobservable. This poses particularly difficult problems because interest rates fall during recessions. All their key effects are driven by an unobservable rise in the cost of equity capital.

On theoretical grounds it is also unclear why the cost of equity capital exceeds market borrowing costs for the firm. According to the theory, corporations are forced to take debt. But even for marginal borrowing, it appears that market rates for debt finance are below those on equity capital. Is the essence of recessions that firms are forced to borrow too much cheap capital? Not all finance theories predict that firms are forced into debt finance. Another well-known tradition suggests that because interest payments are deductible for tax purposes while dividends are not, firms borrow "too much" to economize on tax payments. Cross-country comparisons usually suggest the United States has a relatively high cost of capital because firms rely too extensively on equity financing. Are marginal capital costs better measured by the after-tax cost of debt in the market?

Greenwald and Stiglitz would respond that the cost of debt finance is not measured by the marginal borrowing cost in the market but that the presence of additional debt creates shadow costs as well. But this simply highlights both the difficulties of testing their theories because of the key role of unobservables as well as the need to develop a more complete theory of business cycle.

A related literature which has been developed more rigorously emphasizes the role that equity plays in reducing agency costs, that is, the costs of monitoring and supervising managers of firms. Bernanke and Gertler (1986) and Williamson (1987) develop general equilibrium models in which the financial structure affects the real equilibrium of the economy and have the features that increases in internal finance reduce the agency costs in the economy.[4]

These models revolve around an insight of Townsend (1979) that debt contracts emerge naturally in a world of asymmetric information. Suppose that entrepreneurs have to obtain funds beyond their own resources in order to undertake investment projects but that the returns to their projects are private information. Moreover, investors have to incur a cost to discover the true returns to the project. In this framework, Townsend proved that contracts resembling debt arrangements would be efficient. As long as the investor was solvent, a fixed payment would be made to investors. If the investor declared himself insolvent, the investors would pay the cost to "audit" the project and would also appropriate all the returns.

With asymmetric information, it is necessary that auditing occur in some states of the world, otherwise the entrepreneur could always lie and say that the return of the project was zero. In states in which auditing does not occur, the payment to investors must be constant because there is no additional information on which to base the payment schedule. Finally, once auditing occurs, the entire payment should accrue to investors. Otherwise, the fixed debt payment would be higher and auditing would become more frequent.

Contracts of this form minimize expected auditing costs. This is the appropriate criterion for risk-neutral investors and entrepreneurs. In "most times" the auditing cost is not incurred and fixed payments are made to investors but the auditing cost is incurred in bad times. The larger the amount of internal finance an investor brings to a project, the lower will be the probability of insolvency and thus the lower will be expected auditing or agency costs.

It is not difficult to see how these ideas can fit into a business cycle context. Suppose the economy is shocked in such a way that insiders' equity is reduced. This will raise expected agency costs in the economy and can thereby reduce investment which, in turn, can cause further movements in insiders' equity. Expected agency costs will thereby be higher in recessions. This provides an explanation for sluggish investment during downturns.

Bernanke and Gertler also analyze the effects of disturbances which mimic the "debt deflation" of Irving Fisher that was discussed in chapter 4. An unanticipated fall in the price level can dilute firms' equity holdings and force them to borrow more from external markets. These additional borrowings raise expected agency costs in the economy and can propagate a downturn in the economy. Moreover, relative price shocks which redistribute equity can have real effects in this model as in the Greenwald–Stiglitz models.

One difficulty with these models is that they seem best suited for discussing the plight of small business than large corporations that can have access to capital market. Indeed, Bernanke (1983) argued that farmers and small firms were the ones most significantly devastated during the Great Depression because of the bank or credit failures. For farmers and small business, bank credit was their only source of external finance and the dilution of internal equity combined with the collapse of their sole external credit markets was devastating.

However, for large corporations with access to credit markets, it is not evident how increases in "expected audit costs" manifest themselves. The difficulty of pinpointing auditing costs raises issues similar to those regarding the cost of equity capital in the Greenwald and Stiglitz model. Bernanke (1983) suggested that increased costs of financial intermediation could be observed as the widening of the spread between safe assets, which require no monitoring, and risky assets that require monitoring. Thus, increased spreads between Treasury bonds and AAA corporate bonds would indicate increased costs of intermediation in the economy. Yet, this same increase in the spread between yields on securities during recessions would be predicted by anyone who believed that corporate bonds are more risky than government bonds and that the risk spread increases during recessions. It is difficult to find an independent measure for "expected auditing costs" so that the theory can apply to the large corporate sector.

These new models suggest that the fate of financial institutions can matter for the behavior of the economy. But aside from warnings, they do not yet provide sufficient information to distinguish the consequences of bank failure from failures of other large corporations. Tobin (1987) argued that the failures and financial crises of the 1980s differed from those of the 1930s in that the 1980 difficulties were not runs on currency but were simply shifts of deposits from threatened financial institutions to others. These shifts did not destroy reserves or threaten the solvency of the banking system. Indeed, the Fed's efforts in bailing out large banks such as Continental Illinois increased reserves substantially and had to be coupled with open market sales.

The United States political system is now structured so that potential failures of large financial institutions are handled by the Federal Reserve system and other financial regulatory bodies while bail-outs of large corporations must take the politically more difficult route through Congress. Yet, if the failure of a large bank, as Tobin believes, need not cause macroeconomic dysfunction, why should there be special treatment for financial institutions? The new macro literature suggests that the destruction of specific capital in the form of private knowledge may raise the cost of financial intermediation. Yet, the failure of any business is accompanied by the disappearance of specific capital in the form of special relations with suppliers and purchasers. The new macro literature correctly emphasizes these effects for financial institutions but has yet to provide the quantitative tools to address these difficult questions. Mark Gertler (1988, p. 38), a proponent of these models, concurs in this assessment: "The theoretical models developed thus far are highly stylized and capable of generating only qualitative predictions. Due to methodological limitations, there currently does not exist a unified framework which can directly confront the data."

5.4 Efficient Markets?

Through most of the 1970s, it would have been difficult to find economists who did not subscribe to the notion of efficient financial markets. Although there were plenty of skeptics concerning the efficiency of markets for goods or labor, critics of efficient financial markets were much fewer in number. Part of the reason that rational expectations theory grew in popularity was the apparent success of the similar notion, efficient markets, in financial theory.

Careful reviews of the efficient market literature always stressed that tests of the theory were always *joint* tests of a particular model of the determination of the returns on assets and the rational expectations assumption that market participants knew the distributions of returns. Faith in the rational expectations assumption was such that failures of the tests led to the development of new models of equilibrium returns. "For better or worse, they [researchers] have embraced efficient markets or rational expectations as a *research principle* or tool for deciding the validity of models of equilibrium price determination" (Sheffrin, 1983, p. 150; italics in the original).

This is no longer the case. The shift in mood probably began with Shiller's (1981) work on "excess volatility" of financial markets. Although there has been substantial controversy concerning Shiller's tests, there is now a consensus that models of stock price behavior based on a constant expected required return to holding equity are totally inadequate to capture stock market dynamics.

The most recent research on the returns from holding stock strongly reject the hypothesis that expected returns are constant over all time horizons. Stock price changes are apparently random over short time horizons. But as Fama and French (1988) have documented, returns to holding stock are strongly negatively correlated over longer time horizons extending to several years. High returns now imply low returns in the future. The negative correlation in stock returns arises because there is a slow mean-reverting movement in stock prices. To put it simply, when stock prices have been high, they tend to fall; when prices have been low, they tend to rise. Movements in stock prices seem random over short intervals but over longer periods, this mean reversion is evident.

How should this mean reversion in stock prices be interpreted? Fama and French offer one interpretation that is consistent with efficient markets. Suppose that required returns in the stock market are highly serially correlated but they eventually revert to a constant long-run level. In this case, a shock to expected returns that does not effect long-run dividends will not change the price of stocks in the long run. This is because both dividends and required returns will be unchanged in the long run. However, in the short run, stock prices will have to change immediately because of the shock to expected returns. This change will only disappear as required returns slowly revert to their long-run value. Expectations can be rational but changes in required returns can cause the mean reversion in stock prices.

Summers (1986), however, offers an alternative and radically different story that can account for the same mean reversion in stock prices. Suppose that there are simply "fads" in the market in which investors become inexplicably bullish or bearish for stretches of time. If these fads eventually die out but only do so slowly, then market prices will exhibit mean reversion. This theory, of course, fits closely to popular notions. The market can feed on itself for extended periods of time, driving the market either higher or lower than fundamental values would warrant. The expected value of the fad component gradually dies out over time but new shocks to the fad component keep the market almost always away from fundamental values.

The notion that the market can diverge for substantial times from fundamental value has been given impetus by the concept of "noise traders" in financial markets pioneered by Fischer Black (1986). Black postulated the existence of noise trades, individuals who irrationally participate in markets, in order to explain a wide variety of phenomena in capital markets.

Black argued that noise traders were needed to explain the sheer volume of trading activity that occurs in financial markets. Without noise traders, traders who erroneously believe they are trading on correct information, there would be virtually no trade in individual shares and little asset turnover in the market. Rational investors trading with each other would realize that the other person is only willing to pay a higher price for an asset if that person has superior information. This realization will limit the trading of rational traders who trade on information. Without much trading in individual shares, it would be difficult to correctly price mutual funds or other broad hedging vehicles.

Without noise traders, markets would not be "liquid" enough to facilitate trade. Noise traders are necessary in order to provide the liquidity for healthy markets. But since noise traders operate on spurious information, they necessarily bring irrational forces to the market. The necessary existence of noise traders also implies the necessary inefficiencies of financial markets.

Not all traders, of course, are noise traders. Sophisticated traders bring correct information to the market and trade with the noise traders. The presence of noise traders provides the incentives for the sophisticated investors to gather information, as Grossman and Stiglitz (1976) emphasized in a related context. Sophisticated traders move asset prices towards fundamental values; the cumulative effects of noise traders push asset prices away from these values. Sophisticated traders act more aggressively when prices deviate too far from fundamental value thereby limiting the extent of divergences between price and value. Yet, at any time, noise traders prevent prices from equalling value. Black offered this rather outrageous definition of efficient markets: "However, we might define an efficient market as one in which price is within a factor of 2 of value, i.e., the price is more than half of value and less than twice value" (1986, p. 533).

Do sophisticated traders necessarily drive noise traders from the market? Black pointed out that the presence of noise traders makes markets more risky and thereby limits the positions that sophisticated traders are willing to take. Although a stock may be overvalued, noise traders could make it even more overvalued over short periods of time. DeLong, Shleifer, and Summers (1987) studied this issue in detail with a simple model of sophisticated traders and noise traders. They found that if noise traders took larger risky positions on average, they could profit in the market despite their erroneous beliefs. The essential reason was that noise traders created their own risk and raised the return to holding risky assets. By holding larger risky positions on average, they could earn high returns on their wealth and remain in the market.

The spectacular rise and fall of the United States dollar on world foreign exchange markets in the 1980s also provided fuel for the notion that markets were not efficient. Krugman (1988) argues that the behavior of the exchange rate not only violated the behavior predicted by the simplest efficient market model but did so in such a way as to cast doubt on more sophisticated explanations. In models without risk premia, expected depreciation of a currency should be equal to the excess of domestic over foreign interest rates. This implies that exchange rate change *ex post* should, on average, equal interest differentials and that differences between exchange rate changes and interest differentials should be serially uncorrelated.

Krugman presents evidence that the Deutschmark−dollar rate moved in the opposite direction through the first half of the 1980s to the direction predicted by interest differentials and that differences were highly serially correlated over six-month periods. The dollar kept rising on world markets despite no comparable movements in interest differentials. Explaining this phenomenon based on models which feature risk premia would be little help. These models would require that the dollar became more risky as it rose! This puts a large explanatory burden on an unobservable risk premium.

There are other explanations that could possibly account for the exchange rate movement in a manner consistent with efficient markets. The market could have been expecting major events that never materialized in the 1980s, the "peso" problem. Yet, what were these major events? Other explanations rest on unobserved movements in long-run real exchange rates caused by perhaps fiscal policy. But the connections between fiscal policies and real exchange rates are not understood sufficiently to simply adopt this explanation.

This attack on efficient markets is not directly connected to the new

Keynesian economics which, for the most part, strives to provide rigorous and rational foundations for Keynesian theory. It does, however, add to the arsenal of those economists who are not overly fearful of government intervention, particularly in foreign exchange markets.

Lest the critical tone of this chapter be misinterpreted, it is important to stress that the work in the new Keynesian camp has been interesting and provocative. By all means, it should continue and attempt to provide us with new insights and perspectives. As the work continues, however, it is hard not to harbor the suspicion that it will reinforce, not overturn, the older tacit consensus.

Notes

1 However, see Mankiw et al. (1987) and Blanchard (1987a).
2 However, brand loyalty and habit-forming consumption behavior could possibly lead to some stickiness.
3 Recent real business cycle literature has begun to consider the consequences of incomplete markets and externalities. See Williamson (1987) and King et al. (1988).
4 See Gertler (1988) for a recent survey.

6

Strategic Models of Policymaking

6.1 Introduction

Mainstream macroeconomics has traditionally regarded economic policy as a branch of normative economics − that is, as addressing the question of what should be the best or, more pretentiously, the "optimal policy." The most pronounced tendency along these lines was the development of optimal control theory in the late 1960s and early 1970s. Optimal control theory, adopted from engineering, addressed the policy questions in a direct and precise manner. Given a well-specified model of the economy, precisely how should economic controls (monetary variables or fiscal variables) be manipulated to reach the best possible outcomes, where "best" is determined with reference to the policymakers' preferences over alternative outcomes? Once the policy decision had been specified along these lines, optimal control theory could dictate the methods necessary to solve for the optimal policy choices in ever more complicated models and environments ranging from nonlinearities to uncertainties of various types. Chow's book (1975) provides a rigorous statement of these developments.

Control theory divorced optimal policy decisions from existing policy institutions. Indeed, as a normative project, control theory promised to improve policymaking by realistically linking controls, monetary and fiscal policy levers, with ultimate goals such as employment and price stability. Early in its development, however, concerns related to the institutional environment of policymaking did begin to creep into formulations of control problems. Users of control theory quickly found that if policy preferences were solely defined over ultimate outcomes such as employment and price stability, the policy instruments themselves would show a disturbing degree of volatility. Indeed, sometimes the optimal behavior for policy instruments would literally be unstable leading to the delightful term, "instrument instability."

But even if the solutions for optimal monetary or fiscal policy were not literally unstable, they exhibited too high a degree of variability to be deemed as realistic for policymakers.

The solution proposed for this problem was to attach penalties in the policymakers objective functions to fluctuations in the instruments themselves. For example, preferences of policymakers would include, in addition to variables relating to price and employment behavior, indicators of the volatility of monetary and fiscal policy. Optimal solutions would then be forced to trade off greater precision in reaching desired goals against too much underlying volatility in the instruments necessary to reach those goals.[1]

Unfortunately, this compromise diminished the appeal of control theory as a normative tool. Why should the public ultimately care about the degree of variability of policy instruments if such variability were necessary to best accommodate their ultimate preferences? It is understandable that policymakers would not want to engineer rapid and reversible movements in policy instruments. They would fear being viewed as capricious and unreliable by the public if indeed the public was not fully persuaded by the promise of optimal control theory. But incorporating policymaker's preferences against instrument instability into the preference or objective functions negates the explicitly normative thrust of optimal control theory and contaminates it with the hurly-burly world of actual politics and policy choices. Institutional and political concerns then become central to the determination of "optimal policy" but without any serious reflection or understanding of the politics or institutions themselves.

But this incursion of actual policymaking into control theory was not really responsible for the decline in popularity of the optimal control framework of analysis. Rather, two other factors contributed to its lack of favor. The first factor was perhaps the most fundamental – a general, growing disenchantment with the forecasting accuracy of economic models. Optimal control theory can only be as reliable as the underlying economic models. In the early 1970s faith in the product of model builders reached a new low. Stubborn stagflation that eventually led to wage and price controls and the effects of OPEC, which were not really understood at the time, all contributed to the disillusionment with econometric models.[2] Craine, Havenner and Berry (1978) compared the performance of optimal control methods with other alternatives for the period following the first OPEC shock. Optimal control methods did not perform well because the underlying econometric models failed to forecast accurately during the sample period. As the authors observed, the delicate computers in the cockpit of an airplane are not of much use when the wing of the airplane has fallen off! At least at that time, the novelty and severity of supply shocks effectively lopped the wings off the available econometric models.

A second challenge, although perhaps less practical, proved intellectually more devastating. Lucas's criticism of current econometric practice (forever known as the Lucas critique) insisted that traditional optimal control methods would give misleading results for policy analysis. Rational economic agents would base their plans not only on current policy but on future policy. In order for rational economic agents to even formulate consistent plans into the future, they had to be informed of the policy rules that the government intended to follow. Optimal control theory proceeded on the basis that the private sector's behavioral responses (such as the relation of consumption to income) would be independent of the choice of policy. Lucas forcefully argued that this would in general not be the case.

Lucas's preferred method of analysis was different from the traditional optimal control method but still fell squarely within the camp of normative analysis. Lucas advocated that policy analysis should be conducted as the analysis of alternative policy rules with the assumption that the public would understand these rules and adjust their behavior accordingly. The welfare of the agents under alternative rules could then be compared and the rule chosen that maximized some appropriate index of the welfare of agents. Technically this meant a different style of policy analysis than under optimal control theory but the normative posture towards policymaking was similar.

Although Lucas's observations were heralded and generally accepted within the profession, they eventually were met with criticism along essentially three lines. First, it was not evident that Lucas's methods were very useful when the economy was in the process of changing to a new regime. During a transition period, the agents would not understand the full general equilibrium consequences of the new policy rule and a period of learning would transpire. It was not evident that during such a learning period ad hoc rules of thumb might fare just as well as more sophisticated learning strategies, nor was it evident that an econometrician could not do equally well in forecasting by assuming that agents at least temporarily use their old rules to forecast the future. Lucas (1978) eventually conceded these points and restricted his methods to stochastic steady states where agents have already adjusted to the new rules. While this admission limited the scope of policy analysis, in Lucas's view there really was no respectable scientific alternative. Econometricians and policymakers were helpless during a transition to a new policy regime.

Two other criticisms of Lucas's methods from his own camp stimulated work which eventually led to a resurgence of interest in positive as opposed to normative policy analysis. Kydland and Prescott (1977) observed that in many circumstances, optimal policies (even when discovered by Lucas's methods) would be *time-inconsistent*. The notion of time inconsistency means that a policymaker in the midst of implementing his optimal plan would prefer to change his plan. For example, a policymaker may have offered patent protection in order to stimulate inventions. However, once the inventions have been discovered, the same policymaker would love to strip away this patent protection in order for competitors to copy the technology and compete away the monopoly profits.

Kydland and Prescott argued that policies which were time-inconsistent would not be *credible*, that is, they would not be believed by the private sector. The implicit hypothesis in their charge is that policymakers will always act in their best interest as perceived at the current time. While they may state that they will carry out their original intentions, they cannot be trusted to keep their word. It is important to stress that this is an empirical proposition and one which has been challenged – after all, as Taylor (1983) pointed out, governments do not regularly renege on patent protection. Nonetheless, Kydland and Prescott helped to change the focus from abstract normative analysis to policy analysis which focused on rules which were time-consistent or "credible" according to their definition of the term.

The final challenge to Lucas's normative framework also inspired positive policy analysis. In Lucas's famous paper (1976) which popularized the econometric policy critique, there were two classes of examples. In the first class, a policy rule was changed and economic agents changed their rules in response. As an example, if the government was able to change the stochastic process governing income, the parameters of the consumption function would change. In all the examples in this class, the policy rules would be changed once and for all and consumers would optimally respond.

However, Lucas considered another example in his paper in which economic policy was stochastic and followed stable probability rules. In his example, the government could offer an investment credit which, when in effect, would persist with probability p to the next period, and, if not in effect, would be implemented with probability q in the next period. The public understood this (stochastic) policy rule and their investment plans included the expected capital gains and losses implied by the stochastic behavior of the investment credit.

Now in this particular example, the policy rule followed a stochastic process which was independent of economic conditions. But it is only a short step to consider stochastic policy rules conditioned on the economic environment. Congress is more likely to enact investment credits when it perceives investment is too low. A rational public may grow to anticipate these tendencies and, for example, postpone investments during some phase of a downturn in order to take advantage of the expected implementation of the credit.

Notice, however, the subtle transformation of policy analysis that has occurred. Instead of a normative posture towards the evaluation of policy, we instead see an emphasis on positive theories of policy-making and efforts to predict the behavior of politicians.

Game theoretic models of policymaking have recently become popular for macroeconomics. As we will discuss later in this chapter, game theoretic models of policymaking neatly encompass two of the criticisms of the Lucas critique; namely, that the rules policymakers follow should be time-consistent or credible and the insight that economic policy is not formulated in a vacuum but perhaps can be predicted by the private sector. These two factors have contributed to its popularity.

But not all economists are sanguine about this development. Sargent (1984) stresses that a thoroughgoing game theoretic, positive approach to economic policymaking would mean the end of the type of nor-mative analysis which Lucas prescribed and which Sargent believes holds substantial promise. If the government is viewed as an entity with constant objectives and playing a dynamic game with the private sector, then it is hard to envision what a "regime change" or "rule change" might be. Why should the government, according to this view, want to change anything? Furthermore, there would be no room for a policy advisor in this world except perhaps to fine-tune implementation of the government's strategy against the public. Normative analysis, the traditional province of macroeconomics, would be dead. In Sargent's words, "This method of understanding past government policy leaves no room for improving government policy in the future" (1984, p. 413). Barro and Gordon (1983b), who are advocates of positive economics, are quite explicit, "In our model the economist has no useful day-to-day advice to offer to the monetary authority" (p. 608).

Sargent, Blinder (1984) and others recognized that this debate was another skirmish in the old free will versus determinism conflict. Rational agents need to understand the policy process to choose their optimal strategies. Governments in turn are choosing strategies, con-ditioned on economic outcomes, to achieve their objectives. If this is an accurate description of private sector and government interaction, then the system is determined and it does not make sense to discuss the consequences of hypothetical policies (normative analysis) in this context. Only if the government were free to "change its mind" would normative analysis have foundation.

While the resurgence of game theoretic models of the macro policy process perhaps stimulated this debate, the underlying tension between positive and normative analysis is old. There has been and continues to be a branch of political science whose purpose is to provide positive analysis of policy choices. If that area of research is taken seriously, it provides precisely the same challenge to normative policy analysis as do the newer game theoretic models.

Grand philosophical debates are never really resolved but they are usually discussed sufficiently so that perspectives can be gained to restore sanity. And what is the commonsense view on the free will−determinism discussion that allows ordinary mortals to sleep at night? Social scientific research is based on causal models as a regulative principle of analysis. This means that social scientists search for causal patterns in data governed by theories of more or less precision. The goal of this research program is to obtain causal, positive descriptions of behavior. At the same time, individual action is predicated on the assumption that the individual can freely make choices and that these choices are not in any strong sense determined by history or the environment.

For the most part, these two conflicting views never collide except in rare circumstances such as the predictability of behavior under hypnosis. The basic reason they never collide is that in practical situations our causal models are sufficiently imprecise to be taken seriously. If indeed, psychologists, economists, or political scientists had accurate causal, predictive models then individuals' self-image as autonomous actors would be seriously challenged with accompanying bouts of sleeplessness.

This discussion suggests that before agonizing over the possibility of normative policy analysis, we first closely examine positive theories of policy behavior to determine whether they pose a serious threat to policy autonomy. This is the task of this chapter. The discussion is divided into three parts. The first part looks at the attempts of political scientists to explain macroeconomic policy choices, with their emphasis on elections and party competition. Then we turn to the literature on game theory and policy and survey recent developments from the perspective of empirical applicability. The final section looks in some more detail at the literature that merges the concerns of political scientists with game theory and provides new evidence on some of these models.

6.2 Elections, Parties, and Policy

In the large literature on the interaction of elections, parties, and macroeconomics outcomes, there are broadly two classes of models. The first, which we shall call *cynical apartisan manipulation theories*, suggests (as their name indicates) that politicians use all the levers at their disposable to achieve re-election with little regard for the general electorate or even their party. The second class of theories, *partisan models*, emphasizes that political parties represent different constituencies that may be differentially affected by macro policies. Actual macroeconomic policies follow the interests of the parties while they are in office.

Cynical apartisan political manipulation theories have been the most popular among journalists and political pundits and form the basis of the notion of a "political business cycle." The two most well-known contributions to this literature are the paper by William Nordhaus (1975) entitled "The Political Business Cycle" and Edward Tufte's book (1978) *Political Control of the Economy*. Both generated substantial interest and critical comment.

Tufte's view is quite simple. Politicians will use any tool they can do to aid their re-election efforts. Increasing transfer payments before an election is one tactic while others consist of stimulating the economy before the election to bring down unemployment. Part of the charm of Tufe's book is the apparent "smoking gun" evidence of politicians in action including a copy of a letter sent to Social Security recipients on the eve of the 1972 election by President Nixon informing them that their benefits had been increased. But is there really hard evidence for the political cycle?

Tufte presents three principal pieces of evidence in support of his view. First, in twenty-seven democratic countries during the period 1961−72, nineteen of these countries had more frequent accelerations in disposable income in election years than in years without elections. Although he did not examine each episode, he argued that manipulation of transfer payments was probably the main factor behind the increases in accelerations in disposable income. Second, he argued specifically that government transfer payments in the United States tend to reach their peak in October or November during election years. Finally, he argued that the unemployment rate is lower around election time than either before or after elections.

How has this evidence been received? Further research has been quite critical of most of these findings, especially the results about unemployment. Tufte's own evidence on unemployment was weak to begin with as he omitted two elections taking place during the Eisenhower administration from his calculations on a priori grounds. Tufte stressed that the unemployment rate was lower in the 1964 and 1968 elections than during the months prior to the election but this is a very weak test because unemployment fell virtually throughout the 1960s. Moreover, the first election after the publication of his book, the Carter−Reagan contest in 1980, failed to support this theory about unemployment or disposable income as Carter managed to engineer a recession in the last year of his presidency.

The cross-country evidence on accelerations of disposable income has also come under attack. Alt and Chrystal (1983) note that in some cases, the timing of the election was at the control of the party in power. This suggests that the evidence might more likely represent political good sense than political manipulation of the economy. Taking this into account, the 19−8 verdict in favor of his theory could easily disappear. Barry (1985) found Tufte's evidence suggestive but noted that the countries for which the evidence is strongest are the ones for which unemployment movements fail to indicate any evidence of political cycles. Finally, Tufte failed to present any evidence of the economic significance of differences in disposable income accelerations; this makes it difficult to judge the statistical validity of his conclusions.

Finally, even the "heaping" of transfer payments before elections is not fully persuasive. Years other than 1972 show little or no difference in the timing of transfer payments (Alt and Chrystal, 1983). Perhaps even more devastating is Hibbs's observation (1987, p. 265) that the 20 percent increase in Social Security benefits that was principally responsible for the spike in transfer payments at the end of 1972 was the result of legislation, passed in September, by a Democratically controlled Congress despite "vague threats of a presidential veto." This election year conspiracy must have had a large membership!

Nordhaus's (1975) model of political business cycles is quite simple. Politicians can take advantage of a short-run Phillips curve in which expectations are slow to adjust. Before elections, politicians can thus "buy" sharp reductions in unemployment with little increase in inflation. After the election, as expectations of inflation adjust, inflation rises and popular discontent forces politicians to slow the economy, reduce expected and actual inflation, and prepare for the next electoral cycle. There are two key assumptions in this analysis. First, expectations are slow to adjust and, second, voters are myopic and do not understand the electoral cycle and do not take into account the consequences of future inflation in their voting decisions.

Nordhaus tried to test his theory by determining whether unemployment tended to rise in the first half of incumbencies and fall in the second half. His evidence in support of his theory was extremely weak. Only three of the nine countries he examined (the United States, West Germany, and New Zealand) fit his pattern. As noted above, the evidence for the United States was fragile; the Carter administration provided a ready counter-example and most of the movements in unemployment were dominated by long swings in trend rates.

Except for perhaps Tammany Hall or Mayor Daley's Chicago, politicians do not directly control unemployment but rather have certain instruments at their control. Attempts to find any evidence of pure election cycles in appropriately measured instruments such as full-employment deficits (Golden and Poterba, 1980) or monetary policy (Beck 1982) have been unsuccessful. Finally, studies of voting behavior (Chappell, 1983) reject a model of simple-minded myopia for the voters although positive economic conditions are surely favorable for incumbents.

Evidence for the cynical apartisan manipulation theory is surprisingly weak given the popularity of the theory among journalists. The evidence just does not provide support for the theory. As Weatherford wrote after a extensive review of the literature, "The conclusion is inescapable: however attractive the abstract rationale behind the simple pre-election boom, few chief executives have acted upon the argument" (1988, p. 107).

Models based on differences in policies of political parties, the partisan models, have fared somewhat better. One of the earliest studies was by Hibbs (1977), who used time series analysis to argue that unemployment tended to be lower in Democratic administrations. Technically, he used "intervention analysis" which is essentially a sophisticated dummy variable technique in the Box–Jenkins framework to isolate the effects of Democratic administrations.

Beck (1982) was the most vigorous critic of Hibbs's time series work. Re-analyzing the data, using somewhat different assumptions, Beck found much smaller differences in outcomes from different parties. Perhaps more significantly, he argued that differences between administrations of the same party were just as significant as purely partisan differences. By entering dummy variables for each administration it is possible to reject the hypothesis that all administrations of the same party behave the same towards unemployment. As Beck noted, "only Truman and Johnson look like the Democrats described by Hibbs; similarly, only Ford really fits Hibbs's Republican pattern" (1982, p. 91). And, of course, the Carter administration continues to pose problems for all political theories; in this case, the worries about inflation at the end of his administration had a distinctly Republican flavor. Beck, in fact, argues from his findings that partisan differences in the United States are small, largely because parties themselves are floating coalitions of voters and not direct representatives of class interests.

One difficulty with a pure time series analysis of unemployment rates is that an unemployment rate of 4 percent in 1960 is quite different from an unemployment rate of 4 percent in 1986. Almost all estimates of the natural rate of unemployment have risen over time for the United States. Since policymakers grew to embrace the natural rate idea, it is not clear what a pure time series analysis on unadjusted unemployment rates means. "High unemployment" during an Eisenhower administration would be the same as "low unemployment" during the Carter administration.

In a 1987 book summarizing his work on the United States, Hibbs took an alternative and more persuasive approach to the problem. He first postulated that the parties would have different unemployment goals, measured relative to the natural rate of unemployment. At any point in time, the party in power would slowly adjust the unemployment rate to its goal. Using these assumptions and a series on the natural rate of unemployment, Hibbs estimated an unemployment equation which enabled him to uncover estimates of the differences in unemployment goals between the parties as well as the speed of adjustment to these goals.

Hibbs estimates that the difference in goals between Democrats and Republicans is about two percentage points; that is, if the natural rate is 6 percent then Republicans might have an unemployment goal of 7 percent while the Democrats have an unemployment goal of 5 percent. The results can also be interpreted as differences in the perceived natural rate among policy advisors to the two parties. The speed of adjustment from actual to target unemployment rates, however, is quite slow, in the order of 7 percent per quarter or 30 percent per year.

Hibbs acknowledges that there are differences among administrations of the same party. Alternatively, removing the Johnson or Reagan administrations (aggressively partisan administrations) from the regressions reduces the remaining party differences to between 1.2 and 1.5 percent differences in their targets. These are quite small differences once the slow speed of adjustment is taken into account. Essentially, one year after an election, one would anticipate less than one-half of one percentage point in unemployment from partisan differences. This is small relative to movements in unemployment over the postwar era.

Other evidence in his book also points to distinct but small differences in partisan policies. Based on Gallup poll data, Hibbs reports (1987, p. 177) differences in implicit trade-offs between inflation and unemployment for voters identified as Democrats or Republicans. According to his estimates, Democratic voters would be willing, on the margin, to trade a one point increase in inflation for a one point reduction in unemployment. Republican voters would require a one point reduction in unemployment for a 0.65 point increase in inflation. Moreover, all voters react sharply to increasing inflation. These findings do not give the parties much scope to differentiate their policies to cater to their constituencies.

One way to summarize the evidence that Hibbs presents is that, everything else being equal, Democratic administrations are slightly more willing to take inflationary risks than Republican administrations. But the differences are small enough, less than one-half of a percentage point in unemployment in a year, to be easily dwarfed by other macroeconomic factors. The differences vary by administration and some Democratic administrations look suspiciously Republican in their policies. Moreover, all voters will eventually react adversely to increasing inflation. Partisan differences are perhaps a loose tendency in American political economy but this is far from an iron law dictating policy and forcing an abandonment of normative policy analysis.

One troublesome part of Hibbs's analysis is that behavior of the private sector is not modeled in any serious way. How can the different administrations actually force unemployment rates up or down according to their partisan preferences? Why does the private sector not simply anticipate the partisan policies and incorporate these into their wage-setting decisions thereby rendering it impossible to actually manipulate the unemployment rate? One could object that these hypothesized private sector responses put too much stock in simple rational expectation models of wage behavior. But if there are significant partisan regularities, these are precisely the sorts of effects that should be reasonably included in wage-setting decisions. To put it simply, how is Hibbs's model consistent with rational behavior on the part of the private sector?

The game theory literature on policy takes the challenge of a rational private sector seriously. As we will see in the next section, the most popular model does not lead directly to partisan differences in unemployment. But a marriage of the political models with the game theory models does lead to some interesting testable implications.

6.3 The Inflation Game

The best introduction to literature on game theory and macro policy is to consider a very simplified version of an inflation game played between the Fed and the private sector. After the principles of the game are clear, we will consider more complex versions of the basic model.

. In the inflation game, wage setters must decide upon a nominal wage *before* the Fed chooses the money supply. Wage setters would like to have a target real wage and thus must form expectations about what the inflation will be in the next period. Employment will be demand-determined in the model with actual employment being a decreasing function of the real wage. Thus, if inflation is higher than anticipated, employment will be higher than workers desire. If inflation is less than anticipated, real wages will be too high and employment less than desired. By assumption, workers dislike the alternatives of too high or too low employment equally. For simplicity, workers do not care about the inflation rate itself.

The Fed has different preferences than the workers. The Fed would like to have higher employment than the workers desire. This idea can be rationalized in several ways; perhaps the simplest is to suggest that distortions from taxation cause workers to set too low a desired level of employment. The Fed also likes to have low inflation if possible.

Figure 6.1 contains a payoff matrix to the inflation game following Cuikerman (1986). In the game, workers choose the expected inflation rate while the Fed chooses the actual inflation, either a rate of zero or one. Workers' preferences over each outcome are given by the upper half of each square while the Fed's preferences are given by the lower-half. The workers prefer the outcomes in which their expectations are correct (the elements on the diagonal) and equally dislike the outcomes in which they either have over- or underestimated inflation (the off-diagonal elements). The Fed prefers the situation in which the workers expect zero inflation and the Fed inflates at a rate of one; this is a boom. Their next preferred state is where the actual and expected inflation rate are both zero, that is, no employment gains but low inflation. High inflation and normal employment is the next preferred

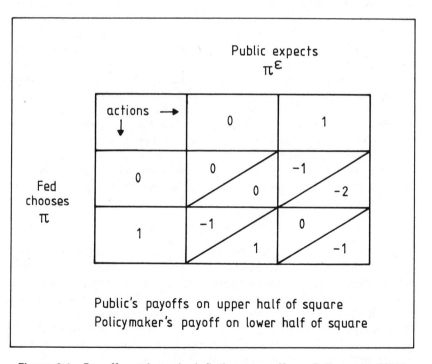

Figure 6.1   Payoff matrix to the inflation game (from Cuikerman, 1986)

outcome (the lower right-hand corner). The worst outcome is the recession resulting from the situation in which workers expect high inflation but the Fed does not inflate.

What is the solution to this game? The solution is actually quite easy to find in this simple model. Take the workers' perspective for a moment. No matter what inflation rate the worker expects, the Fed will always choose to inflate at the high rate. If the workers expect zero inflation, the Fed prefers a boom. If the workers expect inflation at a rate of one, the Fed will want to avoid the recession and also inflate at a rate of one. Choosing high inflation is a *dominant strategy* for the Fed; no matter what the workers expect, its payoff is greatest from inflating at the high rate. Given the Fed's incentives is to always choose high inflation, the workers will maximize their gains by expecting high inflation. Thus, the outcome to this game is the high inflation, normal output case in the lower right-hand corner of the matrix.

There are two important facts to notice about this equilibrium outcome. First, workers' expectations are rational. They expect high inflation and high inflation occurs. This means that output is at its normal level. Second, inflation is in some sense "too high" in equilibrium. Both the workers and the Fed would be willing to swap the actual outcome for the outcome in the upper-left hand corner of the matrix. In that outcome, workers' expectations are also fulfilled and employment is at its normal level but inflation is at the low level. However, there is no way to reach that equilibrium in this game because if the workers were to expect a low inflation rate, the Fed would have an incentive to engineer a boom by generating a high inflation rate. The solution to the game is a Nash equilibrium. Given the action of each party to the game, no one has an incentive to deviate from the equilibrium.

The same principles carry over to more complex theories of the inflation game. Barro and Gordon (1983a) specify the policymaker's objective function as:

$$z = \text{Costs} = (a/2)(\pi)^2 - b(\pi - \pi^c) \qquad (6.1)$$

where the first term is the (quadratic) costs of inflation while the second (linear) term represents the gains from operating above the natural rate of output. Workers are interested only in operating at full employment output and thus prefer to have their expectations ratified.

To find the solution to this game, let the policymakers initially treat the workers' expectations as given. With these expectations fixed, the authorities then choose the inflation rate that minimizes the total costs z. The solution to this optimization problem is:

$$\pi = b/a \qquad (6.2)$$

which is independent of expected inflation. This choice of the inflation rate is again a dominant strategy. Since the workers know this, they will expect the inflation rate to be b/a. Their expectations will be fulfilled and the economy will remain at full employment. Inflation will, however, be at the positive level of b/a. Inflation again is "too high" in this economy; both workers and policymakers would prefer in principle for the economy to remain at full employment but the inflation rate to be zero. There is an inflation bias in this economy.

What determines this bias and the precise inflation that results? With wage contracts set a period in advance, the policymakers gain from having output exceed full employment, that is, by letting the actual inflation rate exceed the expected inflation rate. However, the policymakers also dislike inflation. At a rate of inflation equal to b/a, the gains on the margin from the extra output precisely equal the costs on the margin from higher inflation. Thus, if workers expect that the inflation rate will be equal to b/a, they know that policymakers will have no incentive to engineer either higher or lower inflation.

Before turning to more complex versions of the model, it is time to take stock of the predictive power of the model. The model makes two key predictions:
1 Monetary policy (at least through the mechanisms outlined here) will not move the economy away from full employment.
2 The inflation rate will be greater, the greater the value of b/a. Thus, the higher the benefits from output exceeding full employment and the lower the perceived costs of inflation, the higher will be the equilibrium inflation rate.

Barro and Gordon argue (1983a, p. 114) that the parameter "b", representing policymakers' gains from output, will tend to be high in several circumstances. In their words this occurs
• when the natural unemployment rate is high,
• during a recession,
• during a war or other period when government expenditures rise sharply
• when the deadweight loss from conventional taxes are high
• when the outstanding real stock of nominally denominated public debt is large.

This leads, again in their words, to the following predictions about inflation and monetary policy:
• a rise in the mean inflation rate along with a rise in the natural unemployment rate (as in the United States over the past 10–15 years),
• countercyclical response of monetary policy,
• high rates of monetary expansion during wartime,
• high rates of monetary growth in some less developed countries,
• an inflationary effect from the outstanding real stock of public debt.

These appear to be a rich set of predictions. Unfortunately, under closer examination none of them really follows directly from the basic features of the game theory aspect of the model. First, the fact that governments with a large real stock of debt, unusually high expenditures, or an inadequate tax system, resort to inflationary finance is not surprising. Mankiw's (1987) extension of Barro's (1979) tax-smoothing model to include inflationary finance makes precisely these predictions. According to this model, governments can resort to either explicit taxation or inflationary finance to cover government spending and past indebtedness. There are costs to using both fiscal instruments. As a cost minimizer, the government uses both instruments so as to equate costs on the margin. In this model, higher marginal costs of taxation or higher government spending will lead directly to higher inflation in order to equate the marginal costs of raising revenue from two sources. Thus, the notion of a game between the private sector and the public about "surprise" inflation is superfluous.[3]

The other predictions from the model are tenuous as well. Since recessions do not occur in this model (expectations are always fulfilled), it is difficult to argue that the model predicts countercyclical and inflationary monetary policy. Perhaps, Barro and Gordon had in mind the idea that recessions could occur for reasons other than outlined in the model. But in that case, it is by no means evident that, on the margin, the gains from engineering "surprise output" are increasing as output falls. In Lucas's work (1977), once a negative monetary surprise happens, the damage is done; the capital stock and inventory level have been affected, and it is not evident why "surprise inflation" delivers any more benefits in this circumstance. In any case, these issues are difficult to discuss in models that preclude recessions.

The remaining prediction is that inflation is high when the natural rate is high. This can, in principle, follow from the model. If tax distortions have increased over time, thereby increasing the natural rate of unemployment, then the marginal benefits from "surprise inflation" can increase. But if the natural rate has risen because of lack of capital accumulation, adverse energy shocks, or a change in preferences towards more leisure, then there is no reason to presume that the benefits from surprise inflation have increased. In the United States, changes in the composition of the labor force (towards women and youth) have been cited as important factors in increasing the natural rate; these changes do not increase the benefits from a surprise inflation.

Finally, the evidence in the United States does not point to an inevitable association between high levels of the natural rate of unemployment and high inflation. While inflation increased in the 1970s, it fell in the 1980s. Typical estimates of the natural rate of unemployment were virtually unchanged during the period when the inflation rate fell. Thus, the only prediction that follows directly from the model has no effective explanatory power.

Despite its lack of explanatory power, extensions of the inflation game have delivered some insights on policy problems. These insights are not the type that deliver clear and valuable predictions for the actual conduct of monetary policy but rather help to develop our *grammar* for discussing policy. This work can, in principle, raise new issues concerning the scope of interaction between the public and private sector. The first extension of the model is to investigate whether, in multi-period models, policymakers' concern for their reputation can eliminate the inflation bias that emerged in the one-period version of the game.

In a multi-period, specifically an infinite-horizon model, policymakers have some scope to avoid the outcome of an inflation rate equal to b/a each period. This inflation rate arose, in equilibrium, because there were always incentives for the policymakers to inflate at that rate regardless of workers' expectations. Suppose, however, that the policymakers "promised" the workers that they would inflate at a lower rate and that workers should look at their past performance to justify this belief. If workers were willing to hold expectations of this lower inflation rate as long as the monetary authorities behaved, but returned to expectations of higher inflation if they misbehaved, then there is scope for a lower inflation rate to prevail in equilibrium.

Specifically, let total discounted costs be given by:

$$Z = z_t/(1+r)^t \tag{6.3}$$

where z_t is the one-period costs given in equation (6.1). Workers adopt the following rule governing their expectations. They will expect an inflation rate for the next period of π^* if the current period's inflation is what they anticipated. If, however, they were fooled this period, then they will expect an inflation rate of b/a which was the inflation rate that emerged from the one-period game. Thus.

$$\begin{aligned} \pi_t^\varepsilon &= \pi^* \text{ if } \pi_{t-1}^\varepsilon = \pi_{t-1} \\ \pi_t^\varepsilon &= b/a \text{ if } \pi_{t-1}^\varepsilon \neq \pi_{t-1} \end{aligned} \tag{6.4}$$

These expectations may seem a bit peculiar. If at some point the government breaks its promise and inflates at a high rate, the workers will expect a high inflation rate next period. But if the government then delivers the high inflation rate, the workers' expectation of inflation revert back to the lower level π^*. The idea behind this expectation scheme is that the workers "punish" the monetary authorities for only one period if the monetary authorities break their promise. Longer punishment intervals, including an infinite one in which expectations will always be equal to b/a if a promise is broken, can also be analyzed. But this scheme is a particularly easy one to analyze.

Suppose that the prevailing inflation rate was π^* which was greater than zero but less than b/a. What incentives would the monetary authorities have to increase the inflation rate from π^* to b/a? In the period in which they increased the inflation rate they would gain more from the increase in output then they would lose from increased inflation. But in the next period they would suffer with a higher inflation rate.

Recall that the one-period loss function is given by:

$$z = \frac{a}{2}(\pi)^2 - b(\pi - \pi^\varepsilon) \tag{6.5}$$

Thus, if they maintain the inflation rate at π^* and the public expects this rate, the loss will be :

$$Z^* = \frac{a}{2}(\pi^*)^2 \tag{6.6}$$

If they cheat and raise the inflation rate to b/a, the one-period loss will be lower:

$$Z^{\text{cheat}} = \frac{a}{2}(b/a)^2 - b(b/a - \pi^*) \tag{6.7}$$

The current period gain from cheating will be the difference between Z^* and Z^{cheat} or:

$$\text{Gain} = \frac{a}{2}[\pi^{*2} - (b/a)^2] + b^2/a - b\pi^* \tag{6.8}$$

In the next period, the public will expect an inflation rate of b/a and the monetary authorities will inflate at that rate. Since expectations will be fulfilled, the public will expect an inflation rate of π^* for the following period and thus we return to the original situation. The loss, therefore, is only for one period and will be equal to the difference between the costs of the high inflation rate (b/a) and π^*. These costs come one period later than the gain and thus must be discounted. The costs, therefore, are:

$$\text{Costs} = \left[\frac{a}{2}(b/a)^2 - \frac{a}{2}(\pi^*)^2\right]\left(\frac{1}{1+r}\right) \tag{6.9}$$

The private sector punishment strategy will only work if the costs to the monetary authorities exceed the gains. Using the expression for costs and gains (equations (6.8) and (6.9)), Barro and Gordon (1983a) show that this determines a range for the sustainable inflation rate π^*.

Specifically, an inflation rate π can be sustained by the punishment strategy (equation 6.4) if:

$$b/a \geq \pi^* > b/a \left(\frac{r}{2+r}\right) \tag{6.10}$$

Equation (6.10) gives the range for sustainable inflation rates. The upper bound (b/a) is clearly sustainable because the authorities would choose to inflate at that rate without any punishment at all. The lower bound $\left[b/a \left(\frac{r}{2+r}\right) \right]$ is precisely the inflation rate at which the gains from cheating equal the costs. At any inflation rate below that, the gains from cheating exceed the costs and that inflation rate is not sustainable by one-period punishments.

A zero inflation rate is not sustainable as long as there is a positive interest rate. From (6.7), the gain from cheating at $\pi^* = 0$ is $\frac{b^2}{2a}$. The costs from equation (6.9) are $\left(\frac{1}{1+r}\right) \left[\frac{b^2}{2a}\right]$. As long as $r>0$, the gains will exceed the costs and the one-period punishment rules are not sustainable for zero inflation.

Note that the minimum inflation sustainable rate is increasing in b. Thus, the same predictions concerning times at which inflation will be high follow from this reputation version of the model as follow from the model without reputation effects. The only difference is that the inflation-bias is smaller.

Rogoff (1987) raises serious questions concerning the interpretation of results from this and similar models of reputation. In the model, there was a entire range of sustainable inflation rates generated by one-period punishment strategies. If we enrich the scope of possible punishment strategies, there will be other ranges for sustainable inflation equilibrium. How does the public (1) decide on a particular punishment strategy and (2) decide upon the precise inflation rate within any feasible range? The models are silent on this point but somehow decentralized economic agents must agree on both a strategy and an inflation rate if the equilibrium in the model is to be sustained.

As Rogoff argues, the basic idea behind the inflation game is that there is a lack of cooperation between the monetary authorities and the public sector. Yet, the reputation solutions to the problem require extraordinary coordination among atomistic actors. In a sense, a co-operation problem has been replaced with a coordination problem. This important theoretical issue has yet to be resolved. Even if it is resolved, it will be difficult to find testable differences between reputation and non-reputation equilibria because, as we have observed, both are increasing in b.

Two other other extensions of the inflation game, while not providing any additional substantive empirical insights, do provide insightful treatments into the logic of policymaking. Canzoneri (1985) and Cuikerman and Meltzer (1986) extend the inflation game to include private information held by the policymakers but their models deliver interesting and contrasting policy perspectives.

Canzoneri first considers the inflation game but allows for random and persistent shocks to money demand. These shocks occur after the private sector has formed its expectations and signed its contracts. The Fed or policymaker then gets an unbiased forecast of the shock. Canzoneri then considers a low inflation equilibrium enforced by reputational considerations and the threat of punishment strategies by the private sector. In this equilibrium, can the Fed offset the predictable part of the money supply shock thereby minimizing deviations from full employment, without upsetting the reputational equilibrium?

Canzoneri argues that if the Fed's forecast is public information there are no difficulties in maintaining the low inflation equilibrium. Since the private sector observes the forecast, it knows precisely what the Fed's action should be if the Fed wanted to maintain the equilibrium but offset the shock. If the Fed inflates at a faster rate, the private sector can punish the Fed by changing its expectations precisely as in the previous models. Public information, therefore, does not change the nature of the game.

However, if the Fed's information is private, the public can no longer be sure if the Fed is accommodating the shock or simply trying to inflate. If inflation is higher than normal, the private sector does not know whether the Fed simply overpredicted the shock or deliberately cheated. Canzoneri then considers another equilibrium for the model, one in which the public will maintain its expectations of low inflation until the inflation rate crosses some threshold value. If inflation exceeds this value, the private sector raises its expectations of inflation. The model predicts that there will be periods in which high inflation breaks out in the economy as the result of occasional prediction errors by the Fed. These outbreaks of high inflation and high inflationary expectations by the private sector occur even though the Fed does not cheat in equilibrium.

According to this model, the Fed should attempt to make public as much information as possible. Somehow this fails to accord with the air of secrecy that surrounds the Fed and all central banks. Cuikerman and Meltzer (1986) provide an alternative model with private information that suggests that the Fed will deliberately choose imprecise operating procedures to create ambiguity about the Fed's actions. In their model, the policymaker's objective function is similar to the one used by Barro and Gordon but reflects the private trade-offs of policy-makers, not social welfare. Moreover, the weights placed on inflation and output shift over time reflecting the political pressures applied to the Fed. These political pressures, and thus the weights in the objective function, are the private information of the Fed and the public must try to infer these weights from the actions taken by the Fed.

In the equilibrium considered by Cuikerman and Meltzer, the private sector rationally updates their expectations of inflation given new information about money growth. Although these expectations are unbiased and rational, the Fed still has room to "fool" the public temporarily because the public always observes noisy signals. The speed at which expectations rationally adjust they term *credibility*. If the Fed comes under increasing pressure to increase output, it can engineer an inflation surprise and it will take the public time to learn about the Fed's new preferences. The fact that expectations, although rational, adjust slowly helps the Fed in this case. It hurts the Fed, however, if it wishes to reduce inflation because slowly adjusting in-flationary expectations in the face of reduced money growth rates necessitate a recession and only a gradual reduction in the inflation rate.

Despite these two conflicting factors, the Fed prefers to have some room to maneuver and temporarily to fool the public at times when it is important to the Fed. Cuikerman and Meltzer show that if the Fed can, once and for all, choose operating procedures which will dictate the size of the error between the Fed's planned money supply and the actual money supply, it will want to leave some imprecision in monetary control. This imprecision creates the ambiguity which allows the Fed to pursue its goals at crucial times.

Cuikerman and Meltzer do present an interesting rationale why policy authorities may prefer secrecy and ambiguity even in a rational model. But turning to the actual economy for the moment, it is hard to believe that the minute details of actual operating procedures of the Fed actually matter for the behavior of expectations of inflation of wage setters in the economy. Alternative monetary control procedures may deliver different stochastic patterns for interest rates and the money supply and even lead to differences in money growth over short periods, but should not make much difference over the longer horizons relevant to wage and price decisions. Their model is best taken to be a parable, and an interesting contribution to the logic and grammar of policymaking.

Backus and Driffill (1985) take an alternative approach to the inflation game based on the ideas of Kreps and Wilson (1982). In their model, there are two types of governments. The first type, which they term "wet," has the same preferences as the policymakers in the Barro–Gordon model.[4] Thus a game between them and the private sector would result in a high inflation equilibrium. The second type, or "hard" government, only cares about fighting inflation. These governments do exist but are rare. At the beginning of an administration, the public does not know whether the government is wet or hard but does have some prior probabilities over the two types.

The basic insight of the model is that wet governments have an incentive to pretend they are hard in order to avoid the high inflation equilibrium. Backus and Driffill work out the equilibrium strategies for the public and the wet government according to the principles of "sequential equilibrium" as developed by Kreps and Wilson. (No ad hoc punishment strategies are allowed.) The optimal strategies typically have the following form. Early in an administration, wet governments will not inflate nor will the public expect them to inflate. At a certain point, the public begins to expect some inflation and the wet government adopts a random strategy which inflates with certain probabilities. Once the government actually inflates, the private sector knows it is a wet government (hard governments never inflate) and the high inflation equilibrium results.

The model has several testable implications. First, wet governments (the most prevalent type) will inflate at the end of their administrations. Second, recessions will occur, on average, sometime in the middle of administrations when the public expects some inflation but the wet government fails (randomly) to inflate. These predictions are interesting but do not fit the facts for the United States. Only the Carter administration (the great counter-example to political theories) managed to inflate at the end of its first term. And as we shall see in the next section, recessions have tended to occur towards the beginning of terms but only in Republican administrations.

Nonetheless, the idea of combining the rationality and rigor of the game theory approach with political institutions is sound. The insights of the political scientists can perhaps be combined with the rationality of the game theory models. The next section explores this combination.

6.4 Politics and Game Theory

The basic insight from the political science literature is that elections and political parties do matter for the conduct of macroeconomic policy, although perhaps not in any rigid way. The game theory literature reviewed above was framed in terms of a single policymaker. Extensions to include differences in the preferences of political parties which compete in elections can potentially provide some interesting insights and perhaps testable implications.

Persson and Svennson (1986) offer a timely theory suggesting sub-optimal deficit policies in democracies with alternating parties. Suppose there are two parties which both care about tax distortions but have different preferences for the amount of public expenditure. The conservative government, by assumption, prefers lower levels of the public good than the liberal party. Governments can issue debt in this model and the parties use debt strategically to change the policies of their successors. Specifically, conservative governments will leave a larger debt so that their liberal successors will have to have lower public expenditure in order to avoid too much tax distortion. Conversely, liberal governments will bequeath a surplus to their conservative successors.

While this explanation has great surface appeal for explaining the behavior of deficits and debt under the Reagan administration, it unfortunately only fits this case. The debt as a percent of GNP has declined smoothly in the postwar era and was not increased dramatically during prior Republican administrations. Yet, presumably the same strategic considerations were relevant for those prior administrations.

Moreover, the theory really does not explain the fiscal policy of the Reagan administration. As we argue below, the 1981 recession, which was the primary factor leading to the large deficits, was a surprise both the the public and private sector. Once the deficits had occurred, however, there was some truth to the argument that they were viewed as a blessing in disguise as a means to curb non-defense, non-entitlement expenditure by Congress. But the deficits stemmed more from the irreconcilable conflicts between the parties than as a deliberate tool to reduce social spending in the future.

Perhaps the most salient fact from the political literature was the differences in desired macroeconomic policies on the part of the two parties as documented by Hibbs (1987). But the problem of rationality still remains. Hibbs's model predicts that recessions are more likely under Republican administrations while inflationary surges are more prevalent under Democratic administrations. But if wage and price setters in the private sector are rational, why don't they anticipate tighter money under Republican administrations and adjust their expectations and wage-setting decisions accordingly? Wouldn't this eliminate the tendency for recessions to occur under Republican administrations?

Chappell and Keech (1986), Alesina (1987) and Alesina and Sachs (1988) suggest how recessions could still be more likely under Republican administrations even with rational agents. The key idea is that before an election there is uncertainty as to which party will prevail and wage setters set contracts based on average of money growth under both parties weighted by the probabilities that each party will win the election. If Democrats win, money growth will be higher than anticipated and a boom will occur while the opposite will be true if Republicans win. As Alesina and Sachs emphasize, rational partisan business cycles can only occur at the *beginning* of administrations when there is uncertainty about the outcome of the election; later in the administration, economic agents will anticipate the policies pursued by the government and rational partisan cycles cannot occur.

Specifically, Democrats have preferences that place more weight on output than do Republicans. This leads, in the inflation game, to higher time-consistent, equilibrium inflation rates under Democratic administrations. Uncertainty only occurs before an election; after an election the winning party and, hence, the time-consistent inflation rate is known. Inflation surprises, therefore, can only occur because of elections.

Alesina and Sachs provide a variety of evidence in favor of their view. Perhaps most striking is the fact that all Republican administrations (except for Reagan's second term) experienced negative economic growth in real GNP in the *second* year of their administrations. There were only two other years of negative economic growth in the postwar era and Alesina and Sachs attribute those to oil-related disturbances. Table 6.1, updated from Alesina and Sachs, presents the postwar data.

The one potentially troubling aspect of these facts for rational partisan

Table 6.1   Growth in real GNP

Administration	Year			
	First	Second	Third	Fourth
Democratic				
Truman	0.5	8.7	8.3	3.7
Kennedy	2.6	5.8	4.0	5.3
Johnson	6.0	6.0	2.7	4.6
Carter	5.5	5.0	2.8	−0.3*
Republican				
Eisenhower I	3.8	−1.2	6.7	2.1
Eisenhower II	1.8	−0.4	6.0	2.2
Nixon I	2.8	−0.2	3.4	5.7
Nixon II	5.8	−0.6	−1.2*	5.4
Reagan I	2.5	−2.1	3.7	6.8
Reagan II	3.0	2.9	2.4	

*Oil shocks.
Source: Alesina and Sachs (1988) updated by the present author

cycle theory is that the years of negative growth occur in the second not the first year of the administration. This result could be attributed to details of the lag structure in wage contracts but no hard evidence is available on this point.

We can take a closer look at the evidence in support of rational partisan cycles by looking at the behavior of financial markets after elections. The basic idea is that after a Republican victory, rational agents will anticipate a recession and this recognition should be embodied immediately in the stock market. We first provide evidence that the stock market does have predictive power for movements in real output and construct a predictive indicator based on financial market behavior. This indicator is then used to gauge the extent to which rational agents either anticipate subsequent downturns or are taken by surprise by the downturns in economic activity.

The basic model, which is similar in many respects to Blanchard (1981), can be sketched quite simply. Wage contracts are set one period in advance before the realization of the money supply. Stock prices are equal to the expected present value of earnings of firms which are paid out to owners each period. Earnings, in turn, are procyclical.

Before an election, workers set their contracts based on the expected value of the future money supply which will be higher under a Democratic administration. Contracts are set so that expected output is at the full employment level. Stock prices also anticipate earnings to be at their full employment level. If a Republican is elected, agents immediately know that the money stock will be less than anticipated in their wage contracts and that higher interest rates and lower earnings will follow. This is immediately reflected in lower stock prices which fall both because of the lower earnings and higher discount rates. Note that stock prices fall as soon as the results of the election occur and before the administration has had a chance to reduce the money supply. Thus, the stock market should predict the subsequent recession.

To implement these ideas empirically, it is necessary to first demonstrate that the stock market does have predictive power for developments in future real economy activity and to develop an appropriate predictive indicator from the stock market. Because financial markets react quickly to news, it was desirable to use high frequency data. This led to the choice of the monthly series on industrial production coupled with a deflated index of stock prices (the S&P 500 deflated by the Consumer Price Index).

The predictive equations were developed both for the log of first differences of industrial production and for the stock index to handle the obvious nonstationarities in both series. Sample autocorrelations for the growth in industrial production indicated autocorrelation at low lags as well as at twelve months. Cross correlations indicated that lagged values of the growth of the stock index were positively correlated with the current growth in industrial production. These considerations led to the estimated equation in table 6.2 in which the growth of industrial production is a function of a constant, its first and twelfth lag and a twenty-four-month distributed lag on the growth of the stock index.

Several features about the regression results are of interest. First, the first and twelfth lags of industrial production are significant, with the latter most likely providing information about the pattern of seasonal adjustments. The coefficients on the growth of stock prices are positive and significant (with the exception of the very last few months) and exhibit a smooth declining geometric pattern. This pattern was not imposed on the data as the model was estimated with a flex-

Table 6.2   Real activity and the stock index

Period 1954.04−1985.12

$$GIP_t = 0.002 + 0.346\ GIP_{t-1} - 0.114\ GIP_{t-12} + \sum_{i=0}^{24} a_i \cdot GSI_{t-i}$$
$$3.98 \qquad\quad (7.20) \qquad\qquad (2.43)$$

(*t*-statistics in parentheses)

Lag	Coefficient	Lag coefficients (a_i) t-statistic	Lag	Coefficient	t-statistic
0	0.021	2.58	13	0.008	2.55
1	0.020	3.49	14	0.007	2.04
2	0.019	4.45	15	0.006	1.57
3	0.019	4.98	16	0.004	1.10
4	0.018	4.89	17	0.003	0.87
5	0.017	4.52	18	0.002	0.63
6	0.016	4.18	19	0.002	0.42
7	0.015	3.93	20	0.001	0.25
8	0.014	3.77	21	0.0003	0.09
9	0.013	3.66	22	−0.000	−0.003
10	0.011	3.55	23	−0.0002	−0.03
11	0.010	3.36	24	−0.0002	−0.02
12	0.009	3.02			

$\sum a_i$	t-statistic
0.241	0.431

GIP, growth in industrial production.
GSI, growth in stock index.

ible third-order polynomial distributed lag. These results indicate that cumulative changes in stock prices have significant effects on changes in industrial production where more weights is placed on more recent movements in stock prices.

The estimated distributed lag on the growth of stock prices was then combined with the stock index data to compute a predictive index for economic downturns. The index turns negative and stays persistently negative on or before every official NBER recession since 1952. Table 6.3 displays the official dates of the recessions, the date at which the index first becomes negative prior to the recession, and the number of months the index remains negative. The only peculiar result is for the recession at the end of the Carter administration. The index turned negative early in the Carter administration and remained negative through the recession. The market may have been reacting negatively to the upwards movement in the inflation rate during this period. This recession and the one at the end of the Eisenhower administration do not fit the theory of rational partisan cycles since they occur at the end of administrations.

Paul Samuelson once noted that the stock market is often unduly pessimistic as a forecaster of recession, predicting recessions that fail to materialize.[5] This is also true with our index. The index turns negative and remains negative for at least seven quarters in May of 1962 and May of 1966 which were not followed by recessions, as well as for the period in the early days of the Carter administration mentioned above. However, for our purposes, the market index falls before or with every significant downturn in the postwar era.

Before proceeding to the detailed analysis of Republican elections,

Table 6.3   Recessions and the stock indicator

Date of peak	NBER recessions Date of next trough	Date at which stock indicator becomes negative	Month indicator remains negative
7/53	5/54	6/53	7
8/57	4/58	1/57	18
4/60[a]	2/61	3/60	10
12/69	11/70	3/69	22
11/73	3/75	4/73	27
1/80[a]	7/80	2/77	36
7/81	11/82	7/81	15

[a] Recessions at end of administration.
NBER, National Bureau of Economic Research.

it is useful to recall that on the surface five of the eight postwar recessions possibly can fit the rational partisan cycle theory. Recessions at the end of the Carter and Eisenhower administrations and in the Truman administration (since he was a Democrat) cannot account for the theory. Recessions can occur, of course, for other reasons so a better test is to examine the periods immediately after Republican elections.

In the postwar era, there have been six Republican presidential electoral victories. All but the 1984 Reagan re-election were followed by recessions. Thus, there are five possible elections to examine. Table 6.4 contains the salient data about the stock index and the recessions to examine the theory.

Three of the five elections (1956, 1968, and 1972) appear to be reasonably consistent with the theory. In 1956, the index dropped sharply at election time and turned negative in January of 1957. The recession did not actually begin until August of that year. Thus, the market appeared to anticipate the recession precisely at the time that the uncertainty of the electoral outcome was resolved.

Table 6.4   The stock index and Republican elections

Republican election	Value of index May of election year	Value of index Dec. of election year	Date index becomes negative	Recession peak	Comments
11/52	0.20	0.15	6/53	7/53	Index remainded near 0.16 until March; fell sharply in April
11/56	0.35	0.06	1/57	8/57	Fell near election
11/68	0.12	0.15	3/69	12/69	Dropped sharply 1/69
11/72	0.18	0.21	4/73	11/73	Index started to fall 2/73
11/80	−0.17	0.19	7/81	7/81	Index rose in March and April
11/84	−0.02	−0.03	None	No recession	

The elections of 1968 and 1972 also are broadly consistent with the theory but not so precisely as for 1956. The index dropped sharply in January of 1969 but did not turn negative until March. The recession, however, did not officially begin until December. Thus, the market gave early indications at the beginning of Nixon's first term that a recession was imminent. Following the election of 1972, the index began to fall in February of 1973 and turned negative in April. The recession did not begin until November. Note that the index turned negative well before the Yom Kippur War and the resulting crises in world oil market which are often blamed for the recession.

Other political factors were perhaps at work in the 1972 election. This election is often cited as the prototypical example of the traditional business cycle and some commentators have argued that Nixon put extreme pressure on Arthur Burns, Chairman of the Federal Reserve, to increase the money supply before the election. The money supply did increase dramatically before the election. Woolley (1984) discusses the conflicting interpretations of this episode, including the peculiar pressures that Burns was subjected to with his role in wage and price controls. Regardless of Burns's motives, the money supply grew rapidly in late 1972 and it was natural that some tightening was to occur in the next year. Our market index may have been anticipating the consequences of this tightening.

Advocates of the oil crisis explanation of the recession could argue that the stock market indicator was a "false positive" that coincidentally was followed by an oil shock. It is not possible to refute this interpretation except to note that the index responded quickly after the election and that there were rational grounds for several reasons (rational partisan cycles and the considerations outlined above) to expect a tighter monetary policy.

Three Republican elections do not appear to fit the theory. Reagan's re-election in 1984 was not followed by a recession. The recessions of 1952 and 1980 also do not provide support for the theory. In both cases, it appeared that the recession took the stock market by surprise. In 1953, the index remained high through March, fell in April, and did not turn negative until June. The recession began in July of that year. Under the most generous interpretation, it took until April before the market began to anticipate any downturn.

The recession following Reagan's election in 1980 appears to be even more of a surprise. The index actually rose in March and April of 1981 and did not turn negative until July which was precisely the beginning of the recession. The stock market failed to provide any early warning in this case. In the other "successful" tests of the theory, the market anticipated the recession by a minimum of seven months and the index turned negative no later than April following the election.

One perhaps could argue that a recession following the 1984 election would not be anticipated because the outcome before the election was virtually certain. However, only one Republican victory, Nixon over Humphrey in 1968, was close. In all the other Republican victories, the winner received over 400 electoral votes. Moreover, the 1972 election was as one-sided as the 1984 election. In some cases, there may have been additional uncertainty. In 1956, for example, medical reasons led Eisenhower to postpone his decision to run until February of that year. Nonetheless, there do not appear to be any obvious salient political differences between the successful and unsuccessful episodes for the theory.

Other evidence also suggests that the recessions following the 1952 and 1980 elections may have taken the private sector by surprise. The Korean War ended in July of 1953 which is the same month as the beginning of the recession. Defense expenditures had reached a peak in the second quarter of 1953 and fell by nearly 20 percent in the next twelve months. An abrupt end to a war would precipitate a fall in output in either Keynesian or equilibrium models of the business cycle. As Blyth (1969) recounts, monetary policy had also tightened early in 1953 with an increase in the discount rate in January. "The authorities were concerned about the possibility of inflation, especially the removal of wage and price controls at that time, and adopted a policy of restraint" (1969, p. 31). Nonetheless, the dramatic drop in military spending following the end of the conflict, as well as the market's failure to anticipate the recession (even in the face of clear evidence of Fed restraint in January) suggests that the recession reflected a difficult transition to peacetime and took the economy by surprise.

The recession that began in July of 1981 also appears to have been a surprise to the private sector. First, it followed on the heels of the very brief recession at the end of the Carter administration and no other postwar recession had followed as closely on its predecessor. Second, the private sector was skeptical of the forecasts being produced by the Reagan administration but most forecasters at the time were predicting less dramatic real growth, not a recession. Finally, many commentators argued that the proposed tax cuts would cause an inflationary boom, not a recession. Finally, our stock index actually rose through March and April and did not turn negative until the month the recession began. This recession does appear to have been a true surprise.

The theory of rational partisan business cycles should apply to other democracies besides the United States. However, there have been no tests of the theory outside the United States with its relatively scarce number of critical observations. In Sheffrin (1988b), I examined the evidence from other countries.

Tufte (1978) presented a list of twenty-seven democracies. Using this list and standard political reference books, I developed a sample of ten countries in which liberal and conservative parties alternated and each group had at least two postwar electoral victories. When coalition governments were formed, the coalitions were examined to determine which party was in effective control.

The empirical strategy that was followed was to estimate second-order autoregressive models for the growth rate of real GNP for each country including a measure of the world growth rate and to test for the significance of alternative political dummies. The world growth rate variable was designed to capture international linkages.

Before discussing the results, two issues require discussion. First, some tests of traditional political cycle theory have been critized because election dates are endogenous in some governments. This does not cause a problem for testing rational partisan cycle theory. Governments may choose to have elections in "good times" but the uncertainty of the process remains. The sample includes only those countries for which there was considerable political rivalry. Second, for part of the sample, the countries were on fixed exchange rate systems. With perfect capital mobility, there are substantial limits to independent monetary policy. However, capital mobility increased substantially during the 1970s, the period of flexible rates. Most countries could conduct independent monetary policy in the prior period.

For half of the sample, five countries, there are no significant political effects whatsoever. Regardless of the timing of the political variables or the inclusion of additional variables, such as the inflation rate, no effects could be detected.

There are significant political effects for the other five countries but, for two of those countries, the results are opposite to what is predicted by rational partisan cycle theory. Australia experienced booms after victories of their conservative Liberal Party. Indeed, it appears GNP grows faster the year after any election in Australia. In Austria, there is also a boom after conservative victories with GNP growth on average 2.6 percentage points higher. No effects were noticeable for liberal victories. The experience of these two countries clearly contradicts the theory.

Three countries did have experiences that were more consistent with the theory. Iceland, Sweden, and the United Kingdom all exhibited slower growth after conservative victories. The prediction of booms after liberal victories, however, is not supported by the data.

The two tests of rational partisan cycle theory in this chapter are not kind to the theory. Using evidence from the financial markets, at most three of six episodes following Republican victories in the United States are potentially consistent with the theory. A recession failed to materialize following President Reagan's successful re-election bid and, in two other cases, the recessions appear to have been surprises despite clear evidence of tighter money. The international evidence is far weaker. In ten potential tests cases, only five countries appear to exhibit significant political effects. Of these five, two countries have significant booms after conservative victories and, for the other three, booms fail to follow liberal victories. Clearly, there are not iron or even bronze laws dictating rational partisan cycles.

At least for the United States, one of the problems with the theory is that partisan differences are not always that strong. Uncertainties about the behavior of the parties limit the scope of the theory. To dramatize this point, consider two hypothetical descriptions of the 1988 US election.

First hypothetical Imagine a country that has recently accumulated a large public debt and still has persistent deficit problems. The incumbent is not up for re-election and both parties have tough primary fights in which their most partisan supporters exert considerable influence. The voters have repeatedly expressed dissatisfaction with any mention of the word "taxes." While both parties have middle-class constituencies for spending programs, the leftist party inherits an ambitious wish-list for spending programs. Members of this party are less fearful of inflation than their rivals.

Second hypothetical For the first time in many years, both political parties have nominated individuals not associated with the extreme wings of their parties. The Democrat nominee ran successfully against a more leftist opponent through the primary and played to the political center. His opponent, a longstanding member of the moderate wing of this party, attempted to place some distance between himself and the current popular but more conservative incumbent. Key economic advisors to both candidates have made careers of promoting national savings and investment. The last Democratic president was defeated, in part, by allowing inflation to accelerate sharply.

Given these two possible interpretations, would one expect wage setters to make potential national political developments a primary concern in their decisions?[6]

6.5 Conclusion

The lack of a powerful, positive theory of macroeconomic policymaking does leave plenty of room for traditional normative analysis and policy debate. Game theory does provide a useful discipline for thinking about certain policy problems such as credibility and private information. But it is also clear that the most popular models of policy behavior deliver surprisingly little in terms of useful empirical predictions about the conduct of macro policy.

There are at least two views of the failure of game theory to deliver clear predictions about the course of policy. The first stresses that policymakers and politicians can play a variety of "games" and are not forced to adhere to a fixed set of rules. The proliferation of alternative solution concepts in game theory arises precisely because of this problem. Changing the rules is a key element of political entrepreneurship. My next chapter's story, about the origin of the Gramm–Rudman legislation, illustrates this point.

The second view stresses that games take place in specific political contexts and, until recently, this has been neglected. Traditional political analysis which focuses on political parties and electoral competition can provide some empirical basis for the assumptions necessary to develop game theory or other positive models. Rogoff (1987) developed a model based on imperfect information which would rationalize manipulation of the economy or budgets even with a rational electorate. The key idea is that voters, although rational, are imperfectly informed about the competency or some other aspects of the current administration and its competitors and the incumbent will then have an incentive to pursue actions which would signal its competency. However, the evidence on macroeconomic manipulation at election time is quite weak. While there may be more budget or financial manipulation at election time, careful studies will be necessary to document whether this is a phenomenon worth explaining.

There is slightly more evidence for partisan differences in policies and, as we have seen, they can provide the basis for macro policy models with a bit of explanatory power. But partisan differences in the United States are simply not that strong and can be easily dominated by events or simply administrative differences within the same parties.

Partisan differences, however, do suggest some limitations to the scope of useful normative advice that can be offered to governments. Republican and Democratic administrations will have different overall values. One would never see a Democratic administration official make a cavalier statement about unemployment nor a Republican official minimize the risk of inflation. The explains why the composition of the Council of Economic Advisors is not a random draw from top applied economists in the profession. Within each administration there are always wide-ranging and often profound debates that mirror much wider concerns. Normative analysis lives within this framework.

Notes

1 Under special circumstances, including policy instruments in the objective function can be rationalized as a back-door method for dealing with uncertainty.
2 Chapter 8 documents our lack of understanding of the effect of OPEC shocks as they occurred.
3 Poterba and Rotemberg (1988) find little support for Mankiw's model in data for other countries.
4 According to Margaret Thatcher, "wet" governments hold a damp finger to the wind to detect the latest political breeze.
5 Peek and Rosengre (1988) provide a recent assessment of the stock market as a predictor of recessions.
6 The 1988 presidential election provides another data point. As of May 1989, a "Bush recession" had not materialized.

7

Constitutional Rules and Macro Policy

7.1 Introduction

Prior to the beginning of the Reagan administration, a common theme began to emerge among some conservative economists and policymakers. The poor economic performance of the last part of the Carter administration was not viewed simply as a consequence of badly chosen priorities or poor implementation of economic strategies but as endemic to the normal operation of economic policy in the United States. The fundamental problem concerned the incentives that the institutional framework provided policymakers. Under the system that prevailed, these conservative thinkers argued that the system inevitably produced too high an inflation rate and a tendency towards permanent fiscal deficits. These problems could not be solved simply by changing the personnel inhabiting the offices of the government. Fundamental, institutional change was required to change the incentives that faced policymakers. These institutional changes essentially involved reducing the scope of discretionary policy by placing constitutional or similar restraints on policymakers.

The previous chapter developed several game theoretic models which implied that there would be persistent inflation. While they were useful for illustrating some of the challenges of policymaking, these models were ultimately not persuasive. However, deficits and persistent inflation emerge from another mode of analyzing policy: the public choice approach.

Brennan and Buchanan (1981) in *Monopoly in Money and Inflation: The Case for a Constitution to Discipline Government*, outlined the case for constitutional rules governing monetary policy. Their argument began with a parable of an alchemist who devised a procedure to create gold while living in a country with a gold standard. The alchemist noticed that when he took his newly created gold to buy goods, he was able to acquire goods for the gold but the prices of all other goods rose and the other citizens in the country were made worse off by the alchemist's discovery. In Version A of the story, the alchemist exploited the profits from his discovery and lived a life of luxury in his castle. In Version B of the story, the alchemist decided not to use his gold-creation process because it reduced the welfare of the other citizens of the land.

Brennan and Buchanan asked which version of the parable a ten-year-old girl would find most plausible. Through introspection they argued that their ten-year-old girl would find Version B to be implausible. Assuming this is indeed the case, why should a government in a position, say, to create money through open market purchases, be expected to refrain from the inflation tax? Brennan and Buchanan argue that governments will not be able to refrain from using the inflation tax with the result that excess inflation will result from an unconstrained government with the ability to create money. The remedy for this problem is some type of constitutional restraint on the government's money creation ability. In their words, "Only by restraining the discretionary powers of the monetary authorities through enforceable constitutional rules will the inflation be controlled. It is *monetary regime*, not *monetary policy*, that must be modified" (1981, p. 65).

The argument for the emergence of persistent deficits in a democracy rests on the power of special interests, especially coalitions of special interest, to use the legislative process to provide benefits to themselves at the expense of general taxpayers. The benefits of special interest legislation are highly valued to the recipients while the costs of any one of these benefits to the general populace appears small. The result is a proliferation of spending. Coupled with the electorate's aversion to tax increases, the result is persistent deficits.

Stubblebine provided a succinct account of this process.

> For each of us, government spending on a program offers the least-cost-way of providing that service. Classic examples, of course, are programs whose benefits accrue to a narrow group of people, but which are funded by general taxation. The tax price of the marginal costs to the individual beneficiaries appears to be zero. That they should demand unlimited numbers of those programs, each of un-limited size, should come as no surprise. And this is true of all of us. We are all beneficiaries of some program, and so increased spending has its proponents. At the same time, taxes are painful and we prefer total lower taxes ... The conjunction of these two factors − opportunity to intervene and support for this or that intervention − leads to budget deficits. (1980, p. 51)

The only way to prevent this phenomenon is some type of constitutional restraint on either spending or the budget.

In "Principles of Fiscal and Monetary Policy," Robert E. Lucas, Jr (1986) sketches his ideal framework for the conduct of monetary and fiscal policy. He develops this framework within a simple model economy. Money is introduced into his model of the economy by requiring that agents hold some cash in advance in order to purchase a subset of goods ("cash" goods) while other goods can be paid for by credit. Government spending is exogenous (and possibly stochastic) and no lump-sum taxation is possible, that is, all taxes create distortions. Labor is the only factor of production and there is no capital.

What principles of monetary and fiscal policy emerge in this model? First, unless the nominal rate of interest is zero, agents will face a cost of holding cash balances. As Milton Friedman first pointed out, this cost can be eliminated if there is a deflationary policy so that nominal interest rates are zero. This property also emerges in Lucas's model. The second general principle is that tax rates should be set to minimize dead weight losses. According to the familiar "Ramsey rules" of optimal taxation, this means that goods which are close substitutes (such as leisure across periods) should face similar tax rates. This provides a justification for using debt finance when government spending is higher than usual. Finally, in the long run, any coherent plan for money creation, taxation, and expenditure must be such that the present value of expenditure is equal to the present value of taxation and the revenue from money creation.

Lucas recognized, however, that important political factors posed difficulties with his framework. What would prevent a government, at any point in time, with abandoning or inflating away the existing currency and thereby obtaining additional resources? A similar problem would occur if the model contained capital. A government could, at any point in time, simply announce that all returns from past capital investments would be taxed at 100 percent but that new capital would be free from taxation. Both policies, rapid inflation and confiscatory taxation, would be efficient for the government because they would enable it to reduce other distorting taxes in the economy. But it is clear that, as in the inflation game of the previous chapter, time-consistency is a problem. Individuals deciding to save in the current period will know that governments will also find it efficient to tax old capital at 100 percent rates in future periods and will thereby be discouraged from investing.

Lucas perceived these problems to be fundamental to understanding economic policy over the past several decades.

The tendencies towards permanent deficit finance and inflation that have emerged in our economy in the last fifteen years have much deeper roots that [sic] a succession of transient external shocks and internal mistakes. They arose, I believe, because the implicit rules under which monetary and fiscal policy is conducted have undergone a gradual but fundamental change. If this diagnosis is accurate, then the situation will improve only if new rules can be found that bind policy decisions without committing them to permanent inefficiencies. (1986, p. 133)

The last phrase in the Lucas quote is important. Rules which bind economic policy decisions can prevent policymakers from taking necessary actions in the face of unexpected circumstances and events. Situations will naturally arise in which *all* parties recognize that a discretionary response which violates an existing rule will improve welfare. How can binding rules be designed so as to allow policymakers the opportunity to take decisive steps in the face of undesirable economic circumstances?

Much of the literature on constitutional restraints on economic policy fails to address this point. This literature often presumes that the advent of rules will put an end to "politics as usual." As Allen Schick expressed this point, "Recourse to the constitution is an attempt to negate or limit political action" (1982, p. 96). Political pressures for desirable outcomes do not simply disappear. Faced with "permanent inefficiencies" or even obvious temporary inefficiencies, the political process will generate pressure to sidestep or avoid rules. Any constitutional or statutory scheme to limit policy choices must confront this problem.

During the Reagan administration, both monetary and fiscal policy were subject to controls that, in principle, were designed to limit discretionary policy choices. Monetary policy was subject to a monetary targeting regime from the beginning of the Reagan administration. Fiscal policy choices were restrained through the Gramm–Rudman process during Reagan's second term. This chapter examines the economics and politics of monetary targeting and the Gramm–Rudman process from the perspective of living experiments in rule-constrained economic policy. It examines both the particular circumstances in which the rules developed as well as the influence of the rules on the actual policy choices that were made during the period. By considering two diverse experiments in rule-constrained policymaking, we can look at the common features and difficulties that necessarily emerge in any rule-constrained political environment.

Some supporters of constitutional restraints on economic policy would want to ignore evidence from these two episodes because Gramm–Rudman was a statutory restraint and monetary targeting was partly statutory and partly administrative restraint. But the difference between these types of restraints can be easily exaggerated. As

Allen Schick (1982) noted, New York City plunged into bankruptcy under a constitution that explicitly prohibited deficit financing for operating expenses and pulled itself out of financial disaster through statutory controls on its budget. More generally, to the extent that the same types of problems emerge from all rule-governed policy experiments, the lessons from monetary targeting and Gramm—Rudman should inform the larger debate on rule-constrained political systems.

The next two parts of this chapter analyze the US and other countries experiences with monetary targeting and the US experience with Gramm-Rudman. The final part of the chapter addresses the viability of the constitutional approach based on the experience under the Reagan administration.

7.2 Monetary Targeting

History prior to the Reagan administration

Monetary targeting officially began in the United States in 1975 with the passage of House Concurrent Resolution 133. Although some economists hailed the bill as a triumph of monetarism, the legislative history, as Woolley (1984) recounts, suggests less than a resounding victory. The bill began in the House of Representatives as a move to lower interest rates during the 1975 recession and then was changed in the Senate to call for increased money growth in the first half of 1975 as well as to have the Federal Reserve report to Congress every six months on its plans for the economy. As the final resolution was debated in the House, sponsors of the resolution indicated that concerns about interest rates, not just the money supply, were expressed in the resolution.

Until 1978, the Federal Open Market Committee (FOMC) responded to the resolution by announcing target growth ranges for several monetary aggregates every quarter. Each quarter, the target growth ranges would begin from the current level of the money supply. This policy led to what has been termed "base drift": if the money supply exceeded its target in any quarter and the growth targets were not changed, the deviation of the money supply from its target would be permanent.

With the passage of the Humphrey—Hawkins Act of 1978, the FOMC was required to target growth ranges every February for the remainder of the calender year. Instead of quarterly base drift, the system was subject to possible annual base drift. It is a fair assessment that at least until 1979, meeting the targets was not the Fed's top priority. Targets for M1 were exceeded both in 1977 and 1978.

The situation changed dramatically in 1979. In the midst of deteriorating economic conditions and increased political vulnerability, President Carter made numerous cabinet changes and placed G. William Miller, who was then Federal Reserve chairman, into the position of Secretary of the Treasury. The search for a new Fed chairman eventually resulted with the appointment of Paul Volcker. Volcker was faced with surging inflation, due both to increasing nominal wage demands and the effects of the second major OPEC price rise, a falling dollar, and growing perceptions of a financial crisis.

In October of 1979, Volcker announced a major shift in policy. Prior to this time, the Fed had been using the Federal Funds rate (the interest rate on short-term interbank loans) as the vehicle to meet its money supply targets. Essentially, the Fed estimated what interest rate in the Federal Funds market would be consistent with their money targets and then used its open market operations to hit this interest rate. Under this operating procedure, the Funds rate could, in principle, have to move quite substantially as conditions in the money market changed. As a practical matter, however, the Fed was not willing to let the Funds rate move that dramatically and the result was that the money supply would be allowed to deviate from its targets.

The new policy that the Fed announced involved using bank reserves (technically, reserves not borrowed from the Fed) as the intermediate targets. In practice the Fed now set a wide range for the Federal Funds rate in order to generate a target level of bank reserves which would be consistent with the monetary targets. Although the Fed was critized in some quarters for not moving fully towards reserve targeting, it is clear that the Fed was now willing to tolerate sharp gyrations in the Federal Funds market and in short term interest rates to try to meet its monetary targets.

From a technical point of view, one can make a case for either the old or new operating system based on the underlying structure and nature of the money market. Applying the well-known framework of William Poole (1970), if shocks or disturbances to the supply of reserves are more prevalent than shocks to the demand for reserves, then controlling interest rates will be more effective than controlling reserves. On the other hand, if shocks to the demand for reserves are more important, then reserve targeting will be superior. But, in practice, the Fed's failure to move the Federal Funds rate as required made this academic distinction moot.

In switching to a new operating procedure in 1979, the Fed was, in effect, announcing that it now would take the monetary targets seriously and was willing to change its procedures in order to meet these goals. This was, in part, the price the Fed had to pay to restore credibility and try to limit fears of continuing increases in inflation.

Another, perhaps inadvertent, effect of the change in the operating system was to limit some of the blame for high interest rates and thus to allow the Fed to raise interest rates substantially. As long as the Fed said it was just controlling reserves, it could argue that the "market" was effectively setting interest rates. Of course, the level of interest rates was inversely related to the level of reserves the Fed supplied to the system and thus it could be held responsible for the level of interest rates. Nonetheless, at least some of the Governors felt that the new system had provided "political cover" for raising interest rates.[1]

With the Fed's switch to the new operating stragegy, short-term interest rates were allowed to rise through February and March of 1980. In March of 1980, President Carter promulgated credit controls. These controls had immediate effects in the financial markets and the economy. The economy soon plunged into an extremely sharp but very short recession. As loan demand fell both because of dampening economic activity and the effects of the credit controls, and as depositors moved some assets from deposits to interest bearing assets, M1 fell dramatically in April. The new operating system dictated that the Fed should allow the Federal Funds rate to fall in order to stimulate the growth of bank reserve in order to meet the monetary targets. The Fed did indeed allow interest rates to fall and the Funds rate fell from a high of 17 percent in April to near 9 percent by midsummer.[2]

By midsummer, however, a recovery from the recession had begun (perhaps due to the elimination of controls and easier monetary policy), and the money supply began to soar again. Now the Fed was faced with the less pleasant consequence of its operating procedure – interest rates had to rise to limit money growth. The Fed pushed the Federal Funds rate upwards through the election until it reached over 18 percent by year's end.

The last year of the Carter administration had not been a good year for the Fed. The economy had entered a recession but was still plagued by high inflation and fears of increasing inflation. Interest rates had fallen from very high levels only to rise again. And the Fed still had not achieved credibility in its fight against inflation.

Targeting in the Reagan administration

The first full statement of economic policy from the Reagan administration came in the bold White House publication *America's New Beginning: A Program for Economic Recovery* (1981). This document outlined in considerable detail the economic strategy of the administration and discussed specific budget and tax changes. There was also some discussion of monetary policy which emphasized two key points.

First, there was to be a gradual reduction in the inflation rate engineered by a gradual reduction in the growth of the money supply. Second, it was important for the Fed to hit its monetary targets in order to restore credibility to monetary policy and alleviate fears in the financial markets.

Although the Reagan program has been often criticized for embodying inconsistent goals, the stated inflation and money growth goals of the administration were not that radical. The inflation goals for the five years following 1981 were:

Year	1981	1982	1983	1984	1985	1986
Inflation	9.9	8.3	7.0	6.0	5.4	4.9

These goals were to be accomplished by gradual reduction in the growth of money and credit to one-half the levels that prevailed in 1981.

The statements about monetary targeting were also quite reasonable. "In that connection, success in meeting the targets the Federal Reserve has set will itself increase confidence in the results of policy. Otherwise, observers are likely to pay excessive attention to short-run changes in money growth and revise anticipations upwards or downwards unnecessarily" (p. 22). At the same time, there was a clear recognition of the inherent difficulties of monetary targeting. "A number of factors — such as the introduction of credit controls and their subsequent removal and frequent shifts in announced fiscal policies — have contributed to pronounced fluctuations in interest rates and monetary growth over the past year. At the same time, we need to learn from the experience with the new techniques and seek further improvement."

The sharp divisions among economic advisors in the early days of the Reagan administration, documented by Office of Management and Budget Director David Stockman in his book *The Triumph of Politics* (1986), carried over to monetary policy. While the language about the Fed in *America's New Beginning* may have been rather mild, harsher language echoed in the halls of the Treasury and the Old Executive Office Building. The Reagan administration economic team included two strong advocates of monetarism. Beryl Sprinkel, Undersecretary of Treasury of Monetary Affairs, and Jerry Jordan, of the Council of Economic Advisors, believed that the Fed had not gone far enough in October of 1979 and was still failing to take all the measures necessary to control the money supply.

The full monetarist agenda included a number of institutional reforms and changes. Instead of controlling unborrowed reserves, the monetarists urged the Fed to control total reserves. The discount rate should be pegged slightly higher than market rates and a penalty rate should accompany excessive borrowing. The monetarists also advocated that reserve requirements should be changed so that required reserves would depend on contemporaneous deposits, not deposits that the bank held two weeks prior. Although the Fed later adopted some of this program, they resisted changes early in the Reagan administration which provided opportunities for attacks by monetarists.

Monetary targeting moved to central focus in the early period in the Reagan administration. The central economic challenge for the administration was to reduce inflation without suffering through a recession. If the Fed could consistently meet its targets, administration theorists reasoned, the private sector would then believe that the Fed was indeed embarking on a gradual deceleration of money growth which would imply lower inflation. Inflationary expectations would then gradually be reduced and the economy could manage the transition to lower inflation rates without suffering through a recession; instead, it would be possible to grow rapidly through supply-side stimulus. If the Fed erred on either side, either too rapid or too slow money growth, this delicate expectational game with the public would be upset and with it the prospects for painless disinflation. This partly explained the preoccupation with monetary targeting.

At the same time, the financial markets were also preoccupied with monetary targeting. Economists studied in detail the effects on financial markets when the Fed announced on Friday the weekly money supply numbers. When the money supply exceeded what the market anticipated (and these anticipations were actually circulated in the financial community), interest rates rose. The most plausible explanation for the increase in interest rates following the announcement was that under monetary targeting, higher money growth now meant lower growth later and thus the market was anticipating future Fed tightening.[3] The only problem with this argument was that interest rates on long-term bonds as well as implicit five-year and beyond forward rates rose on the basis of one week's money supply announcement. Is it plausible that noisy data about one week's money supply can cause a revision about the level of interest rates five years in the future? Psychological factors clearly played a role. Clearly, the financial markets were also preoccupied with monetary targeting which in turn reinforced the administration's concerns about the Fed's performance.

Perhaps the key issue with monetary targeting is whether its presence forced the Fed to take actions that it would not have taken without the existence of the targets. Carl Walsh (1987a) examined this issue using econometric methods over the entire targeting period from 1975 to 1985 for M1 and found little effect from the targets. But as Walsh recognized, the Fed's own allegiance to targeting and its own operating procedures changed several times over the sample period thereby reducing the scope for econometric analysis. The approach taken in this chapter is to look carefully at four key episodes in money management during the Reagan administration. In the first two episodes, April of 1981 and February of 1982, it appears that monetary targeting contributed directly to the Fed's decisions. In the latter two episodes, July of 1982 and May of 1984, the Fed proceeded in its own direction.[4]

During the first few months of 1981, the Fed kept the money supply at moderate levels and reduced the Federal Funds rate gradually. In April, the Fed was faced with very rapid money growth rates. On May 6, after a conference call to the FOMC, the operating desk in New York was instructed to raise the funds rate to reduce the expansion of reserves. At the FOMC meeting of May 18, they decided to continue to tighten to bring the money supply under control. The Federal Funds rate rose sharply from 15.7 percent in April to 18.5 percent in May and remained above 19 percent through July. The money supply responded promptly and money growth was negative through May and June and at extremely low rates through November. The National Bureau of Economic Research (NBER) dates July as the start of the severe recession which eventually led to unemployment rates exceeding 10 percent.

A strong case can be made that the Fed would not have been inclined to raise interest rates so dramatically in the absence of monetary targeting. The rise in the money supply occurred in April when income tax transactions can cause distortions in the money figures. Perhaps more important was the introduction of NOW (Negotiated Order of Withdrawal) accounts. The Fed had to create a new monetary measure "shift-adjusted M1−B" which attempted to purify the M1 measure by removing the estimated savings components from the NOW accounts from M1. The FOMC directive to the New York Bank even went so far as to note that "shifts into NOW accounts will continue to distort measured growth in M1−B to an unpredictable extent, and operational reserve paths will be developed in the light of evaluation of these distortions."[5] Faced with these uncertainties, why did the Fed respond to the April increase in the money supply even though money growth earlier in the year had been modest?

White House pressure for meeting the targets, the preoccupations of the financial markets with M1 and M1 targeting, and a desire to build credibility all combined to lead the Fed towards tightening in May of 1981. At this point, there was a consensus among the Reagan economic team that Fed credibility was essential to their progam and that credibility could only be established by meeting the targets. The same philosophy emanated from Wall Street. The Fed had been accused of tolerating too much volatility in M1 growth in the prior recession (which some blamed for the short recession) and had an interest to try to prevent a surge in money growth, even when the causes were extremely unclear. For the year, the target for M1 growth was in the 3.5 to 6 percent range; the actual growth for the year was 2.3 percent.

The second major decision point came for the Fed in early 1982. At this point, the economy had already entered into a recession and the Consumer Price Index in late 1981 had already begun to increase at a slightly lower rate. By the end of the year, interest rates had begun to fall with the Federal Funds rate down to near 12 percent from a summer high near 19 percent and short-term Treasury securities falling from 15 percent to near 11 percent. Beginning in November, the money supply began to increase at a rapid rate and continued to increase through January and February. Despite the fact that the economy had now entered a recession and money growth in the previous year had been below target, the Fed was now faced in February with the prospect of increasing interest rates to stem the increase in the money supply.

Pressure from the White House this time was quite direct; at a press conference on January 19, President Reagan expressed dissatisfaction with the recent increase in the money supply which he feared would send the wrong signals to the market. With the Fed subscribing to monetary targeting, President Reagan was not viewed as abusing the independence of the Fed but specifically asking the Fed to adhere to its own targets. This gave additional legitimacy and concreteness to this event. According to William Greider (1987, p. 443), some Republicans on Capitol Hill, including Senator Howard Baker, had been urging Volcker to lower interest rates but the call from the White House was for control of the money supply.

In reaching a decision about monetary policy in February of 1982, the FOMC had to weigh the risks of deepening the recession against those of losing its credibility and abruptly ending the recession, as in 1980, with no lasting effect on inflationary expectations. Based partly on their belief, reported in the FOMC minutes, that a recovery would begin in the second quarter, the Fed chose to sharply limit money growth and its directive called for no further M1 growth in the first quarter of 1982 and even indicated that declines in M1 would be tolerated.

In June of 1982, it appeared that the February episode was about to be replayed. Since April of that year, money growth had exceeded the Fed's growth ranges and growth in early June appeared to be very rapid. Fed watchers quoted in the *Wall Street Journal* were also predicting further increases in M1 in July accompanying a large cost-of-living-increase for Social Security recipients which, at least temporarily, would be parked in assets belonging to M1. The same Fed watchers anticipated that the Fed would be forced to tighten; in mid-June the bond market nervously studied the money figures.

But several factors made the situation quite different from the previous February. First, the recession had been under way for ten months and the spring recovery had failed to materialize. The Congress was quite vocal about the effects of the Fed's tight money policies and grew concerned about the upcoming elections. But two other factors were perhaps more important: sharp policy divisions among the Reagan economic advisors and the emergence of debt problems and financial fragility.

The divisions among the administration advisors can be seen through the pages of the *Wall Street Journal* during June. On June 11 a story on the credit pages (p. 39) expressed Beryl Sprinkel's concerns. "[He] renewed his criticism of the Federal Reserve, charging that money supply growth has been much too erratic. He added he is 'concerned' about the rapid increase in the money supply and the monetary base in recent months." He was also quoted as saying that the administration was against both raising the targets for money growth or the base for the targets.

On Friday, June 21, a page three story appeared in the *Journal* entitled "Treasury Studies Curbs on Power of Fed on Worry Recovery is Being Undermined." This was a clear attempt to place additional pressure on the Fed. The article quoted Sprinkel as saying that "various options" were being considered about legislation to change the Fed's role. "The major issue is what we mean by independence." Sprinkel went on to complain about the money supply being on a roller coaster. Although the Fed was reducing the money supply on average, which was what the administration desired, there had been too much instability. The Reagan administration "has asked for stable money growth since arriving in office, and we don't think we are getting it." According to Sprinkel, this instability had made the recession deeper. In the context of April through June increases in the money supply and Sprinkel's previous statements, the cry for stability implied that the Fed should raise interest rates to prevent any further increases in the money supply. The article went on to discuss that Secretary of the Treasury Donald Regan felt that the administration had been working hard to resolve budget problems and that current economic difficulties were being caused by the Fed.

These positions, however, were not shared by the rest of the administration. On Monday, advisors Murray Weidenbaum and David Stockman downplayed the implied threats to the Fed and also disavowed a policy of immediate tightening. A story on Tuesday, June 25, in the *Journal* (p. 3) minimized the significance of the Treasury study on the Fed and stressed it dealt solely with highly technical issues. More important, however, was the different slant on the desired course of monetary policy. Weidenbaum, Chairman of the Council of

Economic Advisors, stated that the administration wants a "gradual pace" for monetary growth because it worries that above average growth generates fears of inflation. "At the same time, however, the White House wants the Fed to avoid a sharp tightening of monetary policy, designed to bring the growth rate quickly down to the target range ... An abrupt contraction could create a 'liquidity crunch' Mr. Stockman said." In other words, they wanted precisely the opposite outcome that resulted from the similar situation in February. In addition to Weidenbaum and Stockman publically disowning a strict monetarist line, Greider reports that Chief of Staff James Baker also lost faith in monetarist prescriptions and did not want the Fed to tighten any further.[6]

With the obvious divisions among the White House economic advisors, Volcker and the FOMC were under less pressure to take actions to bring money growth in line with the target ranges. The Fed now was witnessing visible strains in the financial system. Mexico was experiencing the first of several financial crises in the 1980s and Volcker was involved in the first of many rescue attempts. The failure of Penn Square exposed the fragility of other major money center banks and raised the prospects of failures for major banking enterprises which were later realized in the failures of Seattle First and Continental Illinois.

Most economists and Fed officials point to a major shift in Fed policy in October of 1982. Stephen Axilrod, former staff director for the Fed, stated that less importance began to be placed on M1 in October of 1982. "The precipitating event for the de-emphasis of M1 was the maturity of a very large volume ($31 billion) of All Savers Certificates in October 1982, and uncertainty about how M1 might be affected in the process of the public's reinvesting those funds in other instruments" (1985, p. 18).

But the real changes occurred in early July as the Fed raised its target range and began liberally supplying reserves to the system by lowering the Federal Funds rate.[7] Short-term interest rates started falling in July and by October, rates had fallen to 7.7 percent from 12.5 percent in June. The stock market began to rise in the summer as it began to understand that the Fed had eased. The bond market rallied as long-term rates fell nearly 300 basis points from June to October. A strict application of monetary targeting, such as in February, would not have allowed these dramatic decreases in interest rates and the double-digit money growth rates beginning in August.

The last episode under review indicates that strong White House pressure on the Fed without the support of the monetary targeting framework was not sufficient to change Fed policies. In early 1984, the economy was now in the recovery phase and growing at a rapid rate.

The Fed was clearly worried that the expansion was proceeding too rapidly and tightened slightly in late March allowing the Funds rate to rise above 10 percent for the first time since 1982.

The White House was dismayed by this action as they wanted nothing to potentially interfere with the President's re-election bid in the fall. In May, an increase in the prime rate by large banks was taken as an opportunity to citicize the Fed for not allowing the money supply to grow sufficiently to accommodate the expansion. This effort was orchestrated by James Baker who was aided by advisors Richard Darman, Larry Speaks, and Treasury Secretary Donald Regan.[8] But without any justification from a common, shared framework such as was provided by monetary targeting, the pressure from the White House was perceived as simply an election year attempt to influence the Fed and the White House's efforts were denounced on Wall Street and in the press. Reagan was forced to hold a brief press conference to pledge support for the Fed's efforts in difficult times. The Federal Funds rate remained high and there is no indication that the Fed's policy was changed by the White House efforts.

The Fed continued to target M1 until 1987 when it totally abandoned M1 as a target and only announced targets for broader aggregates. But M1 targets did not appear to constrain the Fed's behavior after July of 1982 in the sense of forcing policy shifts that the Fed would not have been inclined to make. Most observers argue that the Fed essentially based policy, certainly after October 1982, on its general readings of the financial markets and the economy. When monetary targets became inconvenient, some device was found to eliminate their effects on fundamental policy choices. In July of 1983 and 1985, for example, faced with too rapid growth in M1, the Fed simply set a new base for its target range, without trying to counteract the prior growth.

Financial deregulation had so fundamentally changed the monetary landscape that M1 targeting was no longer feasible. In 1986, the target growth ranges for M1 were 3–8 percent. Actual money growth for that year was 15.2 percent! The Fed still announced targets for broader aggregates but by 1985 even monetarists were doubting the wisdom of continued monetary targeting in any form.[9]

Although generalizations from one extended episode are inherently dangerous, there appear to be four lessons that emerge from the experience with monetary targeting:

1   Although monetary targets were "on the books" since 1975, it took a serious financial crisis and loss of confidence to force the Fed to take actions which treated the targets seriously. Adherence to the targets was the price that was paid for loss of confidence in the Fed.

2 The explicit guidelines and commonly accepted framework provided by monetary targeting became a useful vehicle through which the White House could exert pressure on the Fed. Without reliance on the device of monetary targeting, White House efforts to pressure the Fed could more easily be perceived as attempts to limit the Fed's independence.

3 Rather than eliminating political influence on the Fed, the effectiveness of monetary targeting as a vehicle to influence the Fed depended dramatically on the ongoing political battles within the administration. When profound and transparent divisions appeared among White House advisors, the effectiveness of monetary targeting disappeared.

4 Institutional changes caused by a sustained period of high interest rates and rapid financial deregulation eventually led to the end of targeting for narrow aggregates. Although at the end of the period, this deficiency in monetary targeting was obvious to all parties, similar difficulties, although on a smaller scale, plagued monetary targeting from the beginning.

Experience of other countries with monetary targeting

The United States was not the only country that embarked on a program of monetary targeting in the 1970s. Isard and Rojas-Suarez (1986) and Fischer (1987) have reviewed the experience of Canada, West Germany, France, Italy, Japan, and the United Kingdom with monetary targeting. The experience with monetary targeting in these countries provides additional information on both the issue of feasibility of targeting as well as credibility.

Perhaps the most noticeable similarity among these countries was the difficulty experienced with finding a suitable target during periods of financial innovation. Canada, which had previously met its monetary targets, abandoned monetary targeting after 1982 because the Bank of Canada no longer felt comfortable interpreting monetary aggregates. France changed the aggregate which it targeted in 1986 again after experiencing difficulties of interpretation with its aggregates. The United Kingdom in 1982 supplemented its targets of sterling M3 with two other aggregates but abandoned the latter targets after two years.

Another common theme from the experience of these countries is that success in meeting monetary targets was often not associated with achieving desired inflation goals. Canada was successful in meeting its target ranges but in the late 1970s its inflation began to outstrip the rapid inflation in the United States. France experienced a similar situation from 1977 to 1981. The United Kingdom at one point had the opposite experience. Although it overran its targets through the early 1980s, the overall impact of monetary restraint eventually brought inflation down.

Several countries modified their monetary targeting procedures in the face of developments in the foreign exchange market. In 1978, both Germany and Switzerland raised monetary growth to avoid a recession after their exchange rates rose in world markets. Germany faced precisely the opposite situation in 1979−81. The mark fell against both the dollar and the yen over that period and the Bundesbank aimed for the lower part of its target range to avoid the inflationary consequences of a depreciating currency.

There appears to be no simple link between achievement of monetary targeting objectives and successful disinflation policy. As described above, Canada and France met their monetary targets over an extended period but inflation increased. The United Kingdom and the United States brought inflation down in the 1980s while generally missing their targets. Blanchard (1987a) argued that there appeared to be some evidence for an increase in the credibility of the disinflation policy in the United States towards the end of 1982. He estimated a standard Phillips curve for wages and found that it began to overpredict inflation in late 1982. However, there are a number of alternative explanations for the breakdown of the simple Phillips relation. Exchange rate effects may have limited wage growth, the delayed effect of breaking the union of air traffic controllers might have been reflected in other wage negotiations, or there may simply have been important non-linearities in the effects from cumulative unemployment in a very deep recession. In any case, this "breakdown" occurs at precisely the time that strict monetary targeting was abandoned by the Fed. Simply meeting monetary targets does not guarantee a credible central bank.

7.3   The Gramm−Rudman Experience

Background

Monetary targeting was adopted in a time of economic crisis with growing panic in the financial markets over inflation. Gramm−Rudman was adopted more in the midst of a political crisis than an economic crisis. Economists had been warning for some time about the pernicious effects of persistent deficits and these warnings had become a veritable litany in Congress, especially in the Senate. Martin Feldstein, successor to Murray Weidenbaum as Chairman of the Council of Economic Advisors, had articulated the case against deficits from within the administration. Deficits first raise short- and long-term interest rates as the additional government bonds compete with private financing. The higher domestic interest rates lead to both "crowding-out" of domestic investment and an appreciated dollar as foreign investors attempt to purchase domestic securities. An appreciated dollar leads to trade deficits as the relative price of US goods increase in world markets.

Although the litany was well understood in Congress, there was considerable debate in the academic community about its accuracy. Perhaps the weakest link in the chain of reasoning was the very first, the connection between deficits and interest rates. This issue had been analyzed by economists in some detail. A Congressional Budget Office review of the literature revealed that the evidence connecting budget deficits and interest rates was weak with as many studies failing to find links as those finding connections.[10] The actual pattern of long-term nominal interest rates exhibited declines as deficits rose and it is notoriously difficult to estimate long-term inflationary expectations to determine the behavior of long-term real rates. Perhaps most disconcerting for the theory was the behavior of the stock market. If government deficits were raising real interest rates in the bond market, then prices in equity markets should be falling in the face of higher required yields. Yet, the US stock market was booming.[11] Indeed, the rising stock market and the trade deficit could be jointly explained by theories that stressed the attractiveness of investment in the United States relative to abroad, assuming no effects from government deficits at all.

The boom in the stock market was indicative of a phenomenon that was more important than mere academic discontent with the traditional deficit story. It did not appear to the general public that the deficits were actually hurting the economy. To be sure, workers in firms in the tradeable goods sector were suffering from the higher dollar (just as they would be benefiting from the falling dollar several years later − with only a mild reduction in the deficit). However, total employment continued to grow, unemployment fell, trips to Europe and foreign goods in general were cheap, and the stock market continued to increase. Some economists warned that the effects of deficits would only be felt in future years in terms of either a diminished capital stock or a transfer of the ownership of domestic capital to foreign residents. But these dangers were abstract; in 1985, the US economy looked quite strong.

The strains on the political system in Washington from the deficits, however, were growing severe. There was a general feeling that the deficits had to be brought under control. This feeling was embraced by traditional conservatives, such as the Senate Republicans who were now in control and the majority of the Reagan economic team. Democrats also favored deficit reduction. They had seen, over the past few years, how persistent deficits led inevitably to pressures to reduce spending, particularly on nonentitlement, nondefense programs. Reduced deficits, particularly through higher taxes, would alleviate pressure on these programs.

The first half of 1985 witnessed a complex three-ringed battle over deficit reduction with the key participants being the Senate Republicans, led by Senator Domenici, head of the Senate Budget Committee, the White House and the Democrats from the House of Representatives.[12] The Senate Republicans, after promises of White House support, pushed through a budget resolution that froze defense spending for one year, eliminated many programs, and also suspended cost-of-living-adjustments (COLAs) for Social Security for one year. They won this fight with Vice-President George Bush breaking a 49−49 tie after Senator Peter Wilson from California was wheeled in from the hospital. The Democratically controlled House, however, put together their own budget resolution which had higher defense cuts, less cuts in domestic spending, and also removed the freeze in COLAs.

The House−Senate Conference was deadlocked. Domenici initially proposed to give up the COLA adjustment for increased taxes on high income Social Security recipients, a proposal that he believed House Majority Leader Tip O'Neil had previously proposed. But the House Conferees rejected taxes on Social Security and the deadlock continued. On July 10, David Stockman, whose credibility and effectiveness had been limited for some time by his previous disclosures in an *Atlantic* magazine article, resigned. President Reagan met with conferees and agreed to a package which eliminated the COLA freeze and was closer to the House position than the position of the Senate. The Senate Republicans felt betrayed by the President. They had taken what they believed to be a responsible and certainly politically risky course by supporting the COLA freeze but had been undercut by Reagan.

It was in this atmosphere of political deadlock and frustration that Gramm−Rudman originated. The key precipitating event was a required vote on a new debt ceiling limit for the federal government, one which would allow the debt to exceed $2 trillion. The House had adopted procedures which obviated the requirement for a separate debt ceiling vote (it was part of their final budget resolution) but in the Senate, a separate vote was required.[13]

Senator Phil Gramm, who had offered budget limitation proposals before, took this opportunity to place binding controls on Congress. He brought on as co-sponsors a Republican moderate, Warren Rudman, and Senator Hollings from the Democratic party. To gain passage of the bill, Social Security was eliminated from any budget cutting procedures. Although, in principle, defense could be cut severely in the final outcome of the process, the President supported the bill perhaps largely to take symbolic action against the deficit and avoid partisan attacks associated with raising the debt limit.

The bill passed the Senate easily and also gained considerable support in the House. Although the House Democratic leadership did not like the bill, they hoped to change it substantially in conference. Indeed, the bill was effectively written in conference and, as we will see below, the House did exert important influence over its final structure.

The Logic and Structure of Gramm–Rudman

Is it ever rational for a person or group to deliberately decrease the options they have available? If an individual or group knows in advance that it is likely that they will make incorrect or unadvised decisions under duress, then it may be valuable to limit the scope for decision-making. Gramm–Rudman was a grand experiment in this tradition. Congress essentially imposed a series of rules that would automatically take over if certain deficit targets were violated. Like Ulysses, Congress tied itself to the mast.

How did Gramm–Rudman work? Table 7.1 contains deficit targets that Congress set for itself under both the initial Gramm–Rudman law and the second Gramm–Rudman law. Unless the Congress adopted

Table 7.1 Deficit targets for Gramm–Rudman

Fiscal year	Gramm–Rudman I	Gramm–Rudman II
1986	171.9	
1987	144	
1988	108	144
1989	72	136
1990	36	100
1991	0	64
1992		28
1993		0

binding budget resolutions to meet these targets (or, in some cases, come within $10 billion of the target), and automatic budget cutting procedure known as sequestration would automatically go into effect. Borrowing the terminology from Dr Strangelove, this was essentially a doomsday machine.

The heart of the Gramm–Rudman law was the automatic sequestration procedure and there were many subtleties involved in its design, both from a political and budgeting perspective. The first step in implementing the first law was to determine the target deficit reduction required under the law. This deficit reduction included any surpluses or deficits for Social Security and other off-budget activities. Then the budget was divided into two parts: defense and nondefense. Exempt activities including interest on the debt, Social Security payments, and a group of low-income programs, were then excluded.

The next step was to reduce defense and nondefense programs equally after eliminating the automatic cost of living adjustments to retirement and disability programs. In addition, a series of adjustments for special programs were made for the nondefense part of the budget. There were also special rules for health programs which limited their reductions and also required the reductions to be made in payments to health providers. Also exempt from both defense and nondefense were prior legal obligations incurred by the government. All these adjustments determined the necessary reduction in *outlays* to meet the targets.

The next step was to determine the uniform percentage reductions to apply to the spending resources in defense and nondefense programs. Spending resources included previously unobligated *budget authority* and any new budget authority. Congress actually determines budget authority, the right to spend money, not outlays. Since the actual sequestrations applied to budget authority and not outlays, the Congressional Budget Office (CBO) and the Office of Management and Budget (OMB) were required to estimate the link between reductions in budget authority and outlays necessary to meet the deficit targets. For fiscal year 1986, the sequestration percentages were 4.9 percent for defense and 4.3 percent for nondefense. These percentages were applied at the program, project, and activity level in all accounts subject to sequestration.

Although there was a general intention to have an "across the board" philosophy and have most programs subject to the sequestration procedures, it is evident from this description that Congress modified this procedure to meet certain Congressional priorities. In addition, the rules for 1986 were also modified. As an example, the President was given authority to remove military personnel accounts from the sequestration base. Congress also put in language protecting "Congressional interest items" ensuring that no military bases were closed. We can, in part, explain some of the structural features of Gramm—Rudman by considering the problem of designing an ideal doomsday machine.

The designers of Gramm—Rudman did not wish to put the government totally on automatic pilot but designed their mechanism to force the Congress and the administration to make choices between tax increases and various forms of spending cuts. Designing a mechanism that would actually work, however, is not an easy task. An ideal mechanism would have to meet two essential tests in order to force a compromise agreement:

1   The outcome if an agreement is not reached must be well defined so that its consequences can be readily foreseen and distasteful enough to most parties so that an agreement is desirable. In other words, it must be *unpalatable*.
2   The default provisions must be *credible*. They cannot be so draconian that no one believes they would be allowed to remain in force if the deficit targets were not reached.

These two considerations strongly influenced the actual structure of the first Gramm—Rudman law. The across the board thrust of the law was essential so that proponents of both military and domestic programs would fear implementation of the sequestration provisions. The detailed sequestration procedures allowed interested parties to calculate the precise impacts if the automatic provisions actually went into effect. No major players looked forward to a major sequestration for fiscal year 1987.

At the same time, many features of the law could best be explained by the need to make the automatic features of the law credible, or in the language of the game theorists, a "perfect" equilibrium. First, fiscal year 1986 had already begun by the time the law went into effect which left very little time for any negotiations that first year. Thus, a limit was placed on the total funds to be sequestered. Second, there were special provisions in place just for fiscal year 1986 including, for example, additional flexibility within defense department accounts. Third, Social Security and interest on the national debt were exempt from all cuts. Fourth, there were safety valve features for both recessions and wars. One can plausibly argue that all these features were necessary in order to prevent Congress from simply passing a new law if the automatic cuts went into effect. If, for example, Social Security were not exempt, many members of Congress would not feel the automatic cuts would be credible because they would anticipate overwhelming pressures for them to adopt a new law. And if they believed that, there would be no real incentives to reach an agreement.

As we will discuss below, the first Gramm—Rudman law was ruled unconstitutional by the Supreme Court. A second Gramm–Rudman bill was passed in 1987. This second bill also had features reflecting the notion of "perfect" equilibrium. The maximum amount cut or sequestered was severely limited for the first two years. This meant that the bulk of the deficit cutting effort was postponed until after the 1988 presidential election. While this could be viewed as mere political escapism, one could argue that foreknowledge of election year pressures led all parties to soften deficit cutting demands to reflect the maximum cuts that were feasible.

Not all of the important features of the law could be explained with reference to our two basic principles, which are to make the automatic features unpalatable but credible. Many low income programs were exempt and there were special rules for health programs and retirement programs. Many of these features, for example the additions to the list of exempt programs, were added by House Democrats in the bargaining process in conference. To explain these features of the law, it is useful to borrow another concept from game theory, the notion of a "threat point."

In cooperative bargaining models, the threat point is the outcome if the parties fail to agree. In general, the nature of the threat point or fallback provisions will be an important determinant of the final outcome. The intense bargaining that occurred in conference between Democrats and Republicans reflected an awareness of the importance of the threat point. Even if everyone anticipated that a bargain would be struck, the threat point would still partially determine the outcome. The 50 percent defense and 50 percent nondefense cuts in Gramm–Rudman were reflected in the budget negotiations for fiscal year 1987, indicating the importance of the threat point.

This brief description of the Gramm–Rudman law gives some feel for its extraordinary complexity. Two areas (in addition to the intricate design of the actual sequestration mechanism) posed special problems for the designers of the legislation. These were the provisions for adjustments in the face of economic downturns and the baseline definitions for determining the actual size of the projected deficits.

Critics of balanced budget proposals have always raised the Keynesian stabilization argument that, in the event of a downturn, balancing the budget would just exacerbate the deteriorating economic conditions. This argument played an important role in the debate prior to final passage. In one of the earliest versions of the bill, the recession provisions were virtually non-existent. In the event that the CBO and the OMB forecast a recession at the beginning of a fiscal year, Congress would be given several extra weeks to formulate a response but the deficit targets would still be in force. These recession provisions were perceived to be much too weak.

In the conference committee, the House Democrats proposed that the targets be adjusted depending on economic conditions. If economic growth exceeded 3 percent, the target would be 20 percent per year below the actual fiscal 1985 deficit. However, for every 0.1 percentage point the growth rate fell below 3 percent, the required reductions would be reduced by one percentage point. For example, real economic growth of 2 percent would require a deficit target of only 10 percent below the prior deficit.

The version which came from the Senate side and was finally adopted had fixed deficit targets but two safety valve features. First, if the CBO and OMB predict negative real growth for two consecutive quarters then an automatic vote is taken in both houses on a joint resolution as to whether the deficit targets must be met. Second, the automatic vote is also triggered if real economic growth falls below 1 percent for two consecutive quarters.

Both the House plan and the final law provided some protection from the Keynesian stabilization dilemma. The final law had the danger that economic growth could be sluggish but not quite fall to only 1 percent for two quarters. In this case, the actual deficit would increase and to meet the targets would require larger cuts during weak economic conditions. The House plan would have avoided this problem but would have created considerable ambiguity as to the precise targets that would be required, thereby making it difficult for all parties to focus on concrete alternative plans.

Charles Schultze (1987) argued that there were serious flaws in the recession escape clauses in Gramm–Rudman. The central problem he identified, which also applies to the House alternative, is that the escape mechanisms were geared to the *rate of change* of GNP rather than the deviation of GNP from some fixed target or forecast. Essentially, slow or erratic growth could lead to cumulative shortfalls of GNP and large budget deficits without triggering the escape clauses.

Schultze performed two interesting experiments to "test" the recession clauses in Gramm–Rudman. He first looked at the last eight recessions in the United States to determine if the escape clauses would have been triggered by two consecutive quarters of negative economic growth. He found that in seven of the eight cases, the law would not have been been suspended in the first year of those recessions and would have been suspended in only one-half of the first years of the recovery periods.

Schultze also examined whether conventional forecasters would have predicted two quarters of negative economic growth in time to trigger the escape mechanisms. Looking at forecasting data for the last three recessions, he found that only in one episode were two quarters of negative growth predicted for the first year of the recession. Schultze concluded that the escape clauses were too weak to be effective. Either Congress would adhere to the targets and inflict substantial harm upon the economy, particularly in protracted recessions, or else it would simply abandon the Gramm−Rudman process entirely by passing another law or resorting to budgetary tricks.

Projections of future deficits require an estimate of what the deficit would be in the absence of any further action. These projections are necessary in order to determine whether the automatic sequestration provisions in the law are to be triggered. Both the CBO and the OMB use *baseline concepts* to project what the budget would be in the absence of changes in policy. But, of course, the term "changes in policy" is somewhat ambiguous. For example, the CBO assumes that no change in policy means that discretionary programs are kept constant in real terms. Baselines are both a statement of the status quo but also involve predictions of what Congress will do within the current policy framework.

The first Gramm−Rudman law developed its own baseline concept. On the revenue side, the current tax law was assumed to remain in force and provisions scheduled to expire were assumed to expire except for excise taxes dedicated to trust funds which were assumed to remain unchanged. On the spending side, the enacted levels for annual discretionary appropriations were to be used. If appropriation bills had not been enacted within five days of the reporting deadlines, last year's appropriations were to be assumed to continue but without any adjustment for inflation.

The zero inflation adjustment assumption did not, of course, preclude Congress from developing budgets which would preserve programs in real terms. However, it implicitly set as the norm a situation in which program reductions were required if appropriation bills were not enacted. Compared to using the CBO baseline, it made sequestration less likely but in the event that sequestration occurred, programs were reduced from a lower level. The zero inflation assumption was an attempt to set a tone for budget reduction.

The second Gramm−Rudman law changed the baseline to include inflation adjustments, that is, existing programs were projected to continue in real terms. The reason for the change was to minimize cuts in the event of any sequestration. Although the deficit targets for the first two years were modest and involved limited deficit reduction efforts, in the event a sequestration did occur, there was a common interest among all elected officials to minimize disruptions prior to the forthcoming 1988 elections.

During the debate of the Gramm−Rudman law, many members of Congress expressed reservations about the constitutionality of the process. Immediately after its passage several suits were brought challenging its constitutionality. The law actually contained contingencies (described below) in case the sequestration feature of the law was found to be unconstitutional, as the Supreme Court in fact ruled. The second Gramm−Rudman law was written to preserve the automatic sequestration procedures yet avoid constitutional difficulties.

Shortly after its passage, the District Court in Washington, DC ruled that the law was unconstitutional in Synar vs. the United States. The sequestration for 1986, however, was allowed to go into effect and the case went to the Supreme Court. The Supreme Court's decision followed the logic of the District Court and it is therefore worthwhile to begin with an analysis of the ruling of the District Court.

There were two principal arguments brought before the District Court. First, the plaintiffs argued that the law delegated too much legislative power to the executive branch in the sequestration process in that legislative decisions and priorities were forfeited to the executive branch. Second, they also argued very nearly the opposite position. The law gave the Comptroller General, the head of the Government Accounting Office, special duties including reconciling any differences between the reports of the CBO and OMB and preparing a final sequestration order for the President. The plaintiffs argued that this delegates executive functions to a legislative officer and again violates the separation of powers doctrine. The administration filed a brief in support of the latter argument.

The District Court rejected the first argument that the law delegated too much power to the executive branch. The opinion noted that Congress had carefully spelled out the entire sequestration process including special rules and exemptions and that the executive branch was simply placed in the role of executing the law.

The District Court did rule, however, that the Comptroller General's role did render the law unconstitutional. The Court ruled that the Comptroller General performed executive functions under the Gramm−Rudman law which were not constitutional because the Comptroller General is removable not only by impeachment but also by a joint resolution of Congress. According to the Court's interpretation of prior Supreme Court cases no other branch of government can have removal powers over officers who perform executive functions.

As the Court itself recognized, their arguments on this point were quite scholastic: "It may seem odd that this curtailment of such an important and hard-fought legislative program should hinge upon the relative technicality of the authority over the Comptroller General's removal" (Synar vs. US., p. X-22). It appears that the Court took a very narrow reading on this issue in contrast to its rejection of the first argument.

In fact, one can argue that the executive functions given to the

Comptroller General were very minor and carefully circumscribed by the law. The Comptroller General was designated to resolve differences between the CBO and OMB but the law indicated that these differences are to be resolved by averaging. The court noted that the President must issue the sequestration order precisely as presented by the Comptroller General. However, almost all the work was to be done by the CBO and OMB and careful directions were given for the Comptroller General in this process.

The Supreme Court concurred fully with the District Court ruling regarding the role of the Comptroller General. The majority opinion stressed the continuity between their ruling in this case and the earlier *Chadha* case also involving separation of power issues. In a footnote, the opinion went out of its way to indicate that this ruling was not to be construed as an attack on independent agencies as some observers feared.

The Gramm−Rudman law contained within it provisions in case the Supreme Court found the sequestration procedure unconstitutional. CBO and OMB would now prepare their reports as before but Congress must then vote in order to require sequestration. Sequestration would no longer automatically begin if Congress failed to act in accordance with the deficit targets. This dismantled the doomsday machine.

The second Gramm−Rudman law reinstated the automatic sequestration feature of the initial law and removed the Comptroller General from the entire process. Under the terms of this law, the President would automatically issue a sequestration order based on a report by the OMB Director. The OMB Director's report would take into account a report from the CBO but final authority would rest with OMB.

The operation of Gramm−Rudman

As the Gramm−Rudman law was passed initially, there was much speculation about the incentives created by its features. Some argued that since deficit targets in the early years only had to be met with a $10 billion leeway, this created incentives for compromise. Others pointed to incentives which could lead to delay or sequestration. If an appropriation bill was passed which implemented budget cuts yet sequestration still occurred, the sequestration would start from the new lower figure. Thus, no party would want to have its appropriation cut before everyone else went through the process. This potential problem was addressed in the second version of the law. A more basic problem is that some parties would prefer sequestration if the alternative were more drastic cuts in their favorite programs.

But rather than speculate about the possible incentive effects, it is more instructive to examine how Gramm—Rudman operated in practice. Since the budget process in four fiscal years (1986—89) was affected by Gramm—Rudman, there is at least a modest history which can be analyzed.

When the first Gramm—Rudman law was passed, fiscal year 1986 was already under way. Sequestration occurred on March 1, 1986, and was limited to $11.7 billion by the special rules that were constructed. In that year, sequestration was simply a useful device to obtain some deficit reduction and these reductions were handled with surprisingly little outcry. Some agencies had more administrative difficulties than others — the Department of Agriculture had to make cuts in 13,000 separate field offices. Yet, the 4.3 percent sequestration in nondefense and 4.9 percent sequestration in defense accounts was not difficult for the system to handle.

At the time of this sequestration, Congress was in the midst of budget planning for fiscal year 1987 and faced the prospect of a larger and much more difficult sequestration in the fall if a budget compromise was not reached. However, the initial District Court and then Supreme Court's ruling on the unconstitutionality of the automatic provisions clouded the picture. Congress would now have to vote affirmatively for sequestration. Moreover, economic performance deteriorated slightly over the summer which raised the deficit savings that were required.

Despite the lack of an automatic enforcement mechanism, Congress did adopt a budget plan that fell within $10 billion of the deficit target of $144 billion and thus avoided a vote on sequestration. The public spotlight on Congress from the entire Gramm—Rudman episode coupled with Congressional elections in the fall led Congress to this course. However, in order to avoid a vote, budgetary loopholes in the law were heavily exploited. First, there were asset sales totalling $8.7 billion which did little to improve the overall fiscal picture yet lowered the deficit by that amount because the government is on a cash accounting system. Eliminating prepayment penalties on Rural Electrification loans led to a cash inflow of $1.1 billion. The most outageous trick of all was to pay $680 million in revenue sharing obligations for fiscal year 1987 on September 30, 1986, in order that these payments fell into the previous fiscal year.

As fiscal year 1988 approached, Congress had passed the second Gramm-Rudman law which eliminated many of these budgetary gimmicks and restored an automatic sequestration mechanism. As the fiscal year began, it appeared that substantial sequestration would possibly be required. On October 2, 1987, for example, the Senate Budget Committee prepared a report outlining the consequences of a $23 billion sequester.[14] But the budgetary picture was changed in the face of the dramatic stock market crash of October 19, 1987. Although public pressure forced an agreement, the amount that would have been sequestered set a floor for the first year of the budget plan.

Congress met the Gramm–Rudman targets for fiscal year 1989. With both presidential and congressional elections looming in the fall, no one wanted budget difficulties interfering with the election campaigns. Early in the fiscal year, the budget committees adopted plans which allegedly met the Gramm–Rudman targets. But at that time, the plans were based on assumptions by OMB which were generally viewed as extremely optimistic. At the time the budget committees accepted the OMB forecasts, the Congressional Budget Office was projecting deficits that were $35 billion larger and would not have met the Gramm–Rudman targets. We thus had the ironic spectacle of the congressional budget committees accepting administration economic estimates over those of the CBO whereas attempts to establish an equal role for the Congress in the Gramm–Rudman process was fundamental to the legislative history of the law!

To the surprise of most forecasters, economic growth was very rapid in 1988 and most forecasters raised their estimates for economic growth for fiscal 1989. The forecasts from OMB were no longer much more optimistic than the consensus. On October 15, 1989, OMB officially estimated that Congress met the $146 billion target by a mere $0.5 billion. Informal CBO estimates, however, still placed the deficit for fiscal 1989 at $152 billion, $6 billion over the target. Nonetheless, sequestration was narrowly avoided for fiscal year 1989.

7.4 Final Parallels

Monetary targeting and Gramm–Rudman are impure experiments in constitutional or quasi-constitutional rules but some evidence, cautiously interpreted, is better than none. Three broad conclusions appear to emerge from our review of these experiences during the Reagan administration.

First, monetary targeting and Gramm–Rudman emerged in times of crisis. In the case of monetary targeting, a financial and credibility crisis led the Federal Reserve to adopt procedures signalling that it was serious about meeting the targeting procedures that were already on the books. Gramm–Rudman was born in the midst of a political crisis with all parties denouncing deficits but no concrete action appearing to be possible. Using the leverage provided by a required and potentially embarrassing vote on extending the federal debt limitation, the sponsors of Gramm–Rudman forced a dramatic restructuring of the budget procedures.

Second, both monetary targeting and Gramm−Rudman suggest that constitutional or quasi-constitutional rules are a continuation of politics, not its denial. These rules and laws were used as potent political symbols and means to exert political influence. Gramm−Rudman targets influenced budget outcomes in both fiscal year 1987, when the automatic mechanism was not binding, and in fiscal year 1988 when the stock market crash forced an agreement in any case. Monetary targeting proved an effective weapon at times for the Reagan administration in its attempts to influence the Fed.

At the same time, these rules and laws had limited influence when some parties were in politically weak positions or there was a general consensus to evade the rule or law. The Fed was able to abandon targeting, despite some criticism, in the face of a divided White House. Congress and the President appear to have chosen unrealistic economic assumptions to avoid a budget fight in 1988.

Finally, technical flaws in designing monetary targeting and budgetary control measures became dominant considerations. Although there was heated academic debate about the desirability of monetary targeting of M1 in the early 1980s, financial deregulation eventually forced the total abandonment of targeting narrow aggregates. The government's cash flow accounting system could not have been better designed to provide escape from deficit control measures. Although many of the loopholes from the first Gramm−Rudman law were eliminated in the second law, there is a general understanding that Congress could, through mandated programs, regulations, credit guarantees or new off-budget gimmicks, find ways to evade the intent of budget control laws.

These are sobering lessons for advocates of constitutional mechanisms to control economic policy. There is perhaps one final paradox. Despite the government's continued ability to create money (recall the alchemist parable), inflation was brought under control and appears to be stable. And despite the general belief of the power of special interest over the general welfare, Congress adopted two major initiatives, Gramm−Rudman and tax reform, which placed general interests over specific interests. Perhaps the original diagnosis which led to the constitutional prescriptions was too simplistic.

But perhaps this assessment of macro rules is a bit too bleak. Suppose monetary targeting and Gramm−Rudman are reinterpreted as temporary, strategic initiatives to aid the process of inflation reduction and budget control. Viewed from this perspective, both policies furthered overall goals for at least some period of time. Intermediate-run, strategic initiatives may be the best compromise between constitutional solutions to economic policy and seat-of-the-pants legislation. This topic will be pursued in the next chapter.

Notes

1 This aspect of monetary targeting was recognized, at least after the fact, by several Governors of the Federal Reserve. See Greider (1987), chapter 3, and Kettl (1986) p. 177, particularly the quotes from Henry Wallich and Nancy Teeters.
2 Interest rate and money supply data are taken from appendix B in Greider (1987).
3 See, for example, Roley and Walsh (1985).
4 The narrative descriptions of the four episodes are based on Greider's (1987) detailed treatment as well as reports and stories in the *Wall Street Journal* and summaries of FOMC meetings in the *Federal Reserve Bulletin*. I have also relied on Kettl (1986) for background material.
5 Greider (1987), appendix C, p. 732.
6 Ibid., p. 490.
7 Ibid., pp. 506−4.
8 Ibid., pp. 506−14.
8 Ibid., pp. 621−3.
9 See, for example, McCallum (1985).
10 Congressional Budget Office (1984), pp. 99−102.
11 Blanchard and Summers (1984) discuss this point in detail.
12 Elwood (1987) provides an interesting account of the politics leading to Gramm−Rudman on which part of this account is based.
13 Ibid., p. 14.
14 Senate Budget Committee (1987).

8

Conclusion

Chapter 1 outlined a series of fundamental challenges to the conduct of stabilization policy which have surfaced in recent developments in macroeconomics. Subsequent chapters reviewed the key debates and presented new evidence on the controversies. This chapter first responds to the challenges to stabilization policy and then presents new perspectives on the perennial stabilization debates.

The challenges to stabilization policy consisted fundamentally of two types. There were first challenges to the theoretical and empirical basis underlying stabilization policy, the models and evidence used to support stabilization efforts. They included both historical revisionism as well as new theoretical and empirical work in macroeconomics. Second, there were challenges to conventional views of the proper conduct of policy itself, in particular, whether the traditional normative approach to policymaking was appropriate. Both game theory and public choice theory contributed to this re-examination of traditional policy analysis.

The historical revisionism, led by Christina Romer, questioned whether there was much evidence to support the view that economic fluctuations in the postwar era in the United States were significantly less severe than in the period prior to World War I. While it was recognized that the interwar period, which included the Great Depression, was more volatile than the postwar period, Romer argued that the Great Depression was a unique event and a more appropriate comparison period would be the period before World War I. Leaving out the Great Depression struck many macroeconomists and historians as fundamentally flawed, but setting aside this issue, has the postwar economy been more stable than earlier periods?

A careful review of the historical debate on the data for the United States suggests that Romer was most likely correct in asserting that the earlier work tended to magnify fluctuations artificially. But even allowing for her corrections, the evidence is clear that the postwar economy is more stable than any earlier historical period. The standard deviation of GNP growth was approximately 50 percent greater in the pre World War I period than in the postwar period. Or, to look at the figures another way, the volatility of GNP fell by roughtly one-third. Comparisons with the interwar period would, of course, magnify the reduction in the GNP volatility.

A similar picture emerges with the unemployment data. Romer's revised series for the period 1900 to 1930 is considerably less volatile than the traditional series constructed by Stanley Lebergott. But if the basis of comparison is extended back one decade to include the period 1890 to 1900, the postwar period is far less volatile than the earlier period.

All these comparisons raise the question of what constitutes an economically significant reduction in volatility. Evidence from a variety of countries is useful to gain perspective for the United States. On the whole, data from outside the United States appears to be more reliable than US data for the earlier historical periods. The cross-country evidence reveals a wide variety of experience. Except for Sweden, most European countries exhibit less of a reduction of volatility between the pre World War I period and the postwar era, although the interwar period is substantially more volatile than other periods. Canada, Sweden, and Australia all exhibit sharp reductions in the volatility of GNP for the postwar era. By these standards, the United States does appear to have a considerably more stable economy in the postwar era, even excluding the period of the Great Depression.

In addition to providing a comparison for the United States, the cross-country experience reveals remarkable diversity. The countries that had the most volatile growth in the early periods were also countries with significant railroad expansions. Our research corroborates earlier work by Alexander Field which attempted to explain differences in the volatility of narrowly defined output measures between Germany, the United Kingdom, and the United States by the extent of railroad investment. The United States had considerably more rail investment in the latter half of the nineteenth century than many other countries. Similarly, Sweden had a much more ambitious rail program during this period than either Norway or Denmark and Canada and Australia had vast state-sponsored rail programs during this time.

The striking impact of railroad investment on the volatility of GNP growth perhaps seems odd given the work of Robert Fogel, who attempted to minimize the contribution of railroads to economic growth. Fogel argued that, on the margin, other transportation links (including canals) could have replaced railroads without dramatic losses in productivity. While there would have been some reduction in GNP without railroad investment, the United States economy would have continued to grow at roughly the same rate.

This research, however, suggests that railroad investment affected the *pace* of economic growth. Macroeconomists have long been familiar with the argument that small sectors can contribute to overall volatility – business fixed investment in the GNP is the prime example. A similar argument appears to be true with respect to railroads. A supply-side perspective is perhaps most appropriate to explain the effect of railroads. New rail lines in the United States, Canada, and Australia, opened up new areas for intensive commerce and development. To be sure, development did proceed the rails. But the rails provided an additional influx of inhabitants to the regions and an effective business linkage to older areas. Perhaps these linkages would have occurred at some future time. But the rails most probably concentrated the development efforts and affected the pace of economic growth.

While the rails perhaps were imporant in the latter half of the nineteenth century, their role should not be exaggerated in the full historical sweep of stabilization policy. The dismal economic performance worldwide through the interwar period cannot be blamed on paucity of railroad investment. Other factors have contributed to the overall stabilization record.

Automatic stabilizers also appear to be important in the United States. As Arthur Burns first observed (1960), automatic stabilizers have been so pervasive that disposable income can actually rise in recessions. Simulations to measure the extent of automatic stabilization are naturally subject to a variety of criticisms. Nonetheless, simulations with econometric models indicate that the stabilization mechanisms in the economy can be powerful and perhaps account for at least part of the improved economic performance in the postwar era. Thus, policy-related factors as well as technological factors have affected the stabilization picture.

The sharpest theoretical challenge came from real business cycle theory. Proponents of real business cycle theory put forth models which, in principle, could account for all economic fluctuations solely by means of technological shocks. Monetary factors did not play any role. Moreover, the actual economic fluctuations that did occur would simply be optimal responses to the technological disturbances. Attempts to dampen these fluctuations would just reduce economic welfare.

The rise of OPEC and the associated oil crisis heightened economists' awareness of the potential importance of technological shocks and created a receptive intellectual environment for real business cycle theory. The apparent importance of rail investment in explaining the volatile growth rates in some countries in the late nineteenth century also provides additional indirect evidence in support of technological factors. But the claim that technological factors are the sole source of fluctuations in the postwar era will not stand up to close examination.

Perhaps the most striking evidence against real business cycle theory is the evidence concerning monetary regime shifts. The international evidence is the most persuasive. The shift to a flexible exchange rate regime sharply increased the volatility of real exchange rate regime movements.[1] This change in the stochastic pattern of real rates did not only occur in the 1970s following the breakdown in Bretton Woods but also is apparent during other episodes as well. If real output were truly independent of monetary factors, the composition of Central Bank portfolios would not affect real exchange rates. Other evidence, although perhaps not as dramatic as the international evidence, suggests that domestic monetary regime shifts also affected the pattern of real variables.

Unemployment poses a special problem for the real business cycle models. The original versions of the models simply ignored unemployment and only accounted for fluctuations in total employment. Models were later developed that could explain unemployment but these models had the undesirable feature of complete unemployment insurance and generally implied that the unemployed were better off than the employed workers.

The empirical evidence concerning the consumption behavior of unemployed workers argues strongly against the assumption of full insurance. The consumption of unemployed workers falls sharply when they experience unemployment. The absence of full insurance cuts at the very heart of real business cycle models. Scheinkman and Weiss (1986) have demonstrated that the cyclical properties of models without insurance can be quite different from typical models in the real business cycle literature. Moreover, without complete markets, economic fluctuations are not likely to be efficient responses to disturbances as asserted by the real business cycle literature.

Independent work in the econometric modelling of economic time series initially lent indirect support to the real business cycle models. Real GNP and other economic time series appeared to be nonstationary, that is, disturbances or shocks to real GNP tended to persist for long periods of time. Monetary factors, by themselves, would not be likely to lead to permanent effects. The most plausible models featuring monetary shocks suggested that their effects would eventually dampen and not persist. Models which featured permanent technological shocks, such as the real business cycle models, would exhibit persistent effects from shocks. While other models, such as those featuring hysteresis or multiple equilibria, could also exhibit similar time series properties, real business cycle models nonetheless gained in plausibility.

More extensive analysis and theoretical work began to undermine these conclusions. First, it became apparent that the typical postwar economic time series were not long enough to truly distinguish nonstationary from stationary behavior. It is difficult to determine whether or not a series reverts to its prior trend following a shock. This is fundamentally a question of the long-run property of the data and cannot easily be answered in short time series. Different statistical methods lead to different empirical conclusions. Second, conventional macroeconomic models with long-term contracts could lead to behavior which would be virtually indistinguishable from nonstationary behavior as long as the monetary authorities tend to smooth interest rate movements. Most observers do feel that the Federal Reserve has engaged in interest-smoothing behavior which makes it impossible to render a definitive statistical verdict on stationarity.

A reinterpretation of the cross-country historical evidence on the time series properties of real GNP actually suggests that stabilization of the economy has occurred. For most of the countries examined, there appears to be more persistence in postwar economic time series for real GNP than for the pre World War I period. In the United States, for example, the hypothesis of nonstationarity cannot be rejected in the later period but can be rejected in the earlier period. Data from other countries also exhibit considerably more persistence in the postwar era.

DeLong and Summers (1988) suggest that the increase in persistence is indirect evidence of the efficacy of stabilization policy. Potential GNP is likely to be nonstationary as it is buffeted by permanent changes in labor force behavior and technological change. But deviations of output from potential output, cyclical fluctuations, are likely to be stationary. If cyclical fluctuations have been reduced in the postwar era, then the time series would increasingly reflect movements in potential output. Thus, with successful stabilization policy, we would expect to see more persistence in economic time series. Real business cycle models have no obvious explanation for the observed increase in persistence in the postwar era for a wide variety of countries.

Not all the criticisms of conventional economic models have come from new classical economics or real business cycle theory. Traditional Keynesian or monetarist economic models operate with the assumption that limited wage and price flexibility is the cause of output fluctuations. With perfect wage and price flexibility, shocks to demand would translate only into movements of prices, not output. Recent work, however, suggests that too much wage and price flexibility could be destabilizing. If this argument were true, it would mean that conventional models were misguided on their most fundamental aspects. DeLong and Summers (1986b), in fact, attribute the bulk of the increase in output stability in the postwar era to a decrease in wage and price flexibility.

The empirical evidence, however, does not provide much evidence for this view. Careful studies do not reveal that the short-run response of prices and wages to movements in output has decreased over time. Broader price indices show a remarkably stable correlation with output movements over historical periods. By this measure, wages and prices have not become more inflexible over time.

The models that were developed to explore destabilizing price flexibility were primarily based on the Mundell–Tobin effect. For price flexibility to be destabilizing, a demand shock which raised prices must also raise expectations of inflation; in other words, there must be a hump-shaped response of prices to output. This hump-shaped response is a consistent feature of postwar economic time series for a wide range of countries but is absent from the data prior to World War I. Price flexibility could not have been destabilizing in the earlier period without the hump-shaped pattern to prices.

Finally, the evidence from the Great Depression lends support not to models which feature Mundell–Tobin effects but to ideas, stemming from Irving Fisher, which stress the problems of debt and deflation. Fisher's views highlight the damaging effects of actual deflation in a world with nominal debts, not the Mundell–Tobin mechanism of higher real interest rates stemming from expected deflation. It is hard to find evidence that the dramatic deflation of the early years of the Great Depression was anticipated. Yet, there does appear to be evidence that reflation spurred economic recovery during this period. Critics of conventional models do have a legitimate point that a massive deflation, such as transpired during the first years of the Great Depression, are more likely to hurt rather than help the economy. But there is little evidence that increased price flexibility in less dramatic times would destabilize the economy.

Not all recent theoretical work was aimed at overturning conventional wisdom. A "new Keynesian economics" in fact had precisely the opposite goal, namely, to provide better theoretical foundations for existing beliefs. Although this work is relatively new and thus difficult to judge, there are grounds for skepticism concerning some of its ultimate contributions. Early attempts to rationalize wage or price stickiness by appealing to costs of adjustment or near rational behavior proved difficult to generalize to dynamic behavior. Indeed it was shown that in some cases, rational "stickiness" of prices at the micro level would disappear at the aggregate level. Lawrence Summers offered a pessimistic assessment of this aspect of the new Keynesian economics: "It is difficult to think of any anomalies that Keynesian research in the 'nominal rigidities' tradition has resolved, or of any new phenomena that it has rendered comprehensible" (1988, p. 12).

Another branch of the new Keynesian economics was its emphasis on incomplete markets and incomplete contracting. This work does show promise and can potentially account for rich interactions between real variables and financial structures. but it is, at this time, quite removed from empirical implementation. Part of the popularity of the new classical economics in recent years was a related econometric research program. The new Keynesian economics has yet to provide a comparable program.

Finally, there is growing skepticism about the validity of the efficient markets or rational expectations assumptions even in financial markets. The concept of "noise" introduced by financial theorists and the volatile behavior of stock markets and foreign exchange markets all contribute to this skepticism. Distrust of the signals provided by key financial markets naturally invites policy intervention.

Conventional normative policy analysis came under attack from two different directions. Some economists suggested that game theory approaches should be used to characterize the strategic interactions between the public and private sector. Positive analysis from the theory of games would replace normative analysis of alternative policies. Public choice theorists argued that hard-nosed political realism demanded that we adopt a view of policy based on the self-interest of politicians. They argued that this could both explain persistent inflation and deficits and lead to prescriptions for constitutional rules for macro policy.

Both approaches promised much more than could be delivered. Game theory models were plagued with a plethora of alternative solution concepts that could lead to sharply differing empirical predictions. Methods to choose among the solution concepts were very limited. This naturally put a tremendous burden on empirical testing of alternative models. As Marianne Baxter commented: "Without an idea of the quantitative importance and relevance of models of purposive policymaking, these theories are likely to end as a collection of intellectual dinosaurs: consigned to a dusty corner of the history of economic thought, interesting in their own way, but of little practical relevance" (1988, p. 149).

Unfortunately, the empirical content of current game theoretic macro models is very slim. The most popular model that forms the basis of work in domestic and international macro, the inflation game, has provided little research of substantial empirical import. Other models, "interesting in their own way," succeed in illuminating some of the nuances of policymaking but fall short on empirical content.

One approach to the plethora of alternative solutions concepts was to delimit the assumptions in game theory models by using detailed information on political structure. In short, there would be a marriage of game theory approaches to policy and empirical political science. Political scientists have explored the interactions between parties, elections, and economic performance. At one point, political business cycle theory − the view that incumbents cynically manipulated the economy for re-election − took center stage. But close empirical work has concentrated on documenting inherent differences in the economic policies of conservative and liberal parties. Some promising recent work combines game theory with partisan models of the political process. But closer examination of these models suggests that they have limited explanatory power. The promise of game theory in macroeconomics remains unfulfilled.

Public choice theory suggests that without binding rules for monetary and fiscal policy, the result will be persistent inflation and deficits. Yet, this view cannot account for the diversity of deficit and inflation policy over the postwar era. More importantly, a detailed examination of recent political "rules" for monetary and fiscal policy reveals the sheer technical difficulty of finding rules that can have more than a transient existence. Financial innovation, budgetary complexities, and political guile all conspire over time to emasculate rules.

The recent experiments in the political economy of rule-governed policy can, however, be seen in a different light. Rather than seeking to prescribe policy for all times, monetary targeting and Gramm− Rudman can be seen as strategic devices to cope with pressing political and economic difficulties. They were successful in focusing political attention on the problems and forcing policymakers to face the problems directly. Seen in this light, the two policies were moderately successful.

Despite these challenges from history, theory, and politics, stabilization policy survives. The postwar economy is more stable than earlier periods; economic fluctuations are not simply optimal responses to technological shocks; normative policy analysis is certainly still possible. The tacit consensus, outlined in chapter 1, should still govern our thinking, albeit modified with a deeper understanding based on the material in earlier chapters.

But what has been missing from this account has been a defense of hands-on, activist, fine-tuning of the economy. To some readers, this would amount to an inadvertent attack on stabilization policy.

Currently, in the United States, fiscal policy is an ideological battleground for diverse partisan views of spending and taxation with deficits as the symptom of political compromise. Traditional activist fiscal policy simply cannot survive in this environment. Activist, hands-on macro management has by default become the sole province of the Federal Reserve. The Fed must weigh inflation, unemployment, and exchange rates − internal and external balance − with essentially one policy tool although sometimes it is aided by actions of foreign central banks. The Fed must manage this awesome task at a time of rapid financial innovation and with little help from the economics profession by way of a consensus model of the economy. The Fed performs its taks using a variety of inputs including commercial forecasts and econometric models of the early 1970s variety. Close attention to data and recent developments in the national and international picture also play an important part in the Fed's deliberations.

What role can economists play in this environment? Two immediate suggestions come to mind. First, economists can help interpret recent events and data; or, in less charitable terms, sort through the tea leaves. Second, economists can work to develop empirically useful models of the economy to guide the Fed's deliberations. Although both activities are useful, neither one will result in substantive improvements in stabilization policy. Business and government economists have long watched and analyzed recent developments in the economy but improvements in this art are difficult. In a time of the crumbling macro consensus, it is difficult to conceive of short-term progress in developing an empirically useful econometric model of the economy.

Both of these suggestions for the role of economists — interpretation of current economic affairs and model development — still fit the mode of the optimal-control mentality discussed at the beginning of chapter 6. This vision of the role of economists has them concentrating on the details of policy and eschewing broader issues of political economy. These activities are clearly useful. But at this stage of our economic knowledge, the marginal product of at least some economists might be higher in precisely the opposite direction: leaving implementation details to the professional staffs in Washington and instead focusing on the broader, political-strategic aspects of policymaking.

There are two distinct aspects to this new strategy. The first is developing clear but precise, simple conceptual frameworks in which to discuss policy dilemmas in a sophisticated manner. The need for such frameworks is best illustrated with a simple example.

In September of 1974, President Gerald Ford convened a Conference of Inflation. This grand conference consisted of summaries of reports from a number of groups which had previously held their own conferences in preparation for the meeting. The reports were from a wide range of areas including banking, finance, transportation, business, and all levels of government. Perhaps as an indication of the esteem in which the economics profession was held at that time, there was a report from a meeting of economists which was chaired by Alan Greenspan.

The two-volume report of the economists conference (*Economists Conference on Inflation*, 1974), also held in September of 1974, provides a unique glimpse into the state of thinking of the profession at that time. The conference brought together some of the most famous academic, government, and policy economists, including Paul

Samuelson, Arthur Okun, Milton Friedman, George Schultz, Walter
Heller and many others.

Before discussing what actually transpired during the economists'
conference, it will be useful to contemplate what they should have
been discussing at that time. The OPEC cartel began to excercise its
power in late 1973. Real GNP fell slightly in 1974 and very sharply in
1975. Unemployment rose 4.9 percent in 1973 to 5.6 percent in 1974
and finally to 8.5 percent in 1975. As any competent student in under-
graduate intermediate macroeconomics can recite today, the period
1973−6 was a classic episode of a "supply shock" which created difficult output−inflation tradeoffs. The student would cite the textbook
picture showing the aggregate supply curve shifting to the left in the
face of the shocks with the result being higher inflation and lower
output.

What did our conference of economists say at that time? Arthur
Okun provided a summary of the economists' positions. There was a
general consensus that the economy was weak and that monetary
policy should be gradually eased. Long-run fiscal restraint was important
although no strong prescriptions were given for the short run. A
general concern was for improving the supply side of the economy by
removing counterproductive restraints on markets. The economists
divided sharply on the wisdom of wage and price controls. At the
second meeting of the group, they endorsed a list of twenty-two structural reforms for the economy. These included ideas such as prohibiting
resale price maintenance (an idea that never would make such a list
today), ending "voluntary" quotas, repealing the interest rate ceiling
on government bonds, and similar measures.

Okun's summary of the first meeting mentioned oil only in the last
paragraph (*Economists Conference*, 1974, p. 5): "Throughout the discussion there was a recurrent theme stressing the need for international
coordination and cooperation, the United States' role in the world,
and our interest in abetting the recycling of the petroleum dollar and
promoting liberal rather than protectionist trade and capital movements." Okun's summary at the major conference did not mention the
consequences of higher oil prices at all.

A fair reading of the economists' views at that time is that most did
not regard the oil price increase as having any special significance. The
real debates concerned the wisdom of policies of wage and price
controls and the best paths for monetary and fiscal policy.

There were economists at the conference who emphasized the
importance of oil. Walter Levy, an expert on oil markets, stressed the
large amounts of revenue that would flow to the OPEC countries.
Richard Cooper, however, was the only economist at the meeting who
discussed the oil problem in terms which we would recognize as familiar
today. He urged consideration of a tax cut, fearing the decrease in

fiscal stimulus stemming from the large transer of funds abroad. In addition to this demand side effect, he also emphasized that the inflation at that time was not traditional wage inflation and that the OPEC price increase had led to a deterioration of US terms of trade.

Why was Cooper's prescient economic analysis largely ignored at the conference? One answer might be that economists had had little recent experience with supply disturbances and just failed to incorporate them into their forecasts. But a more basic answer is that supply disturbances simply did not fit into any models which the economists used to think through macro problems. Unlike the students today, the economists at that conference did not immediately think in terms of aggregate demand and aggregate supply or demand and supply shocks. Today's students surely are not smarter than the illustrious economists assembled by President Ford. But they do have the conceptual apparatus to understand supply disturbances, unlike the economists at that conference.

The first aspect of the broader task for economists interested in stabilization policy is therefore to develop conceptual models that are easy to work with yet highlight key issues and dilemmas. These models make it easier for economists and policymakers who are engaged in analyzing data and developing policy to discuss ideas within a mutually consistent framework and communicate effectively with each other and with the public.

Once the key issues have been identified, the second broader strategic task for economists is to develop workable coherent strategies to attack the problem. Despite the criticisms levied at monetary targeting and Gramm–Rudman as permanent solutions to monetary and fiscal problems, they were coherent political solutions to the perceived inflation and budget problems.

Political leaders thrive on developing strategic plans. They often can use the plan to further their own political goals. President Reagan's striking political victories in the first year of his administration would not have been possible without the overall architecture of a plan. His plan, of course, did not succeed on all fronts; the inflation reduction program only succeeded with a recession which set the stage for future budgetary difficulties. Other politicians, however, were even less successful with their plans, failing to galvanize Congress and the electorate. The slogans "Whip Inflations Now" and "Project Independence" are reminders of failed political programs.

It is altogether too easy to design irrelevant economic programs and strategies. The classic example is the Humphrey–Hawkins legislation. This was designed to lead to full-employment policies. Yet, it was based on unrealistic goals which were not consistent with modern thinking on inflation and unemployment.

How should effective and workable strategies be designed? There are at least four desirable properties that effective strategies must possess. The first property is that there be a general consensus that a major problem exists. Despite differences of opinions on inflation and budget deficits in the 1980s, there was a political consensus that these problems had to be faced. A second property is that once a policy approach has been agreed upon, there must be some enforcement mechanisms consistent with the goals of the program. The history of Gramm−Rudman suggests some of the difficulties in designing these mechanisms. The third property is that, whenever possible, implementation details should be left to the Washington experts but they should be responsible for meeting clearly defined goals. The complexity of modern fiscal and monetary affairs is staggering and only full-time experts can be truly cognizant of all the necessary implementation details. The history of monetary targeting indicates the pitfalls of micromanagement of tactics. Finally, the strategies must be consistent with basic principles of contemporary economic thinking.

It would be ideal to illustrate these principles with existing policies but no current policies meet all these criteria. Instead, I will describe two distinct plans; one chosen for its political ingenuity, the other for its economic good sense. Future policies can perhaps combine attributes of the two plans.

Although public choice theory may not work very well in describing the inflation process, it does an excellent job in explaining some special interest politics episodes. The problems faced in trying to close military bases provide a classic example. Everyone agrees that there are too many bases but Congressmen have found ingenious ways to prevent any base in their districts from being closed. A Congressman from Texas came up with an excellent solution. Form an independent committee to propose a list of bases to be closed. The President could either accept the entire list or reject it but he could not selectively choose from the list to either aid allies or punish enemies. If the President accepted the entire list, Congress could only prevent the base closings by voting to reject the entire package. This bill clearly affirms the general interest at the expense of special interests and demonstrates that the political process can be made to work.

The economic plan comes from Robert Hall's clever device to address price and output stability (1984). Hall proposed that the Fed be required to hit a price level target but one that would be temporarily adjusted by an agreed upon formula in the face of unemployment. Essentially the Fed would be required to forecast the price level and unemployment one year in advance. The Fed would be responsible for meeting a price level target which would be adjusted by the state of unemployment. As unemployment approached the full-employment target, the Fed would be responsible for meeting the original price level target. The Fed would be free to choose its operating procedure but its forecasts and procedures would be subject to public scrutiny.

Hall's proposal has many desirable economic and political features. Its economic virtue is that it targets a price level as opposed to inflation rate and thus aims at a stable long-term price level. Its political virtues are even more impressive. It recognizes political realities and does not force policymakers to eschew unemployment targets. It also allows the Fed to design its own operating procedures but also provides a mechanism by which the Fed is held accountable. Another domestic inflation crisis might be necessary to force adoption of this or a related plan.

Hall's initial empirical evaluation of his proposal was rather casual and much more work could be done in assessing his policy. Lessons drawn from the earlier chapters of this present work could be useful — the econometrics of tends versus cycles, the interactions of price movements and nominal debt, and the importance of real disturbances should all carefully be integrated into a full evaluation. Indeed, a strong selling point of any proposal should be its robustness to differing economic settings and econometric methods of analysis. Hall's proposal falls squarely within the revised tacit consensus; we should continue to search for ways to reduce economic fluctuations with our deeper understanding of the issues. Analysis of proposals such as Hall's should be at the forefront of our research agenda.

Other macro policies and issues will naturally emerge in the next several years. On the horizon are difficult issues relating to budget deficits and Social Security trust funds. Depending on economic projections, the Social Security trust funds will amass funds as the payroll taxes from the baby boom generation begin to amass. These funds are necessary in order to finance the retirement of this generation without exorbitant and unrealistic payroll taxes on workers. Yet, the current budget includes Social Security surpluses which offset part of the large operating deficits of the rest of the Federal Government. Steps must be taken to ensure the rest of the budget does not simply spend these surpluses and thus prevent the accumulation of the required funds. If the surplus does emerge and the United States does become a high-saving nation, we will be faced with transitional effects as we move towards large current account surpluses. All these contingencies will require strategic macro planning.

This call for macroeconomists to become more actively involved in broad political-strategic policy is neither foreign to macroeconomics nor unrealistic. Keynes, after all, was instrumental in designing the Bretton-Woods agreements and macroeconomists are not strangers to Capitol Hill. Merging macroeconomics with politics may strike many economists today as unscientific. Those economists should continue

*

with normal professional discourse. But politicians will not fail to propose grand plans and schemes. Economists can either leave the broad design of policy to the politicians or participate in its construction. The latter alternative promises both better politics and better economics.

Notes

1 Baxter and Stockman (1988) explore the effects of real exchange rate movements on output measure.

References

Akerlof, George and Janet Yellen, 1985, "A Near-Rational Model of the Business Cycle with Wage and Price Inertia," *Quarterly Journal of Economics*, 1001, 823–38.

Akerlof, George, Andrew Rose, and Janet Yellen, 1988, "Comments on 'The New Keynesian Economics and the Output–Inflation Tradeoff,'" *Brookings Papers on Economic Activity*, 88:1, 66–75.

Alesina, Alberto, 1987, "Macroeconomic Policy in a Two-Party System as a Repeated Game," *Quarterly Journal of Economics*, CII, 651–78.

Alesina, Alberto and Jeffrey Sachs, 1988, "Political Parties and the Business Cycle in the United States, 1948–1984" *Journal of Money Credit and Banking*, 20, 63–82.

Alt, James E. and K. Alec Chrystal, 1983, *Political Economics*. Berkeley and Los Angeles: University of California Press.

America's New Beginning: A Program for Economic Recovery, February 18, 1981. White House, Washington, DC.

Annali di Statistica, Instituto Centrale di Statistica, Rome, 1957.

Arrow, Kenneth J., 1985, "Maine and Texas," *American Economic Review*, 75, 320–3.

Axilrod, Stephen H., 1985, "U.S. Monetary Policy in Recent Years: An Overview," *Federal Reserve Bulletin*, 71:1 (January), 14–24.

Backus, David and John Driffill, 1985, "Inflation and Reputation," *American Economic Review*, 75, 530–8.

Backus, David K. and Patrick Kehoe, 1988, "International Evidence on the Historical Properties of Business Cycles," mimeo.

Baily, Martin N., 1978, "Stabilization Policy and Private Economic Behavior," *Brookings Papers on Economic Activity*, 78:1, 11–60.

Balke, Nathan S. and Robert J. Gordon, 1986, "The Estimation of Prewar GNP Volatility, 1869–1938," NBER Working Paper No. 1999.

Ball, Laurence and David Romer, 1987, "Real Rigidities and the Non-Neutrality of Money," NBER Working Paper No. 2476.

Ball, Laurence, N. Gregory Mankiw, and David Romer, 1988, "The New Keynesian Economics and the Output–Inflation Tradeoff," *Brookings Papers on Economic Activity*, 88, 1–82.

Barro, Robert J., 1977, "Long Term Contracting, Sticky Prices, and Monetary Policy," *Journal of Monetary Economics*, 3, 305–16.

Barro, Robert J., 1979, "On the Determination of the Public Debt," *Journal of Political Economy*, 87, 940–71.

Barro, Robert J., 1981, *Money, Expectations, and Business Cycles: Essays in Macroeconomics*. New York: Academic Press.

Barro, Robert J. and David B. Gordon, 1983a, "Rules, Discretion, and Reputation in a Model of Monetary Policy," *Journal of Monetary Economics*, 12, 101–22.

Barro, Robert J. and David B. Gordon, 1983b, "A Positive Theory of Monetary Policy in a Natural-Rate Model," *Journal of Political Economy*, 91, 589–610.

Barro, Robert J. and Z. Hercowitz, 1980, "Unanticipated Monetary Growth and Monetary Revisions," *Journal of Monetary Economics*, 6, 257–67.

Barry, Brian, 1985, "Does Democracy Cause Inflation? Political Ideas of Some Economists," in Leon L. Lindberg and Charles S. Maier, eds, *The Politics of Inflation and Economic Stagnation*, Washington, DC: The Brookings Institution, pp. 280–317.

Baxter, Marianne, 1988, "Toward an Empirical Assessment of Game-Theoretic models of Policymaking: A Comment," K. Brunner and A. Meltzer eds, *Stabilization Policies* and *Labor Markets*, Carnegie-Rochester Conference Series on Public Policy, 141–52.

Baxter, Marianne and Alan Stockman, 1988, "Business Cycles and the Exchange Rate System: Some International Evidence," mimeo.

Beck, Nathaniel, 1982, "Parties, Administration and American Macro-economics Outcomes," *American Political Science Review*, 76, 83–94.

Berlin, Sir Isaiah, 1966, "The Concept of Scientific History," in William H. Dray, ed., *Philosophical Analysis and History*, New York: Harper and Row, 5–53.

Bernanke, Ben S., 1983, "Nonmonetary Effects of the Financial Crisis in the Propagation of the Great Depression," *American Economic Review*, 73, 257–76.

Bernanke, Ben and Mark Gertler, 1986, "Agency Costs, Collateral, and Business Fluctuations," mimeo.

Bjerke, K. H., 1955, "The National Product of Denmark, 1870–1952," in *Income and Wealth Series V*, London, 123–51.

Bjerke, K. H. and Ussing Niels, 1958, *Studier over Denmaks National Product 1870–1950*. Copenhagen: G.E.C. Gad.

Black, Fischer, 1986, "Noise," *Journal of Finance*, XLI, 529–43.

Blanchard, Olivier, 1981, "Output, the Stock Market, and Interest Rates," *American Economic Review*, 71, 132−43

Blanchard, Olivier, 1986, "Empirical Structural Evidence on Wages, Prices, and Employment in the United States," mimeo.

Blanchard, Oliver, 1987a, "Reaganomics," *Economic Policy*, 5, 15−56.

Blanchard, Olivier, 1987b, "Why Does Money Affect Output? A Survey," forthcoming in *Handbook of Monetary Economics*, eds B. Friedman and F. Hahn.

Blanchard, Olivier and Nobahiro Kiyotaki, 1987, "Monopolistic Competition and the Effects of Aggregate Demand," *American Economic Review*, 77, 647−66.

Blanchard, Olivier and Lawrence Summers, 1984, "Perspectives on High World Real Interest Rates," *Brookings Papers on Economic Activity*, 84:2, 273−334.

Blanchard, Olivier and L. H. Summers, 1986, "Hystersis and the European Unemployment Problem," in *NBER Macroeconomic Annual*, Cambridge, Mass.: MIT Press.

Blinder, Alan S., 1981, "Retail Inventory Behavior and Business Fluctuations," *Brookings Papers on Economic Activity*, 81:2 443−520.

Blinder, Alan S., 1984, "Discussion," *American Economic Review Papers and Proceedings*, 74, 417−18.

Blinder, Alan, 1987, "Keynes, Lucas, and Scientific Progress," American Economic Association, *Papers and Proceedings*, 77, 130−6.

Blyth, C. A., 1969, *American Business Cycles 1945−50*. London: George Allen and Unwin.

Box, George E. P. and G. M. Jenkins, 1976, *Time Series Analysis*. San Francisco: Holden-Day.

Brennan, Geoffrey H. and James M. Buchanan, 1981, *Monopoly in Money and Inflation: The Case for a Constitution to Discipline Government*. Sussex, UK, The Institute of Economic Affairs.

Burns, Arthur, 1960, "Progress Towards Stability," *American Economic Review*, 50, 1−19.

Butlin, N. G., 1964, *Investment in Australian Economic Development 1861−1900*. Cambridge: Cambridge University Press.

Cagan, Philip, 1979, "Changes in the Cyclical Behavior of Prices," in *Persistent Inflation*, New York: Columbia University Press, 69−96.

Campbell, John and N. G. Mankiw, 1986, "Are Output Fluctuations Transitory?" mimeo.

Campbell, John Y, and N. G. Mankiw, 1987, "International Evidence on the Persistence of Economic Fluctuations," mimeo.

Cantor, Richard, 1987, "Increased Price Flexibility and Aggregate Output Stability: A Note," manuscript.

Canzoneri, Matthew B., 1985, "Monetary Policy Games and the Role of Private Information," *American Economic Review*, 75, 1056–70.

Caplin, Andrew S. and Daniel F. Spulber, 1987, "Menu Costs and the Neutrality of Money," *Quarterly Journal of Economics*, 102, 703–25.

Caskey, John and Steve Fazzari, 1987, "Aggregate Demand Contractions With Nominal Debt Commitments: Is Wage Flexibility Stabilizing:" *Economic Inquiry*, XXV:4, 583–97.

Cecchetti, Stephen G., 1986, "The Frequency of Price Adjustment: A Study of the Newsstand Prices of Magazines," *Journal of Econometrics*, 31, 255–74.

Chada, Binky, 1987, "Is Increased Price Flexibility Stabilizing?" manuscript.

Chappell, Henry W., 1983, "Presidential Popularity and Macroeconomic Performance: Are Voters Really So Naive? *Review of Economics and Statistics*, 65, 385–92.

Chappell, Henry W. and William Keech, 1986, "Party Differences in Macroeconomic Policies and Outcomes," *American Economic Association Papers and Proceedings*, 76, 71–4.

Chow, Gregory, 1975, *Analysis and Control of Dynamic Economic Systems*. New York: Wiley.

Clark, Peter U., 1986, "The Cyclical Component of U.S. Economic Activity," Standford Graduate School of Business Working Paper No. 875.

Cochrane, John H., 1988a, "How Big is the Random Walk in GNP?" *Journal of Political Economy*, 96, 893–920.

Cochrane, John H., 1988b, "A Test of Consumption Insurance," NBER Working Paper No. 2642.

The Conference on Inflation, Washington, DC, 1974. Washington, DC: US Government Printing Office.

Congressional Budget Office, 1984, *The Economic Outlook*, appendix A, February, Washington, DC: US Government Printing Office.

Craine, Roger, Arthur Havenner, and James Berry, 1978, "Fixed Rules vs. Activism in the Conduct of Monetary Policy," *American Economic Review*, 68, 769–83.

Cuikerman, Alex, 1986, "Central Bank Behavior and Credibility: Some Recent Theoretical Developments," *Federal Reserve Bank of St. Louis Quarterly Review*, 5, 16.

Cuikerman, Alex and Allan H. Meltzer, 1986, "A Theory of Ambiguity, Credibility, and Inflation Under Discretion and Asymmetric Information," *Econometrica*, 54, 1099–128.

DeLong, J. Bradford and Lawrence H. Summers, 1986a, "Is Increased

Price Flexibility Stabilizing?" *American Economic Review*, 76, 1031−44.

DeLong, J. Bradford and Lawrence H. Summers, 1986b, "The Changing Cyclical Variability of Economic Activity in the United States," in Robert J. Gordon, ed., *The American Business Cycle*, University of Chicago: Chicago.

DeLong, J. Bradford and Lawrence H. Summers, 1988, "Assessing Macroeconomic Performance: An Output Gap Approach," mimeo.

DeLong, J. Bradford, Shleifer Andrei, and Lawrence Summers, 1987, "The Economic Consequence of Noise Traders," mimeo.

Donagan, Alan, 1966, "The Popper−Hempel Theory Reconsidered," in William H. Dray, ed., *Philosophical Analysis and History*, New York: Harper and Row, 127−57.

Driskill, Robert and N. Mark, 1988, "Macroeconomic Variability Across Monetary Regime Shifts," mimeo.

Driskill, Robert A. and Steven M. Sheffrin, 1986, "Is Price Flexibility Destabilizing?" *American Economic Review*, 76, 802−7.

Dynarski, Mark and S. M. Sheffrin, 1987, "Consumption and Unemployment," *Quarterly Journal of Economics*, 411−28.

Economists Conference on Inflation, September 5, 1974, Washington, DC: September 23, 1974, New York, NY. Washington, DC: US Government Printing Office.

Eichengreen, Barry and Jeffrey Sachs, 1985, "Exchange Rates and Economic Recovery in the 1930s," *Journal of Economic History*, 45, 925−46.

Ellwood, John W., 1987, "The Politics of Gramm−Rudman," mimeo.

Engle, Robert F. and C. W. J. Granger, 1987, "Co-integration, and Error-Correction: Representation, Estimation, and Testing," *Econometrica*, 55, 251−76.

Evans, George, 1986, "Output and Unemployment Dynamics in the United States 1950−1985," Center for Economic Policy Research, Stanford, Working Paper No. 81

Fama, Eugene F. and Kenneth R. French, 1988, "Permanent and Temporary Components of Stock Prices," *Journal of Political Economy*, 96, 246−73.

Feinstein, C. H., 1972, *National Income, Expenditure and Output of the United Kingdom 1855−1965*. Cambridge: Cambridge University Press.

Field, Alexander J., 1980, "The Relative Stability of German and American Industrial Growth," *Historisch-Sozialwissenschaftliche Forschunger*, 11, 208−33.

Fischer, Stanley, 1977, "Long-Term Contracts, Rational Expectations, and the Optimal Money Supply Rule," *Journal of Political Economy*, 85, 191−205.

Fischer, Stanley, 1987, "Monetary Policy and Performance in the U.S., Japan and Europe, 1973–86," NBER Working Paper No. 2475.

Fisher, Irving, 1932, *Booms and Depressions*. New York: Adelphi.

Fisher, Irving, 1933, "The Debt-Deflation Theory of Great Depressions," *Econometrica*, 1, 337–57.

Flemming, J. S., 1987, "Wage Flexibility and Employment Stability," *Oxford Economic Papers*, 39, 161–74.

Frickey, Edwin, 1947, *Production in the United States 1860–1914*. Cambridge, Mass.: Harvard University Press.

Friedman, Milton and Anna J. Schwartz, 1963, *A Monetary History of the United States, 1867–1960* Princeton, NJ: Princeton University Press.

Friedman, Milton, 1968, "The Role of Monetary Policy," *American Economic Review*, 58, 1–17.

Gallman, Robert E., 1966, "Gross National Product in the United States, 1834–1909," in *Output, Employment, and Productivity in the United States after 1800*, Studies in Income and Wealth, volume 30. New York: National Bureau of Economic Research, 3–76.

Gertler, Mark, 1988, "Financial Structure and Economic Activity: An Overview," NBER Working Paper No. 2559.

Golden D, and J. Poterba, 1980, "The Price of Popularity: The Political Business Cycle Reexamined," *American Journal of Political Science*, 24, 696–714.

Gordon, Robert J., 1980, "A Consistent Characterization of a New Century of Price Behavior," *American Economic Review*, 70, 243–9.

Greenwald, Bruce and Joseph E. Stiglitz, 1986a, "Information, Finance Constraints, and Business Fluctuations," in *Symposium on Monetary Theory*, The Institute of Economics, Academia Sinica, Taiwan, 299–336.

Greenwald, Bruce and Joseph E. Stiglitz, 1986b, "Money, Imperfect Information, and Economic Fluctuations," in *Symposium on Monetary Theory*, The Institute of Economics, Academia Sinica, Taiwan, 337–66.

Greenwald, Bruce and Joseph E. Stiglitz, 1987, "Keynesian, New Keynesian and New Classical Economics," *Oxford Economic Papers*, 39, 119–32.

Grieder, William, 1987, *Secrets of the Temple: How the Federal Reserve Runs the Country*. New York: Simon and Schuster.

Grossman, Sanford and Joseph E. Stiglitz, 1976, "Information and Competitive Price Systems," *American Economic Review*, 66, 246–53.

Hahn, Frank and Robert Solow, 1986, "Is Wage Flexibility a Good

Thing?" in W. Beckerman, ed., *Wage Rigidity and Unemployment*, London: Gerald Duckworth, 1−19.

Hall, Robert E., 1986, "Market Structure and Macroeconomic Fluctuations," *Brookings Papers on Economic Activity*, 86:2, 285−338.

Hall, Robert E., 1980, "Employment Fluctuations and Wage Rigidity," *Brookings Papers on Economic Activity*, 80:1, 91−124.

Hall, Robert E., 1984, "Monetary Strategy with an Elastic Standard," in *Price Stability and Public Policy*, Federal Reserve Bank of Kansas City.

Hall, Robert E. and F. S. Mishkin, 1982, "The Sensitivity of Consumption to Transitory Income: Estimates From Panel Data on Households," *Econometrica*, 50, 461−81.

Hamilton, James, 1987, "Monetary Factors in the Great Depression," *Journal of Monetary Economics*, 19, 145−70.

Hansen, Gary D., 1985, "Indivisible Labor and the Business Cycle," *Journal of Monetary Economics*, 16, 309−27.

Hansen, Gary D. and Thomas, J. Sargent, 1988, "Straight Time and Overtime in Equilibrium," *Journal of Monetary Economics*, 21, 281−308.

Hempel, C. G., 1966, "Explanation in Science and in History," in William H. Dray, ed., *Philosophical Analysis and History*, New York: Harper and Row, 95−126.

Hibbs, Douglas A., 1977, "Political Parties and Macroeconomic Policy," *American Political Science Review*, 71, 1467−87.

Hibbs, Douglas A., 1987, *The American Political Economy*. Cambridge, Mass.: Harvard University Press.

Howitt, Peter, 1986, "Wage Flexibility and Employment," *Eastern Economics Journal*, 12, 237−47.

Huizinga, John and F. S. Mishkin, 1986, "Monetary Policy Regime Shifts and the Unusual Behavior of Real Interest Rates," in *The National Bureau Method, International Capital Mobility and Other Essays*, K. Brunner and A. Meltzer, eds., Carnegie−Rochester Conference Series on Public Policy, Amsterdam: North Holland, 231−74.

Isard, Peter and Liliana Rojas-Suarez, 1986, "Velocity of Money and the Practice of Monetary Targeting: Experience, Theory, and the Policy Debate," Staff Studies *World Economic Outlook*, International Monetary Fund, Washington, DC.

Johansson, Öslen, 1967, *The Gross Domestic Product of Sweden and its Composition 1861−1955*. Stockholm: Almqvist and Wiksell.

Jonung, Lars, 1981, "The Depression in Sweden and the United States: A Comparison of Causes and Policies," in K. Brunner, ed., *The Great Depression Revisited*, Boston: Martinus Nijhoff, 286−315.

Kendrick, John W., 1961, *Productivity Trends in the United States*,

National Bureau of Economic Research, No. 71, General Series, Princeton, NJ: Princeton University Press.

Kettl, Donald F., 1986, *Leadership at the Fed*, New Haven, Conn.: Yale University Press.

Keynes, John Maynard, 1965, *The General Theory of Employment, Interest and Money*, Harbinger edition. New York: Harcourt Brace and World.

Kiefer, Donald W., 1980, "The Automatic Stabilization Effects of the Federal Tax Structure," in *The Busines Cycle and Public Policy*, Joint Economic Committee, Washington, DC: US Government Printing Office.

King, Robert G. et al., 1988, "Production, Growth, and Business Cycles II. New Directions," *Journal of Monetary Economics*, 21, 309−41.

King, Stephen R., 1986, "Price Stickiness and Output Stability: Conventional Wisdom Restored," Standford University, manuscript.

Kreps, David M. and Robert Wilson, 1982, "Reputation and Imperfect Information," *Journal of Economic Theory*, 27, 253−79.

Krueger, Alan B. and Lawrence H. Summers, 1988, "Efficiency Wages and the Inter-Industry Wage Structure," *Econometrica*, 56, 259−94.

Krugman, Paul R., 1988, Exchange Rate Instability," mimeo.

Kuznets, Simon, 1946, *National Product since 1869*. New York: National Bureau of Economic Research.

Kuznets, Simon, 1961, *Capital in the American Economy*. Princeton, NJ: Princeton University Press.

Kydland, Finn E. and Edward C. Prescott, 1977, "Rules Rather Than Discretion: The Inconsistency of Optimal Plans," *Journal of Political Economics*, 85, 473−91.

Kydland, Finn E. and Edward C. Prescott, 1982, "Time to Build and Aggregate Fluctuations," *Econometrica*, 50, 1359−70.

Lebergott, Stanley, 1964, *Manpower in Economic Growth*. New York: McGraw-Hill.

Lebergott, Stanley, 1986, "Discussion," *Journal of Economic History*, XLVI, 367−71.

Lieberman, Sima, 1970, *The Industrialization of Norway 1900−1920*, Oslo−Bergen−Tromso: Universitetsforlaget.

Lindahl, Erik et al., 1937, *National Income of Sweden*. London: P. S. King & Son.

Lindbeck, Assar, 1974, *Swedish Economic Policy*. Berkeley and Los Angeles: University of California Press.

Lucas, Robert E., Jr, 1972, "Expectations and the Neutrality of Money," *Journal of Economic Theory*, 4, 103−24.

Lucas, Robert E., Jr, 1973, "Some International Evidence on Output−Inflation Tradeoffs," *American Economic Review*, 63, 326−34.

Lucas, Robert E., Jr, 1976, "Econometric Policy Evaluation: A Critique," in *The Phillips Curve and Labor Markets*, Karl Brunner and Allan H. Meltzer, eds, Amsterdam: North Holland.

Lucas, Robert E., Jr, 1977, "Understanding Business Cycles," in *Stabilization of the Domestic and International Economy*, Karl Brunner and Alan Meltzer, eds, Carnegie–Rochester Conference Series on Economic Policy, New York: North Holland, 7–29.

Lucas, Robert E., Jr, 1978, "Asset Prices in an Exchange Economy," *Econometrica*, 46, 1429–45.

Lucas, Robert E., Jr, 1986, "Principles of Fiscal and Monetary Policy," *Journal of Monetary Economics*, 17, 117–34.

Lucas, Robert E., Jr, 1987, *Models of Business Cycles*. Oxford: Basil Blackwell.

Mankiw, N. Gregory, 1985, "Small Menu Costs and Large Business Cycles: A Macroeconomic Model of Monopoly," *Quarterly Journal of Economics*, 100, 225–52.

Mankiw, N. Gregory, 1987, "The Optimal Collection of Seignorage: Theory and Evidence," Journal of Monetary Economcs, 20, 327–42.

Mankiw, N. Gregory et al., 1987, "The Adjustment of Expectations to a Change in Regime: A Study of the Founding of the Federal Reserve," *American Economic Review*, 77, 358–74.

McCallum, Bennett, T., 1985, "On Consequences and Criticisms of Monetary Targeting," *Journal of Money, Credit and Banking*, XVII: 4, part II, 570–97.

McNamara, Ron and Steven Sheffrin, 1989, "Can Econometric Methods Detect Long Run Relationships?" UC Davis Working Paper.

Mink, Louis O., 1966, "The Autonomy of Historical Understanding," in William H. Dray, ed., *Philosophical Analysis and History*, New York: Harper and Row, 160–92.

Minsky, Hyman, 1982, *Can It Happen Again? Essays on Instability and Finance*, Armanh, NY: M. E. Sharpe.

Mishkin, Frederic S., 1987, "Can Futures Market Data Be Used to Understand the Behavior of Real Interest Rates? NBER Working Paper No. 2400.

Mussa, Michael, 1986, "Nominal Exchange Rate Regimes and the Behavior of Real Exchange Rates: Evidence and Implications," in K. Brunner and A. H. Meltzer, eds, *Real Business Cycles, Real Exchange Rates*, and *Actual Policies*, Carnegie–Rochester Conference Series on Public Policy, New York: North Holland, 25, 117–214.

Nelson, Charles R. and C. J. Plosser, 1982, "Trends and Random Walks in Macroeconomic Time Series: Some Evidence and Implications," *Journal of Monetary Economics*, 10, 139–62.

Nordhaus, William D., 1975, "The Political Business Cycle," *Review of Economic Studies*, 42, 169–90.

Peek, Joe and Eric S. Rosengre, 1988, "The Stock Market and Economic Activity," *New England Economic Review*, May/June, 39–49.

Perron, Pierre and Peter C. B. Phillips, 1987, "Does GNP Have a Unit Root? A Re-evaluation." *Economics Letters*, 23, 139–45.

Persson, Torsten and Lars Svennson, 1986, "Checks and Balances on the Government Budget," mimeo.

Poole, William, 1970, "Optimal Choice of Monetary Policy Instruments in a Simple Stochastic Macro Model," *Quarterly Journal of Economics*, LXXXIV, 197–216.

Poterba, James and Julio J. Rotemberg, 1988, "Inflation and Taxation with Optimizing Governments," NBER Working Paper No. 2567.

Prescott, Edward C., 1986a, "Theory Ahead of Business Cycle Measurement," Federal Reserve Bank of Minneapolis, *Quarterly Review*, Fall 1986, 9–22.

Prescott, Edward C., 1986b, "Response to a Skeptic," Federal Reserve Bank of Minneapolis, *Quarterly Review*, Fall 1986, 28–33.

Rogerson, Richard, 1988, "Indivisible Labor, Lotteries, and Equilibrium," *Journal of Monetary Economics*, 21, 3–16.

Rogerson, Richard and R. Wright, 1986, "On the Nature of Unemployment in Economics with Efficient Risk Sharing," mimeo.

Rogoff, Kenneth, 1987, "Reputational Constraints on Monetary Policy," in *Bubbles and Other Essays*, Karl Brunner and Allan Meltzer, eds, Amsterdam: North Holland, 141–82.

Roley, V. Vance and Carl E. Walsh, 1985, "Monetary Policy Regimes, Expected Inflation, and the Response of Interest Rates to Money Announcements," *Quarterly Journal of Economics*, 100, 1011–39.

Romer, Christina, 1985, "New Estimates of Gross National Product and Unemployment," *Journal of Economic History*, XLVI, 341–52.

Romer, Christina, 1986a, "Spurious Volatility in Historical Unemployment Data," *Journal of Political Economy*, February, 1–38.

Romer, Christina, 1986b, "The Prewar Business Cycle Reconsidered: New Estimates of Gross National Product, 1869–1918," NBER Working Paper No. 1969.

Romer, Christina, 1986c, "Is the Stabilization of the Postwar Economy a Figment of the Data?" *American Economic Review*, 76, 314–34.

Romer, Christina, 1986d, "New Estimates of Prewar Gross National Product and Unemployment," *Journal of Economic History*, XLVI, 341–52.

Romer, Christina, 1987, "Gross National Product 1909–1928: Existing Estimates, New Estimates and New Interpretations of World War I and its Aftermath," NBER Working Paper No. 2187.

Rosen, Sherwin, 1985, "Implicit Contracts: A Survey," *Journal of Economic Literatue*, 23, 1114–75.

Rotemberg, Julio J., 1987, "The New Keynesian Microfoundations," in Stanley Fischer, ed., *NBER Macroeconomics Annual*, Cambridge, Mass.: MIT Press, 69–104.

Sachs, Jeffrey D., 1980, "The Changing Cyclical Behavior of Wages and Prices: 1890–1976," *American Economics Review*, 70, 78–80.

Sachs, Jeffrey D., 1982, "The Changing Cyclical Behavior of Wages and Prices, 1890–1976: Reply," *American Economic Review*, 72, 1191–3.

Sargent, Thomas J., 1979, *Macroeconomic Theory*. Orlando, Fl: Academic Press.

Sargent, Thomas J., 1984, "Autoregressions, Expectations, and Advice," *American Economic Review Papers and Proceedings*, 74, 408–15.

Sargent, Thomas J., 1986, "Equilibrium Investment under Uncertainty, Measurement Error, and the Investment Accelerator," Hoover Institution, mimeo.

Sargent, Thomas J., 1987, *Dynamic Macroeconomic Theory*, Cambridge, Mass.: Harvard University Press.

Scheinkman, José A. and Lawrence Weiss, 1986, "Borrowing Constraints and Aggregate Economic Activity," *Econometrica*, 54, 23–45.

Schick, Allen, 1982, "Controlling the Budget by Statute: An Imperfect but Workable Process," in *Reconciliation: The New Budget Process*, Princeton, NJ: Woodrow Wilson School of Public Affairs.

Schultze, Charles L., 1981, "Some Macro Foundations for Micro Theory," *Brookings Papers on Economic Activity*, 1981:2, 251–92.

Schultze, Charles L., 1986, *Other Times, Other Places*. Washington, DC: Brookings Institution.

Schultze, Charles L., 1987, "The Economics of Gramm–Rudman," mimeo.

Schwert, G. William, 1986, "The Times Series Behavior of Real Interest Rates, A Comment," in *The National Bureau Method, International Capital Mobility and Other Essays*, K. Brunner and A. Meltzer, eds, Carnegie– Rochester Conference Series on Public Policy, Amsterdam: North Holland, 231–74.

Senate Budget Committee, 1987, "The Estimated Effect of a 1988 Sequester Under the Amended Gramm–Rudman–Hollings Law," October 2, 1987.

Shaw, William H., 1947, *The Value of Commodity Output Since 1869*. New York: National Bureau of Economic Research.

Sheffrin, Steven M., 1983, *Rational Expectations*. New York: Cambridge University Press.

Sheffrin, Steven M., 1988a, "Have Economic Fluctuations Been Dampened? A Look at Evidence Outside the United States," *Journal of Monetary Economics*, 21, 73–84.

Sheffrin, Steven M., 1988b, "Two Tests of Rational Partisan Business Cycle Theory," U.C. Davis Working Paper in Applied Macroeconomics and Macro Policy, No. 54.

Sheffrin, Steven M. and Liang Yn Liu, 1988, "Historical Changes in Inflation–Output Relations: A Cross-Country Study," U.C. Davis Working Paper in Applied Macroeconomics and Macro Policy, No. 53.

Shumway, Robert H., 1988, *Applied Statistical Time Series Analysis*, Englewood Cliffs, NJ: Prentice-Hall.

Solow, Robert M., 1985, "Economic History and Economics," American Economic Review, 75, 328–31.

Stiglitz, Joseph E. and Andrew M. Weiss, 1981, "Credit Rationing in Markets with Imperfect Information," *American Economic Review*, 71, 393–410.

Stock, James H. and M. W. Watson, 1986, "Does GNP Have a Unit Root?" *Economics Letters*, 22, 147–51.

Stockman, David, 1986, *The Triumph of Politics*, New York: Harper and Row.

Stubblebine, W. Craig, 1980, "Balancing the Budget versus Limiting Spending," in W. S. Moore and Rudolph G, Penner, eds, *The Constitution and the Budget*, Washington, DC: The American Enterprise Institute, 50–6.

Summers, Lawrence H., 1986, "Does the Stock Market Rationally Reflect Fundamental Values?" *Journal of Finance*, 41, 591–601.

Summers, Lawrence H., 1988, "Should Keynesian Economics Dispense with the Phillips Curve," in Rod Cross, ed., *Unemployment, Hystersis, and the Natural Rate Hypothesis*, Oxford: Basil Blackwell, 11–25.

Synar vs. United States of America, Decision printed in *Daily Tax Reporter*, February 10, 1986, X1–X23.

Taylor, John B., 1979, "Staggered Wage Setting in a Macro Model," *American Economic Review Proceedings*, 69, 108–13.

Taylor, John B., 1980, "Aggregate Dynamics and Staggered Contrast," *Journal of Political Economy*, 88, 1–23.

Taylor, John B., 1982, "The Swedish Investment Funds System as a Stabilization Rule," *Brookings Papers on Economic Activity*, 82:1, 57–106.

Taylor, John B., 1983, "Comments," *Journal of Monetary Economics*, 121, 123–7.

Taylor, John B., 1986, "Improvements in Macroeconomic Stability: The Role of Wages and Prices," in Robert J. Gordon, ed., *The American Business Cycle*, Chicago: University of Chicago Press, pp. 639–8.

Tobin, James, 1975, "Keynesian Models of Recession and Depression," *American Economic Review Proceedings*, 65, 195−202.

Tobin, James, 1980, *Asset Accumulation and Economic Activity*. Chicago: University of Chicago Press.

Tobin, James, 1987, "The case for Preserving Regulatory Distinctions," in *Restructuring the Financial System*, Federal Reserve Bank of Kansas City.

Townsend, Robert, 1979, "Optimal Contracts and Competitive Markets with Costly State Verification," *Journal of Economic Theory*, 21, 265−93.

Tufte, Edward R., 1978, *Political Control of the Economy*, Princeton, NJ: Princeton University Press.

Urquhart, M. C., 1986, "New Estimates of Gross National Product, Canada 1870−1926: Some Implications for Canadian Development," in Stanley Engerman and Robert Gallman, eds, *Long-Term Factors in American Economic Growth*, Chicago: NBER, University of Chicago Press.

Walsh, Carl E., 1987a, "The Impact of Monetary Targeting in the United States: 1976−1984," mimeo.

Walsh, Carl, 1987b, "Testing for Real Effects of Monetary Policy Regime Shifts," NBER Working Paper No. 2116.

Warren, George F. and Frank A. Pearson, 1935, *Gold and Prices*. New York: John Wiley.

Watson, Mark W., 1986, "Univarate Detrending Methods with Stochastic Trends," *Journal of Monetary Economics*, 18, 49−76.

Weatherford, M., Stephen, 1988, "An Agenda Paper: Political Business Cycles and the Process of Economic Policymaking," *American Politics Quarterly*, 16, 99−136.

Wegge, Leon, 1982, "The Canonical Form of the Dynamic Rational Future Expectations Model," mimeo.

Weinstein, Michael, 1981, "Some Macroeconomic Impacts of the National Industrial Recovery Act, 1933−35," in K. Brunner, ed., *The Great Depression Revisited*, Boston: Martinus Nijhoff, 262−89.

Weir, David, 1985, "Stabilization Regained: A Reappraisal of the U.S. Macroeconomic Record, 1890−1980," mimeo, Yale University.

Weir, David, 1986, "The Reliability of Historical Macroeconomic Data for Comparing Cyclical Stability," *Journal of Economic History*, XLVI, 353−65.

West, Kenneth D., 1988, "On the Interpretation of Near Random Walk Behavior in GNP," *American Economic Review*, 78, 202−9.

Williamson, Stephen, 1987, "Financial Intermediation Business Failures and Real Business Cycles," *Journal of Political Economy*, 95, 1196−216.

Woolley, John T., 184, *Monetary Politics*. Cambridge: Cambridge University Press.

Index